Beginning Windows 8
Application Development:
XAML Edition

Kyle Burns

Apress·

Beginning Windows 8 Application Development: XAML Edition

ISBN-13 (pbk): 978-1-4302-4566-7

ISBN-13 (electronic): 978-1-4302-4567-4

President and Publisher: Paul Manning
Lead Editor: Jonathan Hassell
Technical Reviewer: George Johnston
Editorial Board: Steve Anglin, Ewan Buckingham, Gary Cornell, Louise Corrigan, Morgan Ertel, Jonathan Gennick, Jonathan Hassell, Robert Hutchinson, Michelle Lowman, James Markham, Matthew Moodie, Jeff Olson, Jeffrey Pepper, Douglas Pundick, Ben Renow-Clarke, Dominic Shakeshaft, Gwenan Spearing, Matt Wade, Tom Welsh
Coordinating Editor: Kevin Shea
Copy Editor: Kim Wimpsett
Compositor: SPi Global
Indexer: SPi Global
Artist: SPi Global
Cover Designer: Anna Ishchenko

Distributed to the book trade worldwide by Springer Science+Business Media New York, 233 Spring Street, 6th Floor, New York, NY 10013. Phone 1-800-SPRINGER, fax (201) 348-4505, e-mail orders-ny@springer-sbm.com, or visit www.springeronline.com.

For information on translations, please e-mail rights@apress.com, or visit www.apress.com.

Apress and friends of ED books may be purchased in bulk for academic, corporate, or promotional use. eBook versions and licenses are also available for most titles. For more information, reference our Special Bulk Sales–eBook Licensing web page at www.apress.com/bulk-sales.

Any source code or other supplementary materials referenced by the author in this text is available to readers at www.apress.com. For detailed information about how to locate your book's source code, go to www.apress.com/source-code.

This book is dedicated to my wife, Lisa, who encouraged me to undertake the endeavor of writing it, and my son, Kolin, who spent a summer knowing me as the guy who came home from work and sat at the computer writing. Thank you both for your support in this and every other aspect of my life.

Contents at a Glance

Contents

About the Author

Kyle Burns is a technical architect with Perficient, living in Indianapolis, Indiana. He first discovered a love for writing computer applications when his father brought home their first Apple II computer and he would spend hours transcribing programs from BASIC magazine to see what they would do. After serving as a tuba and euphonium player in the Marine Corps Band, Kyle realized that people were writing software for pay, and he started his professional career. During his career, Kyle has worked in companies ranging from a six-person start-up to a Fortune 100 company and is constantly looking for new ways to explore solving problems with people, process, and technology.

About the Technical Reviewer

George Johnston is a lead technical consultant for Perficient, living and working out of Indianapolis, Indiana. He fell in love with software development in his early teenage years and quickly became immersed in technology. When he's not developing solutions for customers, he can often be found at home working on personal projects, studying the latest cutting-edge technology, and participating in community software development Q&A forums.

Acknowledgments

The writing of this book is the culmination of knowledge and experience gained over more than a decade of creating software applications professionally. Over the years, I have encountered many individuals who have helped shape my development in some form or another. While it is next to impossible to identify each of them individually, some prominent names come easily to mind.

- To Mark Thayer: Thank you for taking a chance on the kid with enthusiasm instead of education or experience those many years ago.

- To Mike Korzeniowski: Thank you for helping me to see the more pragmatic side of software development.

- To Ramu Kannan, Tim Davis, Steve Gaylor, Raju Eedarapalli, and Kiran Raja: Thank you for helping me understand how to see the bigger picture.

- To Greg Pogue and Kyle Zeronik: Thank you for pulling me out of my comfort zone and helping me learn what being an enterprise architect is about.

Introduction

Welcome to Beginning Windows 8 Application Development: XAML Edition. When I was first asked to produce a sample table of contents for what my Windows 8 development book would include, I spent a lot of time thinking about the aspects of Windows 8 development that I felt would be most important to help a developer just learning to write software in a XAML-based environment. I thought back to when I was first learning to apply BASIC to an event-driven, GUI environment and realized that I would have been most helped by being walked step-by-step through the creation of a simple but complete application. The majority of this book focuses on introducing you to concepts that should be applied to production Windows 8 applications and then integrating those concepts into an application that should be relevant to most readers. I hope that you learn as much reading this book as I did writing it.

Whom This Book Is For

This book is intended for developers who have learned the basics of the C# programming language and the Microsoft .NET platform and are ready to expand their knowledge by learning how to combine these skills with XAML and the new Windows 8 platform. This book will also serve as a valuable resource for developers who have more experience but are new to building XAML-based applications.

How This Book Is Structured

This book can be logically split into three parts. In Chapters 1 through 6, you will learn about the design style used in Windows 8 applications and the tools that Visual Studio provides to create applications in this style. In Chapters 7 through 16, core concepts used in developing Windows 8 applications are unfolded and integrated into a sample application that you will build in exercises. Chapters 17 through 20 introduce additional concepts that were not integrated into the sample application but will be valuable to the developer beginning to write Windows 8 applications.

Downloading the Code

The code for the examples shown in this book is available on the Apress web site (`www.apress.com`). A link can be found on the book's information page on the Source Code/Downloads tab. This tab is located in the Related Titles section of the page.

Contacting the Author

Should you have any questions or comments—or even spot a mistake you think I should know about—you can contact me through my blog at `www.geekswithblogs.com/kyleburns`.

CHAPTER 1

■ ■ ■

Welcome to a Touch-First World

Following the light of the sun, we left the Old World.

—Christopher Columbus

In April 2010, I first heard the phrase that was Microsoft's new strategy: "three screens and the cloud." This referred to a targeted approach to make sure that Microsoft's products were ubiquitous on mobile phones, desktop computers, and television screens and that these platforms provided a seamless experience by being held together with data in the cloud. The products represented on the three screens were Windows Phone 7, Windows 7, and Xbox 360. Microsoft still dominates the television screen with its Xbox line accounting for approximately half of all game consoles sold worldwide and a continued focus to move that platform beyond gaming, but to me Windows 8 brings a different meaning to three screens and the cloud—one where the three screens include phones, tablets, and PCs all running on the Windows 8 core and tied together with cloud services, as shown in Figure 1-1.

Figure 1-1. *Windows 8 vision of three screens and the cloud*

This book is about developing applications in this new environment, but before you start any development, you need to understand the environment and how it will be used. In this chapter, I will discuss some background on the user interface of Windows 8 and how users will interact with applications running on this platform. I will focus mostly on touch, but because Windows 8 is touch-first environment and not a touch-only environment, I will also cover when touch is not appropriate and alternative input methods.

Moving to More Natural Interaction

In 1985 users interacted with PCs primarily using a keyboard, but the first Macintosh was increasing the popularity of the mouse, and Microsoft introduced Windows 1.0, which was essentially a shell that allowed people to point and click to open programs and documents instead of requiring them to remember appropriate commands to type. These mouse-based environments were successful in both the business and consumer markets and made computing accessible to the masses; by the time Windows 95 was released, PCs were not uncommon in people's homes.

Over the years, computer and software makers have flirted with the idea of a computer that could be carried anywhere in a pocket or attached to your belt. Apple attempted to realize this vision as early as 1992, but it wasn't until the mid-2000s that technology really caught up and hardware manufacturers could create small, lightweight computing devices capable of running software comparable to what would be found in the desktop. By the time hardware was ready for prime-time mobile computing by consumers, the Windows brand was firmly entrenched in the market, and Microsoft made several attempts with Windows CE, Pocket PC, and various flavors of Windows Mobile to create a mobile experience that was simply a scaled-down version of Windows. This approach yielded screens that required a lot of precision to interact with, and computers running the mobile version of Windows were largely looked at as specialized devices and not accepted by the average consumer.

The introduction of Windows Phone 7 in 2010, likely driven by the successes of Apple's iPhone three years before and subsequent popularity of Android, discarded the notion of a tiny version of Windows and went with an entirely new user interface concept dubbed Windows design style. Windows design style is based on a set of core design principles focused around the user, and the finger became the primary tool for interacting with the computer. Unlike with previous versions of Microsoft's mobile operating systems, Windows Phone devices no longer shipped with the stylus being a standard component.

With Windows 8, Microsoft has taken the opportunity to hit the "reset" button on user interface expectations and reversed its previous strategy by, instead of taking desktop concepts to the mobile world, bringing the interactions that are natural by necessity in the mobile world to the desktop environment.

Windows 8 Touch Language

With the full incorporation of touch as a first-class citizen in Windows 8, it is important to understand the language of touch gestures recognized by the operating system. This is important not only as a user of Windows 8 but even more so as a developer who wants to make sure users can learn applications as quickly as possible and have a consistent experience. The Windows touch language consists primarily of eight gestures, which I will discuss in this section.

Press and Hold

The *press and hold* gesture, illustrated in Figure 1-2, is analogous to the right-click gesture with a mouse. The gesture is intended to allow the user to learn something about the target or be presented with additional options, such as a context menu. This gesture is accomplished by touching a single finger to the screen and pausing until the system acknowledges the hold, often by outlining the user interface element held.

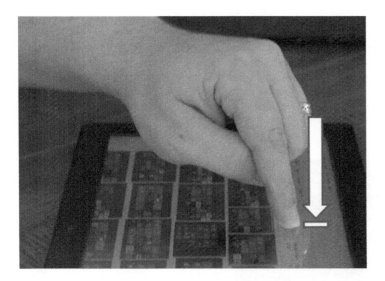

Figure 1-2. *Press and hold*

Tap

While the press and hold gesture can easily be equated to a single mouse gesture, the same cannot be said for the *tap* gesture. The tap gesture, illustrated in Figure 1-3, is intended to invoke the primary action on a user interface element. Often, this will be an action such as activating a button or following a link. The mouse gesture most closely resembled by the tap gesture is the left-click, but the left-click is also used for other tasks that have their own gestures in the touch language such as selection. This gesture is accomplished by placing a finger on the user interface element and then immediately lifting the finger straight up.

Figure 1-3. *Tap*

Slide

The *slide* gesture in the Windows touch language, shown in Figure 1-4, is used for panning or scrolling content that extends beyond the bounds of the screen or a screen section. In a mouse-driven environment this is accomplished using scrollbars, but with touch, the slide gesture is more natural, and the scrollbar would either have to grow to the point of taking up too much real estate on the screen or be a difficult touch target. To accomplish the slide gesture, a finger is placed on the screen and then pulled up and down or side to side depending on the orientation of the content.

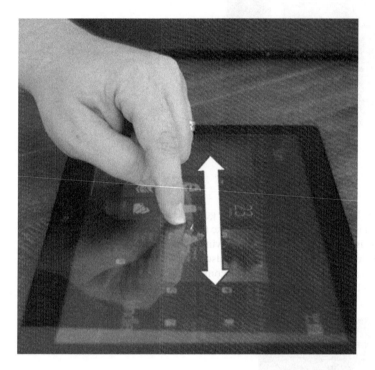

Figure 1-4. *Slide*

Swipe

The *swipe* gesture is used to communicate selection, much like left-click, Control + left-click, and Shift + left-click are used when interacting with the computer using a mouse and keyboard. To achieve this gesture, shown in Figure 1-5, the finger is placed on the screen either on top of or adjacent to the item selected and then drawn through the item. The direction of the gesture depends on the orientation of the content, with horizontally oriented content being swiped vertically and vertically oriented content being swiped horizontally. The gesture going against what would be used to slide sometimes causes it to be referred to as a *cross swipe*. Use of this gesture as opposed to a tap eliminates the confusion that could be created when trying to accomplish multiselect scenarios with no keyboard modifier keys such as Control and Shift that aid in mouse selection.

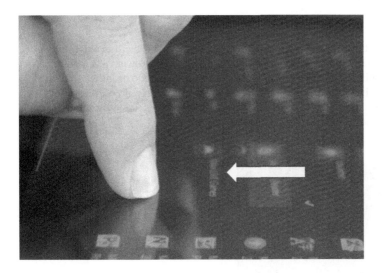

Figure 1-5. *Swipe*

Pinch

The *pinch* gesture, illustrated in Figure 1-6, does not have a direct equivalent in most mice and is considered a "zoom" gesture. The pinch zooms out from a narrow view with a high level of detail to a broader view with less detail. You will see in later chapters that in addition to the optical zoom, applications can take advantage of this gesture at a semantical level as well and use it to navigate summary and detail data. To accomplish the pinch gesture, two fingers are placed separated and roughly equidistant from the center of the element that is the target of the gesture, and then the fingers are slid together until either the desired zoom is met or the fingers meet.

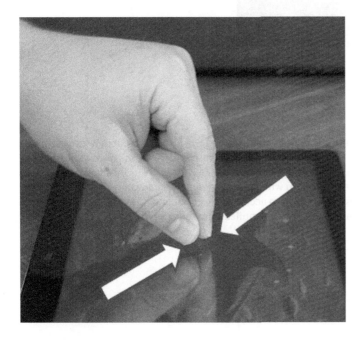

Figure 1-6. *Pinch*

Stretch

The *stretch* gesture, shown in Figure 1-7, is the opposite of the pinch gesture both in its execution and in the results. The stretch gesture is used to zoom in from a broader, less-detailed view to a narrower view with more detail. As with pinch, you will find that applications can be designed to allow the gesture to be either an optical zoom or a semantical one. To accomplish the gesture, fingers are placed together centered on the element to be zoomed and then are moved in opposite directions along the screen until either the desired zoom level is achieved or one of the fingers reaches the edge of the screen.

Figure 1-7. *Stretch*

Swipe from Edge

As you learn more about Windows 8 and the Windows design language, you will find that content is king and anything that distracts from the content is to be left off the screen. You will also find that users need to be able to perform actions with the least effort possible. Windows applications balance these needs by placing less frequently accessed commands off the edge of the screen in what are called *app bars* and *charm bars*. The *swipe from edge* gesture, illustrated in Figure 1-8, is used to access these commands. To achieve the gesture, a finger is placed beyond the edge of the screen and then pulled onto the screen.

Figure 1-8. *Swipe from edge*

Turn

The *turn* gesture, illustrated in Figure 1-9, is used for rotating either the view or the content within the view. One example of where this type of gesture could be used would be in a touch version of the classic video game Tetris, where falling blocks can be rotated to fit together. To accomplish this gesture, two fingers are placed on the screen, and then either both fingers are pulled around the circumference of a circle or one is rotated around the other, which remains stationary.

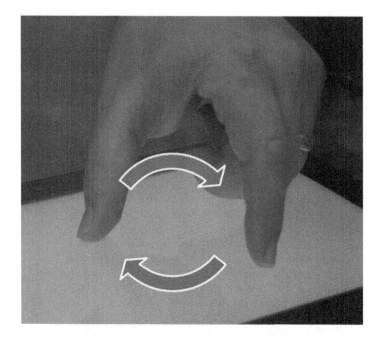

Figure 1-9. *Turn*

Keys to a Successful Touch Interface

Building a successful touch interface requires careful thought and consideration on the part of the designer and developer. Many of these considerations are embedded in the design principles governing the Windows design style, which I will discuss in Chapter 2, but in this section I will discuss a few concepts that are critical to touch interfaces, whether or not they use the Windows design style.

Responsiveness

Although responsiveness is important for any application, it is especially important for users of a touch application to never be left looking at an unresponsive screen. Users are aware, even if only at a subconscious level, that a mouse pointer is a much more precise tool than the end of a finger, so if it is not readily apparent that the user's last command was accepted and is being carried out, the user is likely to feel like they did not hit the target and issue the command again. Responsiveness can be achieved with actions such as giving a visual clue that a long-running process is begun or ensuring that content follows the user's finger as it is dragged across the screen.

Touch Targets

As mentioned in the previous section, the mouse pointer is a far more precise tool than the human fingertip. While nothing can eliminate the possibility of the user missing targets within certain applications, using large touch targets spaced well apart is an important way to minimize missed targets. When at all possible, targets should be no smaller than 7mm square with at least 2mm between them. As a general rule, when hitting the wrong target has severe consequences or is hard to correct, the target should be larger in proportion and should also have more space between it and other targets.

Intuitive Interface

To the end user, the best applications "just work." Usually this is because the application makes it easy for the user to do what needs done, rather than figure out how to do what needs to be done. Many desktop applications today make up for a lack of intuitiveness by providing detailed instructions in tooltips that appear as the user explores the application with their mouse pointer. Touch interfaces can still use tooltips, and the touch language defines the press and hold gesture for this type of learning, but it takes more effort than with a mouse, so more effort should be put into a design that clearly communicates what the user should do.

Beyond Touch

Like Windows 8 does, this chapter has put a lot of importance on the user interacting with the computer through the use of touch gestures. It should be noted, however, that the Windows 8 user interface is referred to as *touch-first* and not as *touch-only*. Windows 8 boasts the ability to run on much of the hardware that ran on Windows XP and Windows 7 and in many cases will perform better because of optimizations that have been made to accommodate mobile devices. This means that even though vendors are rushing to market with innovative touch hardware, for the foreseeable future, application developers need to acknowledge that many of their users will approach the application equipped only with a keyboard and mouse.

In addition to the volume of older hardware that will remain in use, it's also important to understand that some usage scenarios simply do not translate as well to a touch environment. Users sitting for hours doing data entry are going to be much more comfortable and suffer less fatigue and injury using a keyboard and mouse than users performing the same tasks with their arm outstretched to reach a touch-screen monitor set up like most monitors today. Hardware vendors will meet this new need by continuing to innovate, and you will likely see changes such as multitouch trackpads replacing the traditional mouse and monitors that adjust to lie flat or at least angled on the desk. Additionally, I expect to see Microsoft's Kinect device used in even more innovative ways than seen today.

Conclusion

In this chapter, you looked at Windows 8 as the touch-first world in which your applications will live. You learned about the basic gestures that have been defined in the Windows touch language and how end users will expect applications to react to them. You also learned that regardless of what the computer of tomorrow looks like, the computer of today often looks remarkably like computers sold the day before or even five years before Windows 8 released to market and that your applications must take the users of today's computer into account. Regardless of whether the user is interacting with their hands or a mouse, Windows applications should be fluid, intuitive, and responsive.

■ ■ ■

CHAPTER 2

The Windows Design Language

It seems that perfection is reached not when there is nothing more to add, but when there is nothing to remove.

—Antoine de Saint-Exupéry (translated from original French)

Beyond the basic touch principles discussed in the previous chapter, the design teams at Microsoft developed the Windows Design Language, which is used to guide the user interface development for Windows Phone 7, for Windows Phone 7.5, and now for Windows 8. The Windows Design Language was inspired by the simple, easily understood language seen in street signs in metropolitan areas and in mass transit and strives to bring this simplicity and intuitive flavor to computing. In this chapter, I will cover the elements of the Windows Design Language, show examples, and explain how Windows 8 incorporates them. Before jumping into the Windows Design Language itself, I will cover the Swiss design style, whose influence can be clearly seen in elements of Windows.

Swiss Design Style

The Windows Design Language is influenced most by a design style known as the Swiss design style or international typographic style, which began development in Switzerland in the 1950s and really started coming into its own in the 1960s and 1970s.

Influence of Bauhaus

The Swiss style was heavily influenced by the Bauhaus movement, which Walter Gropius founded in 1919 with the establishment of the art school Staatliches Bauhaus in Weimar, Germany. The guiding principle of the Bauhaus movement was that of function over form, favoring concise communication and stark contrast over abstract ideas and gradient transition. It was art and architecture designed for an industrialized society where it could be mass produced. The Bauhaus movement played an important part in the development of modern design and architecture. Today the web site http://Bauhaus-online.de is maintained by the Bauhaus Archive Berlin/Museum for Design, the Weimar Classic Foundation, and the Bauhaus Dessau Foundation (see Figure 2-1) in an effort to preserve information about the school and educate people about the impact of the institution.

Figure 2-1. *Bauhaus building in Dessau, Germany*

Elements of Swiss Design

The Swiss design style is characterized by a number of elements, which I will discuss in this chapter. These elements include typography, photography, iconography, generous use of whitespace, and strict organization. Brought together, the elements produce the distinct look and feel of a work designed in the Swiss style.

Typography

Front and center in the Swiss design principles is typography. The developers of the Swiss style and those who design with it today hold steadily that text should be clear and simple and that unnecessary adornment not only occludes the message being conveyed in the text but also actively distracts from the message. In keeping with the idea that text should be clear, concise, and simple, Swiss designs will typically feature sans-serif fonts with text left justified and jagged on the right. Figures 2-2 and 2-3 are examples of a newsletter designed using justified columns and a serif font (Times New Roman) followed by the same newsletter designed using a sans-serif font (Helvetica) and left justified to align with Swiss design principles. Look at the marked difference specifically in the typeface between the two examples and how the sans-serif typeface produces a cleaner look. The headlines are especially good examples of this.

LEAD STORY HEADLINE

Lorem ipsum dolor sit amet, consectetur adipiscing elit. Integer nec odio. Praesent libero. Sed cursus ante dapibus diam. Sed nisi. Nulla quis sem at nibh elementum imperdiet. Duis sagittis ipsum. Praesent mauris. Fusce nec tellus sed augue semper porta. Mauris massa. Vestibulum lacinia arcu eget nulla. Class aptent taciti sociosqu ad litora torquent per conubia nostra, per inceptos himenaeos. Curabitur sodales ligula in libero. Sed dignissim lacinia nunc.

Curabitur tortor. Pellentesque nibh. Aenean quam. In scelerisque sem at dolor. Maecenas mattis. Sed convallis tristique sem. Proin ut ligula vel nunc egestas porttitor. Morbi lectus risus, iaculis vel, suscipit quis, luctus non, massa. Fusce ac turpis quis ligula lacinia aliquet. Mauris ipsum. Nulla metus metus, ullamcorper vel, tincidunt sed, euismod in, nibh. Quisque volutpat condimentum velit. Class aptent taciti sociosqu ad litora torquent per conubia nostra, per inceptos himenaeos. Nam nec ante.

Sed lacinia, urna non tincidunt mattis, tortor neque adipiscing diam, a cursus ipsum ante quis turpis. Nulla facilisi. Ut fringilla. Suspendisse potenti. Nunc feugiat mi a tellus consequat imperdiet. Vestibulum sapi-en. Proin quam. Etiam ultrices. Suspendisse in justo eu magna luctus suscipit. Sed lectus. Integer euismod lacus luctus magna. Quisque cursus, metus vitae pharetra auctor, sem massa mattis sem, at interdum magna augue eget diam. Vestibulum ante ipsum primis in faucibus orci luctus et ultrices posuere cubilia Curae; Morbi lacinia molestie dui. Praesent blandit dolor.

Sed non quam. In vel mi sit amet augue congue elementum. Morbi in ipsum sit amet pede facilisis laoreet. Donec lacus nunc, viverra nec, blandit vel, egestas et, augue. Vestibulum tincidunt malesuada tellus. Ut ultrices

Figure 2-2. Mock newsletter in non-Swiss style

LEAD STORY HEADLINE

Lorem ipsum dolor sit amet, consectetur adipiscing elit. Integer nec odio. Praesent libero. Sed cursus ante dapibus diam. Sed nisi. Nulla quis sem at nibh elementum imperdiet. Duis sagittis ipsum. Praesent mauris. Fusce nec tellus sed augue semper porta. Mauris massa. Vestibulum lacinia arcu eget nulla. Class aptent taciti sociosqu ad litora torquent per conubia nostra, per inceptos himenaeos. Curabitur sodales ligula in libero. Sed dignissim lacinia nunc.

Curabitur tortor. Pellentesque nibh. Aenean quam. In scelerisque sem at dolor. Maecenas mattis. Sed convallis tristique sem. Proin ut ligula vel nunc egestas porttitor. Morbi lectus risus, iaculis vel, suscipit quis, luctus non, massa. Fusce ac turpis quis ligula lacinia aliquet. Mauris ipsum. Nulla metus metus, ullamcorper vel, tincidunt sed, euismod in, nibh. Quisque volutpat condimentum velit. Class aptent taciti sociosqu ad litora torquent per conubia nostra, per inceptos himenaeos. Nam nec ante.

Sed lacinia, urna non tincidunt mattis, tortor neque adipiscing diam, a cursus ipsum ante quis turpis. Nulla facilisi. Ut fringilla. Suspendisse potenti. Nunc feugiat mi a tellus consequat imperdiet. Vestibulum sapien. Proin quam. Etiam ultrices. Suspendisse in justo eu magna luctus suscipit. Sed lectus. Integer euismod lacus luctus magna. Quisque cursus, metus vitae pharetra auctor, sem massa mattis sem, at interdum magna augue eget diam. Vestibulum ante ipsum primis in faucibus orci luctus et ultrices posuere cubilia Curae; Morbi lacinia molestie dui. Praesent blandit dolor.

Sed non quam. In vel mi sit amet augue congue

Figure 2-3. Mock newsletter using Swiss-style typography

In addition to the focus on simple, sans-serif typefaces, another key element of Swiss design with regard to typography is the use of contrasting font size and weight to draw attention to certain points in the text or to create emphasis. This calls for stark differences in font sizes when different font sizes are used, so while some design schools may allow for 12-point headlines and 10-point body text, the same publication designed using Swiss design may find 18-point headlines and 10-point body text to ensure that there is no question about the difference between the two.

Photography

Swiss design is also marked by the idea that the design should convey a sense of reality and that visual elements will be perceived as "more real" when photographs are used in place of drawn illustrations.

Figure 2-4 shows the sunset over a body of water. The photograph captures the ripples in the water and the effect of the sun's light on the water in a way that feels very real to the viewer.

Figure 2-4. *Sunset over the water photograph*

Figure 2-5 also depicts the sunset over a body of water. Many of the same elements are present, such as the sun's reflection over ripples in the water and silhouetted figures, but the theories driving Swiss design hold that the viewer is not left feeling as though what they are viewing is real when illustration is used instead of photography. Both the photograph and the painting are pleasing to the eye, but the photograph is more in line with the Swiss style.

Figure 2-5. *Sunset over the water painting*

Iconography

While photographs are favored over drawings or other illustrations in many cases, works created using Swiss design often include extensive use of icons either to augment or in place of text. This is particularly the case when Swiss design is used in a setting where information must be conveyed to an international audience or one where you cannot be sure that the viewer needing to consume information being conveyed can read words printed regardless of the language. Rich iconography used in conjunction with other elements of Swiss design made a big show on the international stage during the 1972 Summer Olympics in Munich, Germany. Otl Aicher designed the brochures and leaflets for the Olympic Games in the Swiss style and used what is now a familiar system of figure icons to represent individuals participating in various events for the games. This helped communicate with the international audience present for the games. Additional places where you see prominent examples of Swiss design and iconography are in bus and train stations, on restrooms in public places (Figure 2-6), and as warning signs on many consumer goods.

Figure 2-6. *Familiar Swiss-style design helps avoid an embarrassing mistake*

Generous Use of Whitespace

In Swiss design, content is king. Too much of anything packed haphazardly into a space is considered too cluttered or noisy and a distraction from the information being conveyed. This leads to a design goal that includes plenty of whitespace to ensure that anything appearing within an expanse of whitespace immediately becomes the center of attention.

Figure 2-7 shows a dog that appears to be on watch in a snowy country setting. "The Sentinel" is a descriptive caption, but no particular attention is drawn to either the dog or the caption because the contents are all allowed to run together without any separation and because the trees produce noise that detracts from the message of the caption. While this figure is visually appealing, it lacks the stark contrast pursued when using Swiss design principles. I'll use the natural whitespace present in the expanse of snow to highlight both the portion of the photo where I want attention focused and the caption, as shown in Figure 2-8.

Figure 2-7. *Photo and caption with no whitespace*

Figure 2-8. *Photo and caption with whitespace for contrast*

In Figure 2-8, the only change that I applied was to move the text out of the noise produced by the trees, allowing the caption to sit by itself within uninterrupted whitespace. This narrows the focus of the photograph to exclude more of it that is not that direct subject and really makes the caption stand out. More of the photograph could have been cropped from the top and bottom to bring even more focus to the subject, but in this case enough was left to ensure the winter scene was not lost on the viewer. Neither the first nor the second version should be considered better or worse because there are instances where the intent would be to keep focus on the entire setting and where adhering to the principles of Swiss design is not a goal, in which case the first may be preferred.

Strict Organization

In keeping with the overarching theme of clean simplicity and avoiding anything that distracts from the content, Swiss design is typically marked by strict organization. This is observed in the uniformity of geometric figures as well as in the use of font size to communicate informational hierarchy within text and adherence to a grid system to lay out both text and other visual elements in a structured manner. The use of grids is definitely not limited to the Swiss style and has been around typography design for centuries. With a grid-based design, the design surface is divided into one or more grids that are used to position text and elements with cells. This provides for an organized and aligned look. At times, the use of grid layout may not be quite as evident as at other times because the grid lines need not be perpendicular and parallel with the edges of the design surface, making it possible for a design to use a grid layout while the content appears angled to the viewer.

Figure 2-9 shows the structural organization achieved by using a grid layout, but it also demonstrates the way that typography is used to achieve organization within the Swiss design style by using a stark difference in font size to delineate different levels within the informational hierarchy. At the highest level of the informational hierarchy, the page header is presented in a 56-point font size. At the next level, group headers are given around one-half the font size of the page header. At the lowest level of the hierarchy for this page, the item title is about half the size of the group header.

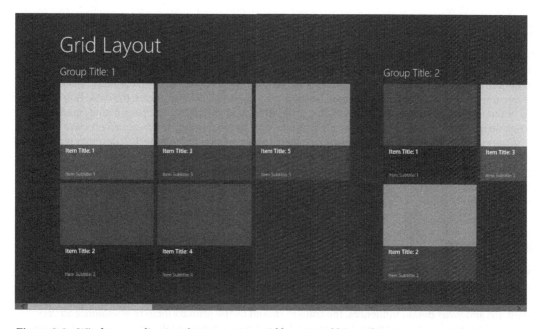

Figure 2-9. *Windows application demonstrating grid layout and hierarchy*

Windows Design Language

Rooted heavily in the Swiss design style that we've just covered, the Windows Design Language guides user experience design for the Windows Phone 7/7.5 and Windows 8 operating systems as well as for current incarnations of the Zune and Xbox 360 user interfaces, striving to give a consistent look and feel regardless of which device you are interacting with.

Windows Design Principles

In the earliest guidance given by Microsoft on the Windows Design Language, the Windows design style was characterized as a confluence of five guiding principles rather than a book of rules or recipes. In this section, I'll cover the principles that you should weigh when making design choices.

Show Pride in Craftsmanship

Not even the smallest detail should be left to chance in your user interface. Everything the user sees and experiences should be part of the plan and work according to that plan. Additionally, information should be presented according to a carefully thought out visual hierarchy and should be laid out using a grid-based design.

Be Fast and Fluid

Applications should allow users to interact directly with the content and should remain constantly responsive by using motion to provide feedback to interactions. Applications should typically be designed with "touch-first" in mind.

Be Authentically Digital

One of the most shining examples of a failed user experience experiment from Microsoft came with the release of Microsoft Bob in 1995. This application was a shell for the operating system that intended to abstract away the whole "computerness" of the computer by providing real-world analogies for different operations. If you wanted to retrieve documents, you clicked the file cabinet. Need to write a letter? Click the pen on the desk! Bob's failure was driven ultimately by two factors. The first was that it was perceived as childish and patronizing (many shells similar to Bob do find favor in preschool classrooms). The second was that it simply was not an effective way for people to interact with the computer, and introducing abstractions intended to hide the computer tended to make interactions much less efficient, especially for people who have to use a computer all day. The Windows design principles acknowledge that people know they are interacting with a computer and call on designers to embrace the medium. This includes using the cloud to keep users and apps connected and effectively using motion and bold, vibrant colors to communicate with the user.

Do More with Less

Windows 8 provides rich functionality to allow applications running both on your device and in the cloud to interact with each other. This allows for applications to focus on doing a very narrowly defined set of things and to do that one thing in an extraordinary manner rather than do several things in a mediocre manner. In keeping with the Bauhaus and Swiss design influences, the content should be the primary focus of attention, and very little else should be present to distract from this content. The full-screen nature of Windows apps even removes the need for window chrome, allowing a completely immersive experience so that when the user is in your application, your application receives all of their attention.

Win As One

One of the keys to working in a Windows style application is that the style has been set. Users of a Windows application will be opening your application with the expectation that they will already have some level of familiarity with the application because they are familiar with the look and feel of other Windows applications. One of the things that can really be harmful to individual applications and eventually to the ecosystem in which the applications reside is design decisions that radically change the design paradigm of the application to give users something "new" and "better" than what they are used to having. You should strive to impress your users with how well your application does the things it is meant to be good at, but trying to surprise those users by changing user interface and navigation paradigms will only confuse them and make them lose trust in your application. Microsoft has provided guidance, tools, templates, and style sheets to make it easy for developers to create Windows applications with a consistent look and feel, and you should make full use of these resources.

Windows User Experience Guidelines

In addition to the more generalized principles that Microsoft has published for Windows applications, a comprehensive set of guidelines has also been made available in order to provide detailed prescriptive guidance in regard to the look, feel, and behavior of applications designed to run in the Windows ecosystem. Although not a comprehensive treatment of these guidelines, which are freely available in their entirety on the MSDN Library web site at `http://dev.windows.com`, this section covers a few of the aspects that are most applicable to designers/developers getting a feel for the Windows experience.

Application Layout

Applications should be designed using a grid layout organized using either a hierarchical navigation scheme or a flat view, as dictated by the content.

When a hierarchical approach is taken, the top of the hierarchy represents the lowest level of detail, and each subsequent level in the navigation hierarchy zooms in with increasing detail. Typically the highest level, sometimes referred to as Hub, is the entry point of the application and reveals one or more groups that the user can drill into (see Figure 2-10).

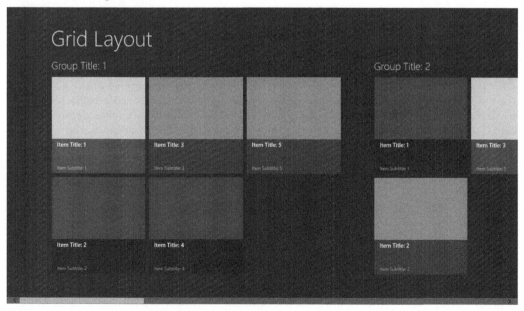

Figure 2-10. *Hierarchical navigation at highest level*

By selecting (note "select" vs. "click" because we're in a touch-first environment where "select" may be a "click", a "tap", or even a keystroke) a group from the main Hub, the next level of navigation (commonly referred to as *Section*) is revealed. The Section page is arranged to provide some context about the Section itself and lists the individual items that are the lowest level of navigation and highest level of detail (see Figure 2-11).

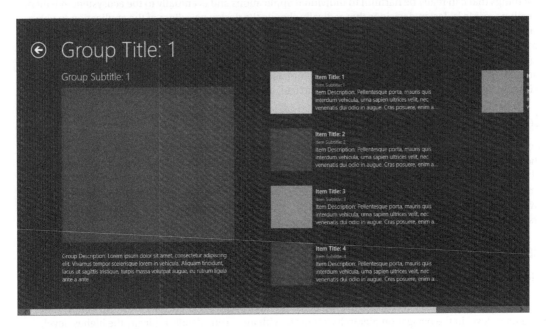

Figure 2-11. *Hierarchical navigation at section level*

From the Section page, the user is offered a way to navigate back up a level, typically through the use of a back arrow, as shown in Figure 2-11, to the Hub; a means to navigate to sibling Section pages through a swipe gesture (if touch enabled) or through the use of arrows at the left and right edge of the screen centered vertically; or items to select in order to continue to the Detail page. At the Detail page level of navigation, a granular view of the item data is presented (see Figure 2-12). As with the Section page, the back arrow is presented to allow for navigation up the hierarchy to the Section page in which the item is organized. As with Section pages, users can choose to navigate between Detail pages within the same section through the use of a swipe gesture on touch-enabled systems or through interaction with arrows at the left and right edge of the screen. The hierarchical navigation is especially well suited for browsing and interacting with information that can be fit into master-detail categorization. For an excellent example of a Windows style application designed with a hierarchical navigation structure running on a platform other than Windows 8, take a look at the Microsoft Zune application running on Windows 7 or at the Windows style user interface on Xbox 360.

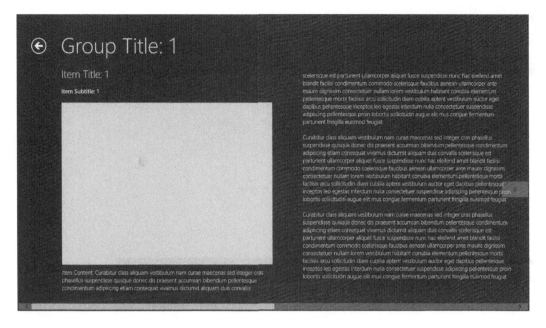

Figure 2-12. *Hierarchical navigation at Detail page*

Many applications do not fit into the master-detail categorization that works well with a hierarchical navigation structure and focus more on the document-based style familiar with Microsoft Word, Excel, or Internet Explorer. For this type of application, a flat navigation system works much better. At the core of the flat navigation is that content is separated into pages with information that is either unrelated or at the same hierarchical level (see Figure 2-13). The Navigation Bar is presented when activated by the user and is used to switch between active documents, often presenting a command that the user can use to add a document to the session (see Figure 2-14).

Figure 2-13. *Internet Explorer's Modern UI design presents a flat view with a single document using an entire viewport*

Figure 2-14. *Internet Explorer with Navigation Bar activated to switch active document*

Typography

With its heavy emphasis on typography and text-centered content, no coverage of the Modern UI user experience guidelines would be complete without providing advice for the formatting and use of text. Following in the tradition of Swiss design, consistent fonts should be used when building applications. Which specific font should be used varies by the purpose of the text. Text that is intended to be used for buttons or labels on UI elements should favor the Segoe UI font, which is used throughout Windows 8 user interface elements (see Figure 2-15).

Figure 2-15. *Segoe UI is used for labels and other UI elements*

Blocks of text that are to be presented to the reader in a read-only fashion, such as news articles, should favor the serif Cambria font because readers are accustomed to extended blocks of text being presented in a serif font (see Figure 2-16). This font should be presented in either 9 points, 11 points, or 20 points depending on the need to draw focus or show emphasis. This is a departure from the Swiss style's preference for sans-serif fonts in all things because the Modern UI design team found serif fonts to be easier on the eyes for extended reading.

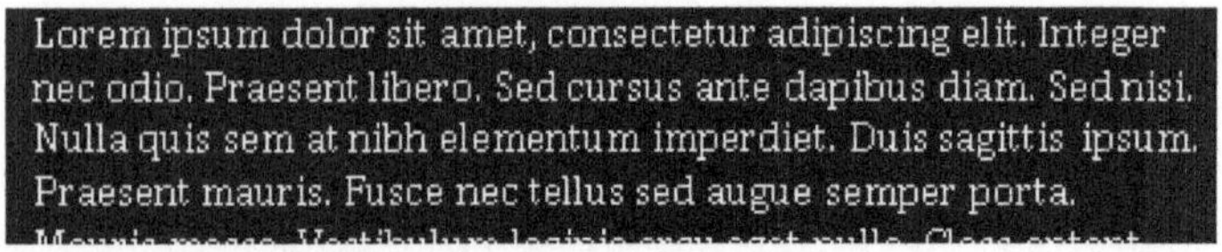

> Lorem ipsum dolor sit amet, consectetur adipiscing elit. Integer nec odio. Praesent libero. Sed cursus ante dapibus diam. Sed nisi. Nulla quis sem at nibh elementum imperdiet. Duis sagittis ipsum. Praesent mauris. Fusce nec tellus sed augue semper porta.

Figure 2-16. *Cambria for read-only text blocks*

Continuous blocks that are intended for the user to both read and edit should favor the sans-serif font Calibri (see Figure 2-17). The recommended size for this font is 13 points, which shares the same height as 11-point Segoe UI, so the two will maintain a consistent appearance when used together on the same line.

Lorem ipsum dolor sit amet, consectetur adipiscing elit.
Integer nec odio. Praesent libero. Sed cursus ante
dapibus diam. Sed nisi. Nulla quis sem at nibh elementum
imperdiet. Duis sagittis ipsum. Praesent mauris. Fusce nec
tellus sed augue semper porta. Mauris massa. Vestibulum

Figure 2-17. *Calibri for read-write text blocks*

Regardless of the font face, when emphasis is needed on certain pieces of text, the appropriate way to produce emphasis is through the use of stark contrast with the font size or the font weight. At the same level within the information hierarchy, weight is used for emphasis, while size draws the distinction between levels. Using text decorations such as underline or italics reduces clarity and should not be used for emphasis in a Windows application.

Other Windows User Experience Guidelines

In this section, I have touched on some of the user experience guidelines but have intentionally focused on those that deal with the visual look of the application, leaving more of the behavioral aspects to topics that will be covered elsewhere in this book when I cover the tools available to developers for building great Windows applications. If you want to see these guidelines all in one place or don't want to wait, I encourage you to take a deeper look at the Metro-style apps section of the MSDN web site (`http://msdn.microsoft.com`).

Styling in the Windows 8 User Interface

With the exception of Desktop mode, which is present in Windows 8 running Intel-based processors, the Windows 8 user interface is largely based on Windows style guidelines and principles. Let's start by looking at the Start screen (see Figure 2-18).

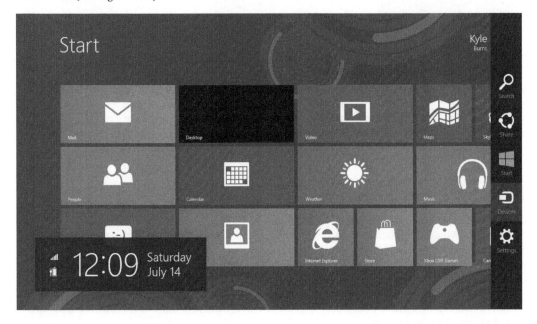

Figure 2-18. *Start screen with charms activated*

The Start screen features a full-screen grid displaying the applications that are most important to the user (indicated by the user selecting the app for inclusion in the Start screen) from which the user selects the application they want to run. This assumes that the first thing the user wants to do is run one of the applications they normally use and is very much laid out to accomplish this very specific task in as efficient a manner as possible. By activating the App Bar (not shown), the user can request that all applications be presented instead of their narrower list of favorites, allowing the user to run any application that is installed on the machine through an additional step. If the user intends not to run an application but to perform some other task such as changing system settings or searching for a file, the user activates the charm bar on the right side of the screen, presenting a list of additional commands.

Earlier in this chapter, you saw how Internet Explorer running from the Start screen is a good example of the flat navigational style. For an example of the hierarchical navigational style, you can look to the Windows Store, where apps are available for purchase or free download. When you enter the application, the Hub is displayed, showing the different categories for which applications are available (see Figure 2-19).

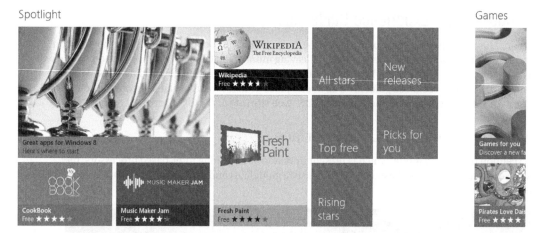

Figure 2-19. *Windows Store Hub page*

From this Hub, users can either directly select certain Detail items or choose to drill down through Section pages.

Throughout the Windows 8 interface and the applications supplied with it, you can see a recurring theme of clean typographic-based interfaces, vibrant colors, and animation to ensure the user perceives the applications as being responsive and providing connectivity to information in other apps and the cloud.

Conclusion

In this chapter, you learned about the Windows Design Language, which is the basis for the Windows 8 user interface and modern Windows applications, and you learned about some of the earlier styles and design paradigms that influenced Windows development. These concepts will remain in either the background or the foreground whenever you are building Windows applications and should influence every design decision you make. Although simple enough in nature that a developer with little design skill can effectively create Windows style user interfaces, the guidelines also provide for much more sophisticated designs created by people skilled in the art and craft of visual design. These skilled designers are encouraged to dive more deeply into Bauhaus, the Swiss style, and Microsoft's user experience design guidelines.

■ ■ ■

CHAPTER 3

Designing Windows 8 Applications

It is easy to fail when designing an interactive experience. Designers fail when they do not know the audience, integrate the threads of content and context, welcome the public properly, or make clear what the experience is and what the audience's role in it will be.

—Edwin Schlossberg

In a "perfect" world, application developers are handed clear, concise packets of paper that lay out exactly how their application should look and everything that it should do. They work from that paper, which from their perspective may have spontaneously generated itself, and produce a working and useful application. While many developers have managed to find such a world, to the majority of people who make their living writing code, this arrangement seems as unattainable as reaching Shangri-La.

Developers who are not handed a completed design have to become more than someone who translates requirements to code and instead have to take on what I view as the much more difficult and interesting task of designing software. This chapter is for developers who either by choice or by necessity will take part in the design of Windows 8 applications and is intended to provide an overview of important steps in this process. In it, I will introduce important concepts related to deciding what an application should do and how it should be presented to the user. My primary focus in this chapter is gathering requirements that serve as the input to the design, because a novice designer who fully understands the problems that need to be solved by an application can produce a more useful application than a skilled designer who does not.

■ **Note** There are many different methodologies for gathering requirements and for designing and building software. While some of the terminology I use in this chapter may lean toward one methodology or another, my intent is to capture concepts that are important and relevant regardless of the methodology (if any) you use to build your software.

Communication Is Key

A colleague of mine once told me that in the development of applications, no truth should be considered self-evident. Years later, this was reinforced by a conversation that I had with a relative. This relative started a conversation by saying "I have a friend who is doing court reporting and needs software to help. How long would something like that take to build?" I started to reply with "You just asked how long it would take to build...," and he quickly interjected, "But I didn't tell you what the darn thing needs to do!" Often, a conversation like this reveals the disconnect between what the person asking has in mind and what the person building the software hears, but in an atypical twist, the relative picked up on something that many business partners have not – namely that if you want something built, you need to clearly communicate your requirements. Figure 3-1 illustrates this disconnect, often referred to as *impedance mismatch*.

Figure 3-1. *Impedence mismatch*

The primary cause of the impedance mismatch that causes developers to often build what is asked for instead of what is needed is that everyone involved in the process sees their own view very clearly and cannot imagine how someone else could see things any differently. The impedance mismatch can be reduced, if not avoided altogether, by starting the design process with an acknowledgment that people will have varying understandings for different topics and by committing to an environment where nothing is taken for granted.

■ **Note**   Developers not participating in building software as part of a team should still separate the roles of developer and user in their minds to force themselves to look at things from the vantage point of the user. Here, forcing yourself to mentally "explain" everything as if trying to avoid impedance mismatch will help uncover hidden requirements.

What Should the Application Be Good At?

It may seem like an obvious point, but the first thing to determine when beginning the task of designing your application is to determine the purpose that it serves. At this point, specifics are not necessary; just create a general statement or description of the application that clearly states the use or purpose of the application. A well-designed application will have one thing that it is really good at, especially Windows 8 applications, which, as you will learn in Chapter 17, can work together to solve problems larger than what each individual application's developers envisioned. It's good to use a template statement such as "This application will _____ so that _____" to help focus your thoughts not only on *what* the application will do but also on *why* the application will do it or the benefit that it provides. If I am building an application to track the gas mileage of a vehicle, the statement may be something like "This application will calculate the fuel economy of a vehicle so that I can better anticipate my fuel costs."

■ **Note**   Be sure to document the high-level purpose of your application in a manner that will be very visible throughout the design and development. This forms the backbone of your application, and you will often refer to it as you decide whether a piece of functionality belongs in the application. If it isn't required for some sort of legal or regulatory means and does not contribute to the application's stated purpose, then it does not belong in the application.

Identify Functional Requirements

Once the primary purpose of the application has been identified as a sort of guiding principle, the work of identifying the requirements necessary to support the primary purpose, known as *functional requirements*, begins. Depending on the type of application you are building and the availability of others to participate in the requirements process, several techniques exist to discover or elicit requirements. Some of the more regularly practiced techniques include the following:

- *Interviewing*: Stakeholders, or people who have some sort of interest either in the software being produced or in the output or benefit produced by the software, are consulted to learn what they expect and need out of the application. During the interview, stakeholders should feel that they can freely express their wants and needs without being told they can't have anything in order to make sure they don't stay quiet about critical requirements.

- *Brainstorming*: Stakeholders and members of the design team work together to come up with ideas for requirements. This session begins with an "anything goes" atmosphere for the same reason stakeholders are not discouraged from voicing wants and needs using the interviewing technique. Brainstorming sessions are often most effective when all of the participants can be in the same room at the same time with tools such as whiteboards and sticky notes available, but a disciplined team can also accomplish this remotely using teleconferencing tools. The key is to get everybody focused and actively participating at the same time.

- *Process mapping*: Existing processes are walked through and thoroughly documented to capture all of the steps that are carried out to meet the goal. This technique requires an existing process and works best when each step can be subjected to scrutiny. It's not enough to know what is currently done, but the motivations behind each step and how it contributes to meeting the end goal are also critical to understand.

■ **Note**   "We've always" and "we've never" are two phrases that can lead to an organization that never improves unless the organization is willing to add "until now" to sentences when starting a beneficial activity or stopping one that brings no value is necessary. This brings to mind an old tale of a woman who was taught by her mother to begin preparing a roast by cutting 1 inch off of each end, just as was done by the woman's grandmother. When the grandmother came for dinner, she noticed her granddaughter cutting the ends off the roast and asked why she was doing that. "Grandma, that's the way you always made yours." The grandmother just laughed and replied, "But my pan was 2 inches too short." Software projects are an excellent opportunity to ask "why" and ensure similar situations don't exist in your organization.

Evaluate Identified Requirements

The techniques for identifying requirements all specify that care be taken not to discourage communication of any requirement that seems important or valid to any stakeholder or member of the team. This doesn't mean that every identified requirement can or should be implemented in the finished product, just that they should all be available to evaluate. Once the realm of potential requirements has been identified, the next step is to review each requirement for appropriateness. The determining factor for appropriateness is simple and straightforward. If you can directly (and honestly) communicate how fulfilling the requirement is necessary to allow the application to meet its goal, the requirement is appropriate. The exception to this rule is that some requirements are driven by outside forces such as contractual obligations and regulatory requirements, and these must be met regardless of whether they contribute to meeting the application's higher-level goal. Figure 3-2 illustrates the decision process used to decide whether to promote a potential requirement to a requirement that will be implemented.

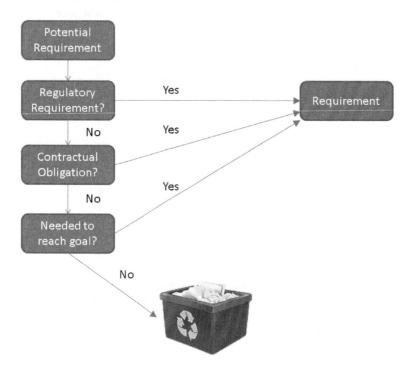

Figure 3-2. *Potential requirement to requirement decision*

Another measurement that is often used to determine whether a potential requirement should become promoted to an actual requirement is to categorize the items as either "must have," "nice to have," or "don't need." The idea is that "must have" items become requirements, "don't need" items are excluded from consideration, and "nice to have" items get considered if additional resources are available after the "must have" items are accounted for. I don't generally like to use this ranking pattern because I prefer an approach to software design and development that calls for spending time, effort, and ultimately dollars only on those items that fall into the "must have" category. In general, I view potential requirements as only "must have" items and "don't need" items, and "don't need" items should not be implemented.

■ **Note** Practitioners of Agile methodologies tend to express requirements in what is called a *user story*. The user story often takes some form of the statement "As a _____, I need the system to _____ so that _____." While the term *user story* is specific to certain methodologies, the idea of identifying the key stakeholder and purpose for each requirement is a valuable practice for any methodology.

The act of measuring requirements against the purpose of the application is not just an exercise in keeping the application true to purpose, but it is also intended to help maintain balance between the three key factors that drive any project whether it is building software or a skyscraper.

- *Time*: When must the project be complete in order to meet organizational goals?

- *Money*: How much can be spent?

- *Scope*: What is the body of work to be completed?

These three factors are often depicted in what is known as the *project management triangle*, as illustrated in Figure 3-3. The triangle is a great way to depict the relationship between these factors because like the sides of the triangle, one cannot be changed without impacting the other two. For example, if more money is available, additional developers may be hired, and the time required to complete the project will be shortened. Often, the easiest way to rein in a software development project is to keep firm control over the scope.

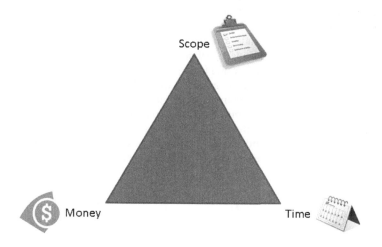

Figure 3-3. *Project management triangle*

In some projects, the "must have" items can't all fit into scope because the project is constrained on time, money, or both. In these cases, the project must be evaluated to determine whether there are items that need to be implemented but can wait for a later time. This prioritization process is a time to really think critically about needs and can make the difference between being able to produce something of value or having to scrap the project because of the requirements process stalling out.

Decompose Requirements

Once the requirements necessary for the application to meet its goals have been identified, an iterative process called *decomposition* begins. Decomposition in software development is when a large problem is broken into individual steps. With iterative decomposition, the steps are then themselves broken into smaller pieces, and this continues either until there is nothing left to break down or until you're "done." *Done* is a bit of a subjective term, but I view it as having reached the point where a developer familiar with the project should have every expectation of being able to sit down and use the requirement as a blueprint for building the application. In organizations where the developers are very familiar with the problems that they are solving, "done" will not be decomposed to nearly as granular a level as when the development work will be performed by developers who are not as familiar with the problems that need to be solved.

■ **Note** Decomposition is an important way to turn big problems that are daunting into a bunch of little problems that are easily solved. Remember the saying about how to eat an elephant: "one bite at a time."

Build Interaction Flows

Up until this point, all of the focus has been on what needs to be accomplished by the application as a whole, and you should have a good idea of what information needs to come into and out of the application to meet those requirements. Once those needs are established, you can turn your attention to determining how the user can most effectively get that information into and out of the application. Here for the first time you start to think about the idea of a screen, but it is still a bit of an amorphous concept because you are trying to determine what goes where. At this point in the design process, I typically prefer to avoid language that suggests decisions have been made about how the screen will be laid out and with what kind of controls. I favor phrases like "and then the user selects the save action" over "and then the user clicks the save button." It's a subtle turn of phrase, but it leaves the focus at this point on determining the sequence of steps needed to accomplish the application's goals and how to organize information into screens for the users' interactions. Coming out of this step, you should have a good idea of what screens the application will have and what will trigger movement between these screens. Figure 3-4 shows a navigation diagram, which is a useful document to help define and document these flows. In it, you clearly see the views that are anticipated within the application and how the user will move between them.

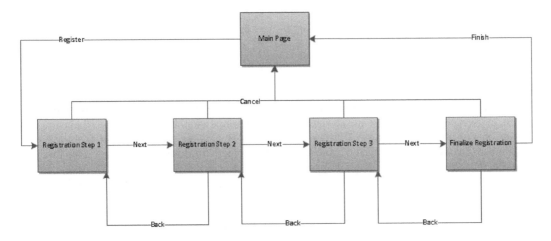

Figure 3-4. Navigation diagram

Wireframes

Once the team has settled on the flow of the application, it's time to work on wireframes. Wireframes are low-fidelity sketches of the application screen that focus on what information and commands the screens will hold rather than worrying about making them pretty and getting bogged down in aesthetic details. Wireframes may be captured on the back of a napkin, a whiteboard (be sure to take a picture), or via tools such as Visio, Balsamic, or SketchFlow in Expression Blend. This is the step where you decide what type of controls will be most effective for the user to interact with the application. In a Windows 8 application, the wireframes should reflect full-screen experiences where the user can focus on content. Figure 3-5 illustrates a sample wireframe. Notice how no effort was put into making it look like a Windows application; it instead focuses on the information and what will happen with different interactions.

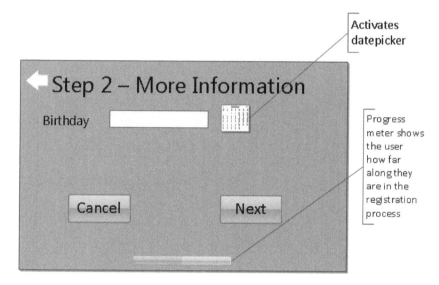

Figure 3-5. *Wireframe*

Visual Design

After the wireframes for the application are agreed upon, some project teams will pass the wireframes to a visual designer, who will use a tool such as Microsoft's Expression Blend to turn the ideas in the wireframes into a visually appealing interface. Ideally, the designer will follow the guidelines in the Windows Design Language and the Swiss design style to produce an application that has a consistent look and feel with other Windows 8 applications. Because Expression Blend is XAML-based and its projects are compatible with Visual Studio, the designer's work can become the base on which the developer adds code to create a finished application.

More often than not, teams will not have a dedicated visual designer. They may have a developer who has a better eye for design than the other developers on the team, or the visual design may just be left up to chance. Unlike like some design paradigms, using the new Windows design guidelines actually gives a developer who is not artistically inclined a chance at creating an appealing user interface. Additionally, Microsoft includes built-in styles in the project templates that can be used to help ensure the application has the new Windows look and feel. These styles will be discussed in Chapter 7.

Conclusion

In this chapter, I briefly introduced many of the concepts and steps that go into designing an application. While the focus has been on what this looks like when the process is executed by a team, all the steps are valid for you to consider when you are working as a team of one creating your applications. The important thing to remember is that with rare exception, great applications are intentional. They are first defined, and then designed, and only when these two are complete are they built. Microsoft has provided guidance for the new Windows-style applications that eases the task of the visual design, but in order to produce an application that is suitable for its intended purpose, the work of requirement definition still must be completed in as thorough a manner as possible.

CHAPTER 4

■ ■ ■

Visual Studio 2012 and Windows Store Application Types

Our environment, the world in which we live and work, is a mirror of our attitudes and expectations.

—Earl Nightingale

In application development, the integrated development environment (IDE) can make the difference between feeling like you can work easily and focus on the problem your application is supposed to solve and feeling like you are so distracted trying to figure out how to maneuver within the IDE that you cannot focus on the real task of producing software. With the last several versions of Visual Studio, Microsoft has increasingly built upon a reputation of having one of the best development IDEs available. Even many developers who don't care to develop for the Microsoft platform will say (if grudgingly) that one is hard-pressed to find a better development environment. In this chapter, you will learn about Visual Studio 2012, which is the latest release in this line-up. While complete coverage of the tools and features would take a book of its own, I will cover in this chapter the topics that I consider to be important to finding your way around the environment well enough to complete the exercises in this book. In addition to learning about Visual Studio in general, you will also learn about the project templates that are used to develop applications designed to run on Windows 8.

Visual Studio Editions

Visual Studio is often used generically to describe the IDE for developing applications built on Microsoft platforms, but rather than a single product, it designates an entire line of products. Including the freely available Express editions, the Visual Studio 2012 line-up includes the following:

- Visual Studio Express 2012 for Windows 8

- Visual Studio Express 2012 for Web

- Visual Studio Express 2012 for Windows Desktop

- Visual Studio Test Professional 2012

- Visual Studio Professional 2012

- Visual Studio Premium 2012

- Visual Studio Ultimate 2012

Visual Studio Express 2012 for Windows Phone 8 has not been released at the time of this writing, but Microsoft has announced that it will be added to the Visual Studio line-up upon the release of Windows Phone 8.

The Visual Studio Express 2012 editions each provide an environment to develop applications for different portions of the Microsoft stack that can be used without having to invest in one of the full Visual Studio 2012 products. Visual Studio Express 2012 for Windows 8 is focused on providing the necessary tools to build and test Windows applications as well as providing support for sharing and selling your applications in the Windows Store. Visual Studio Express 2012 for Windows 8 is sufficient for completing the exercises in this book, and features available in this edition will be the focus of discussion in this chapter. The following are key features of Visual Studio Express for Windows 8:

- Basic analysis of code for errors or practices that could prevent Windows Store certification

- Integrated debugger

- Simulator for running Windows applications

- Profiler to help identify code that requires tuning

- Unit testing support

With the exception of Visual Studio Test Professional 2012, which is designed for people assigned to the testing role in an application development organization, the non-Express editions of Visual Studio 2012 are designed for professional developers. Visual Studio Professional 2012, Visual Studio Premium 2012, and Visual Studio Ultimate 2012 each progressively add features to assist in the following areas of application development:

- Design

- Construction

- Testing

- Analysis

- Troubleshooting

You can find a full comparison of the features that come with each Visual Studio 2012 edition at www.microsoft.com/visualstudio. You can also find Visual Studio Express 2012 for Windows 8 at this site. If you do not already have a Visual Studio 2012 edition installed, I encourage you to install Visual Studio Express 2012 for Windows 8 before reading further.

Getting Started with Visual Studio

When you first open Visual Studio 2012 Express, the default view appears, as shown in Figure 4-1. The most important features in the user interface at this point are the menu bar (labeled A in the figure) and the Start Page (labeled B). The menu bar provides access to many commands, but when first opening Visual Studio, you are most likely going to head for the File menu (shown in Figure 4-2) where you will select either New Project or Open Project. The Start Page offers links to items of interest to developers such as articles on how to be more productive in Visual Studio or perform certain development tasks.

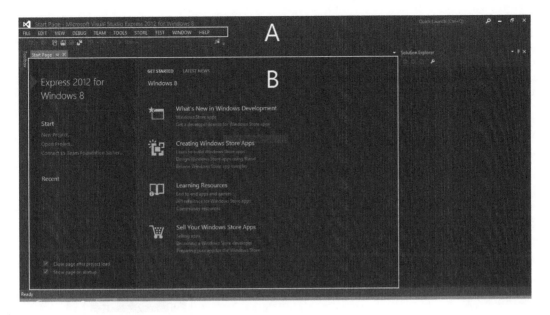

Figure 4-1. Visual Studio initial user interface

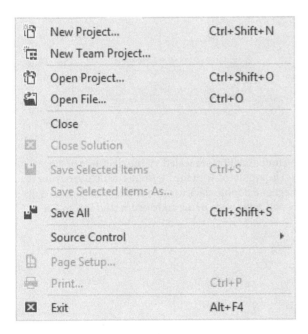

Figure 4-2. File menu

Selecting New Project from the File menu opens the New Project dialog, as shown in Figure 4-3. This dialog presents available project types that are grouped into categories on the left side of the window. Selecting a category shows a listing of the project types within that category in the center section of the window. At the bottom of the windows are fields to assign a name to the project, the location of the project on disk, and the name for a solution to create and add the project to. Solutions are not covered in this book, so at this point I will just describe them as a collection of related projects that are opened and worked with at the same time. The option to create new projects within a solution is enabled by default because many applications will separate the business logic, the data access code, and the code used to present an interface to the user into their own projects to help create a clean division of these duties. Another common use for solutions is to have a separate project within the solution to test the application.

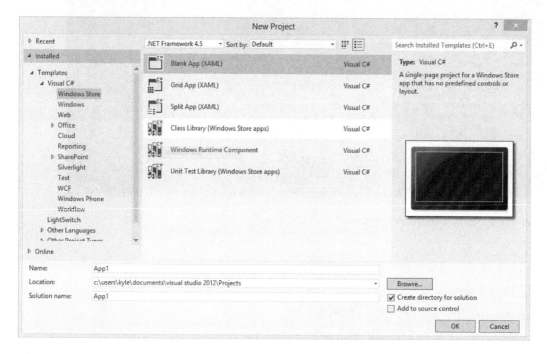

Figure 4-3. *New Project dialog*

Once a project has been created or opened, additional functionality is revealed. At the right side of the screen, the Solution Explorer window (shown in Figure 4-4) is populated with the file/folder structure of your project, allowing you to navigate to any file within the project and double-click to open either a designer or a code editor depending on the type of file. Figure 4-5 shows app.xaml open in the code editor, and Figure 4-6 shows MainPage.xaml open in a designer.

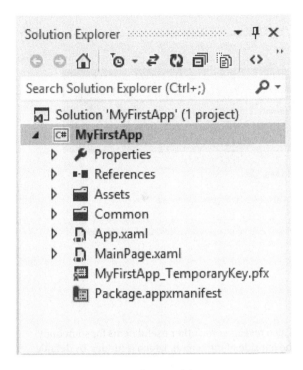

Figure 4-4. *Solution Explorer window*

```
App.xaml.cs  ⊕ X
MyFirstApp.App                                                    ⊕ App()
  using System;
  using System.Collections.Generic;
  using System.IO;
  using System.Linq;
  using Windows.ApplicationModel;
  using Windows.ApplicationModel.Activation;
  using Windows.Foundation;
  using Windows.Foundation.Collections;
  using Windows.UI.Xaml;
  using Windows.UI.Xaml.Controls;
  using Windows.UI.Xaml.Controls.Primitives;
  using Windows.UI.Xaml.Data;
  using Windows.UI.Xaml.Input;
  using Windows.UI.Xaml.Media;
  using Windows.UI.Xaml.Navigation;

  // The Blank Application template is documented at http://go.microsoft.com/fwlink/?LinkId=234227

  namespace MyFirstApp
  {
      /// <summary>
      /// Provides application-specific behavior to supplement the default Application class.
      /// </summary>
      sealed partial class App : Application
      {
          /// <summary>
          /// Initializes the singleton application object.  This is the first line of authored code
```

Figure 4-5. *Code editor*

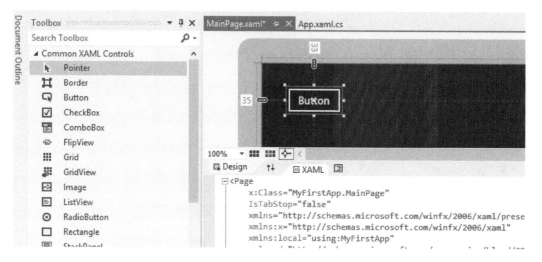

Figure 4-6. *XAML designer*

In addition to showing the XAML designer, Figure 4-6 also reveals some other useful items for somebody learning their way around Visual Studio. The Toolbox on the left side of the screen, which is hidden by default but can be shown by clicking the word *Toolbox*, contains controls that can be dragged onto the design surface to build your screens. Additionally, you may find that dragging controls onto the design surface does not give you enough control over the XAML created by the designer, so you instead might desire to create all or part of the XAML by hand. The designer defaults to a "split view," which enables you to both work directly with the XAML and use the drag-and-drop functionality of the designer. In most real-world applications, you are likely to find yourself using a combination of these two methods.

The Properties window, shown in Figure 4-7, contains different content based on what is actively selected within Visual Studio. If the actively selected item is a control within the XAML designer, the properties and events attached to that control are displayed. If the selected item is a file within the Solution Explorer, the attributes of the selected file are displayed. The Properties window has a convenient feature, a search box, which will filter the displayed items in the list to those whose name contains the criteria entered in the search box. For controls with a significant number of properties, this feature will be a great time-saver over scrolling through the list looking for a particular property name.

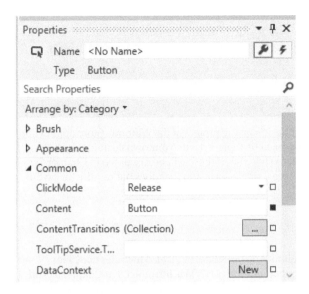

Figure 4-7. Properties window

The final user interface element I will discuss in this chapter is the Debug button on the toolbar, which is shown in Figure 4-8. This button is used to initiate a build and debugging session of your application within either your local machine, the built-in Windows 8 simulator, or a remote machine on your network. By activating the drop-down in this button, you can change the default runtime environment for your application. In general, I prefer to run my applications in the simulator because it gives me easy access to do things such as change orientation and capture screenshots.

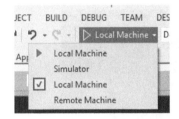

Figure 4-8. Debug button

I have just guided you through a whirlwind tour of the Visual Studio interface, stopping only to show you those features that you will need to successfully work in this book. I strongly encourage you to explore the different windows, menus, and options that are available within Visual Studio and learn how each can help with your development tasks.

Windows Store Application Types

In this section, I will cover the different application types that you can create using the project templates that ship with Visual Studio 2012. You can find these templates in the New Project dialog categorized under Installed ➤ Templates ➤ Visual C# ➤ Windows Store. I will cover only application types, so the following Windows Store project templates, which are beyond the scope of this book, will not be covered:

- Class Library (Windows Store apps)

- Windows Runtime Component

- Unit Test Library (Windows Store apps)

Blank App (XAML)

Blank App is the template that provides you with the most basic starting project of the Windows Store application project template. The project includes a starting set of images to be replaced with your own custom images for the application's logo and splash screen as well as a standard style sheet (these will be discussed in Chapter 7) and a blank page. This project type works well when you have a single-page app that does not require the layout provided by the other templates.

Grid App (XAML)

The Grid App template gives everything provided by the Blank App template, but it also includes code files establishing a basic Model-View-ViewModel (MVVM) implementation (MVVM is introduced in Chapter 9) and provides the screens and application code for an application that drills down through varying levels of detail to browse hierarchical data. The application consists of three pages: a high-level view that shows all groups with a summarized view of the items within each group (illustrated in Figure 4-9), a group detail page that provides additional information about the group and a listing of the items that it contains (illustrated in Figure 4-10), and an item detail page that gives the finest level of detail on a single item within the group (illustrated in Figure 4-11). As you can see in the figures, this project template provides an application that has been practically prebuilt for you, requiring only that you modify it to fit your data. This project type will be the basis for an application that you will start building in Chapter 7 and continue to build across several chapters as you learn more concepts that can be applied to the application.

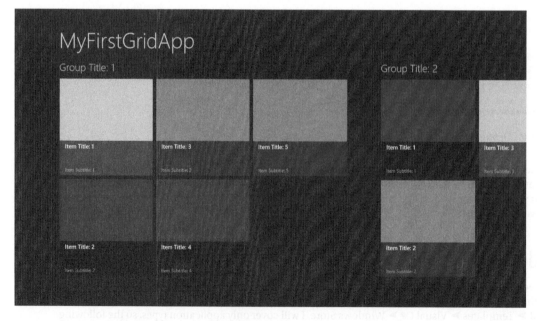

Figure 4-9. *Default Grid App grouped items view*

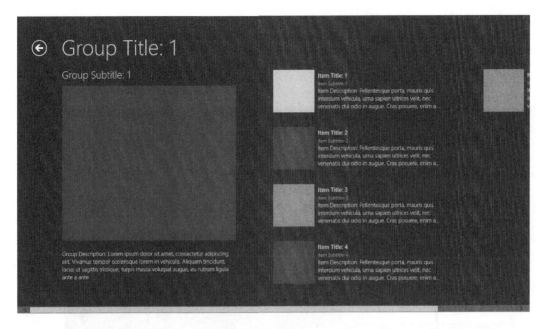

Figure 4-10. *Default Grid App group details view*

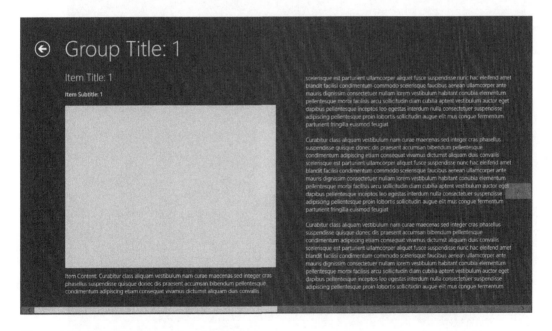

Figure 4-11. *Default Grid App item details view*

Split App (XAML)

The Split App project template, like Grid App, provides a ready-made application designed to browse hierarchical data. The main difference between Grid App and Split App is that Split App uses only two views to display the information. The first view, which is shown in Figure 4-12, displays a list of the groups into which items are categorized. Unlike Grid App, this view contains information only about the groups and does not display any item information. Selecting any group navigates to that group's item screen (shown in Figure 4-13), which provides a listing of the items in the group on the left side of the screen and shows the details of the selected item on the right side of the screen.

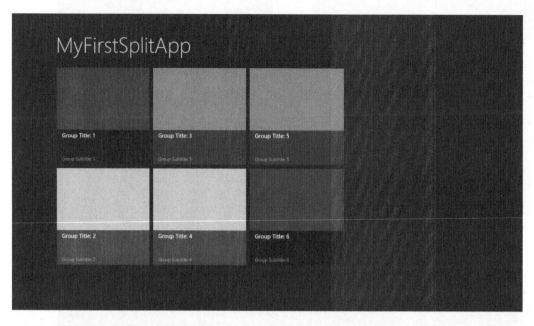

Figure 4-12. *Default Split App group view*

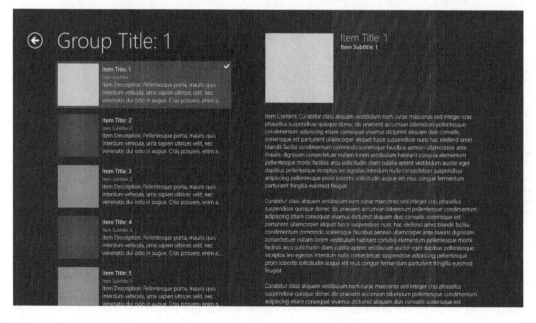

Figure 4-13. *Default Split App items view*

Conclusion

In this chapter, you were introduced to Visual Studio 2012 and to the Windows Store application types that can be built using the built-in project templates. For further learning, examine some existing Windows 8 applications with the Grid App and Split App templates in mind. You may be surprised at how often you see components of these two approaches. For example, the News and Store apps installed with Windows 8 both take the Grid App approach, while the People app was designed based on the Split App template.

CHAPTER 5

■ ■ ■

XAML Controls in the Visual Studio Toolbox: The Common Controls

The expectations of life depend upon diligence; the mechanic that would perfect his work must first sharpen his tools.

—Confucius

One of the keys to becoming a productive developer on any technology stack is to fully understand the tools available to you on that platform. When developing Windows applications using C# and XAML, these tools include the following:

- The C# language features

- The APIs available under the Windows Runtime

- The controls in the Visual Studio Toolbox

In this chapter, I will focus on the controls in the Visual Studio Toolbox and, more specifically, pay attention to the user interface controls that are by default presented on the Common tab. I will focus in detail on these controls because they can be leveraged together to meet the user interface needs of many Windows applications. For each control, I will discuss the following:

- The purpose of the control

- Common usage scenarios

- Important properties and methods of the control

- The XAML used to add the control to a page

Windows design principles and the default functionality of each control are so well aligned that developers can build compelling user interfaces without having to take advantage of the rich customization options presented by XAML controls. Because of this, I will discuss only those aspects of each control that you are likely to encounter regularly as you begin writing Windows applications. Topics covered in this chapter should be considered foundational, so be sure to use the information as a starting point and explore on your own.

Grid

A Grid control in almost any XAML development environment, including WPF, Silverlight, and Windows 8, is not to be confused with the control featured in Figure 5-1, which is more in line with what would be referred to with a name such as DataGrid or DataGridView in some environments and does not exist at all in the tools provided with Visual Studio for Windows development.

Name	Quest	FavoriteColor	
Maecenas cras aenean mauris	Aenean class nam	Nam sed aliquam	▲
Nam nullam	Curae mauris	Integer maecenas quisque	
Praesent aliquam class	Maecenas aliquam integer	Dis vivamus	
Sed integer dis	Sed praesent quisque cras	Mauris est	
			▼

Figure 5-1. *This is not a Grid*

So, now that I have established that a Grid is not what probably came to mind when you saw the word, what is a Grid? The Grid is a member of a class of controls known as *layout controls* or *panels*, whose purpose is to provide a container responsible for the layout and arrangement of controls that they contain. Grids handle layout concerns by establishing one or more rows and columns into which other controls are placed. Each contained control, by default, will be in row 0 and column 0, with the developer or designer laying out the page and needing to specify a nondefault value to land the control in the desired location. Figure 5-2 illustrates a Grid with three rows and four columns ready to be used to lay out content. It is possible to configure the Grid to display gridlines as shown in the figure, but in most cases, a designer would choose not to actually display the lines.

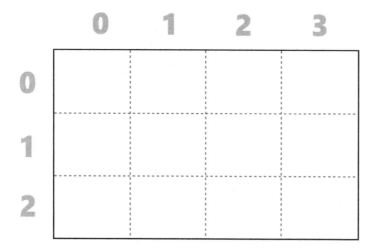

Figure 5-2. *Empty Grid*

The Grid panel is the default layout control in new Windows application pages and provides an excellent balance between effort and control by allowing you a good deal of control over how controls are arranged in relationship to each other without requiring you to specify exact coordinates for each element. In addition to the ease of use, the concept of using a grid layout is very familiar to designers aware of Swiss style. This makes translation from a designer's proofs to a functional page smooth for many Windows designs.

These are some properties that are commonly specified for a Grid control:

- Height and Width: These properties control the size of the container. If these properties are not specified by the page author, the control will size itself appropriately to contain all of its content. When the Height or Width property is specified, any content that would push beyond these bounds is clipped and not displayed.

- Background: This property controls the Brush that is used for the background of the control. Notice that the term Brush is used as opposed to *color*. This is because the Windows Runtime API defines a Brush as an abstract class that defines how a region is to be painted. A Brush is not limited to a solid color but can be configured to output complex renderings such as gradients and images.

- DataContext: This property does not impact the way the control looks but can be important when used with data binding, which I will discuss in Chapter 8.

- ColumnDefinitions: This property contains a collection of ColumnDefinition objects describing the number of columns as well as their sizes.

- RowDefinitions: This property contains a collection of RowDefinition objects describing the number of rows as well as their sizes.

While you are able to place a Grid on a page using a single Grid element, it really makes no sense to have a Grid without the rows and columns that make it useful. The following XAML snippet demonstrates placing a Grid with three rows and four columns onto a page:

```
<Grid x:Name="LayoutRoot" Background="White" Width="500" Height="300">
    <Grid.ColumnDefinitions>
        <ColumnDefinition />
        <ColumnDefinition />
        <ColumnDefinition />
        <ColumnDefinition />
    </Grid.ColumnDefinitions>
    <Grid.RowDefinitions>
        <RowDefinition />
        <RowDefinition />
        <RowDefinition />
    </Grid.RowDefinitions>
</Grid>
```

Placing controls within the Grid requires placing additional controls within the <Grid> </Grid> pair, specifying the Grid.Row and Grid.Column properties to the zero-based desired position. For example, if I want to place a TextBlock in the second column of the third row, I could add the following within the grid:

```
<TextBlock Foreground="Black" Grid.Row="2" Grid.Column="1" Text="App Title"
           FontFamily="Segoe UI" FontSize="48" />
```

If you're following along in a XAML editor, you likely discovered in the preceding code that you did indeed place the TextBlock where you desired, but there was also an undesired effect. The text within the TextBlock was cut off at the end of the column that contains it, as shown in Figure 5-3.

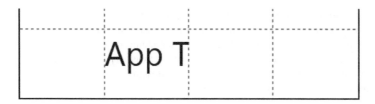

Figure 5-3. *Grid columns cut off content*

This leads me to the final set of properties that I will discuss with regard to the Grid control. When placing content on the Grid, in addition to specifying the Grid.Row and Grid.Column properties, you can also designate that the content will expand beyond the bounds of its contained row and/or column by using the Grid.RowSpan and Grid.ColumnSpan properties. The visual effect originally desired (show in Figure 5-4) is achieved by changing the XAML you used to place the TextBlock on the grid to look like this:

```
<TextBlock Foreground="Black" Grid.Row="2" Grid.Column="1" Grid.ColumnSpan="2"
           Text="App Title" FontFamily="Segoe UI" FontSize="48" />
```

Figure 5-4. Grid.ColumnSpan *allows content to remain visible across columns*

StackPanel

Like the Grid, the StackPanel is a layout control. Unlike the Grid, which requires you to declare the number of rows and columns initially, the StackPanel is used to lay out its contained controls in a linear manner across either a vertical or horizontal plane—one after another until they are all displayed.

The StackPanel has the advantage of being a bit simpler to use than the Grid because the developer does not have to declare the position of each control. This may seem trivial, but in cases where the potential exists for a grid with even as little as tens of rows and columns, the act of inserting a new control or controls somewhere in the middle (or even the beginning, for that matter) of the layout requires updating the RowDefinitions or ColumnDefinitions property of the Grid as well as the Grid.Row or Grid.Column property of each control that is being displaced by the addition of the new control. This makes StackPanel ideal for situations that don't have the layout requirements to make using a Grid necessary.

These are some properties that are commonly specified for a StackPanel control:

- Height and Width: These properties control the size of the container. If these properties are not specified by the page author, the control will size itself appropriately to contain all of its content. When Height or Width is specified, any content that would push beyond these bounds is clipped and not displayed.

- Background: This property controls the Brush that is used for the background of the control.

- DataContext: This property does not impact the way the control looks but can be important when used with data binding, which I will discuss in a later chapter.

- Orientation: This property controls whether the StackPanel expands along a vertical plane, which is its default, or along a horizontal plane.

Because StackPanel does not require the type of layout declaration needed by Grid, placing a StackPanel onto a page is as easy as using the following XAML:

```
<StackPanel Background="White" Orientation="Vertical">
</StackPanel>
```

I've included Orientation = "Vertical" in the XAML to make the orientation clear to the user, but because Vertical is the default value, it doesn't necessarily have to be specified at all in this case. To arrange controls within the StackPanel, we simply include them in the XAML between the < StackPanel > </StackPanel > tags, as in the following XAML:

```
<StackPanel Background="White" Orientation="Vertical">
        <TextBlock Text="Text Block 1" FontFamily="Segoe UI" FontSize="24" />
        <TextBlock Text="Text Block 2" FontFamily="Segoe UI" FontSize="24" />
        <TextBlock Text="..." FontFamily="Segoe UI" FontSize="24" />
        <TextBlock Text="Text Block 100" FontFamily="Segoe UI" FontSize="24" />
</StackPanel>
```

The controls will then be laid out in the order that they appeared in the XAML, as in Figure 5-5.

Text Block 1
Text Block 2
...
Text Block 100

Figure 5-5. StackPanel with Vertical orientation

By changing Orientation = "Vertical" to Orientation = "Horizontal", you change the flow of the display and end up looking more like Figure 5-6.

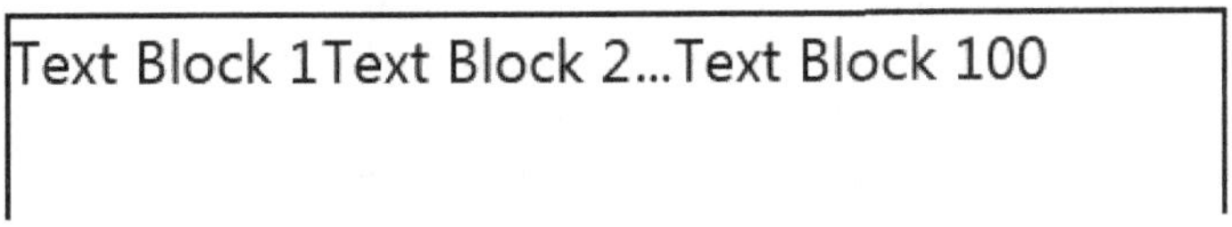

Text Block 1Text Block 2...Text Block 100

Figure 5-6. StackPanel with Horizontal orientation

One very common usage pattern for StackPanel is to nest StackPanel instances within another StackPanel, often using different orientations. For example, if I wanted to create a data entry form, I might use the following XAML to achieve the result shown in Figure 5-7:

```
<StackPanel Background="White" Orientation="Horizontal">
    <StackPanel Orientation="Vertical" Margin="5">
        <TextBlock Text="Last Name" FontFamily="Segoe UI" FontSize="24" />
        <TextBox />
    </StackPanel>
```

```
    <StackPanel Orientation="Vertical" Margin="5">
        <TextBlock Text="First Name" FontFamily="Segoe UI" FontSize="24" />
        <TextBox />
    </StackPanel>
</StackPanel>
```

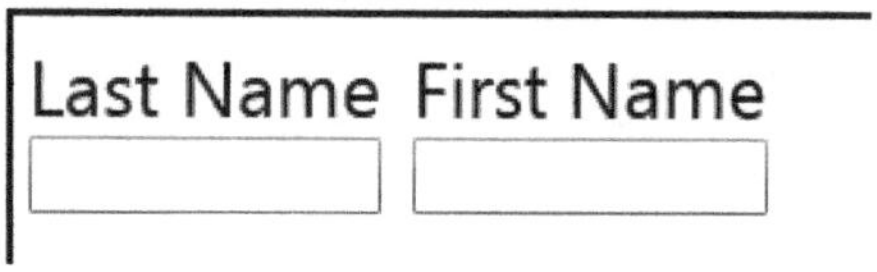

Last Name First Name

Figure 5-7. *Nested StackPanels*

Border

Border acts as a parent containing only one child control. The purpose of Border, as its name suggests, is to draw a border around the contained control. The most common usage scenario for Border is to provide a visual separation between the control within the border and other elements on the screen or—in the case where the single child element is a layout control containing children of its own—to stress that elements within the border are to be considered a logical group.

These are the properties that are most commonly specified for Border:

- Height and Width: These properties control the size of the container. If these properties are not specified by the page author, the control will size itself appropriately to contain all of its content. When Height or Width is specified, any content that would push beyond these bounds is clipped and not displayed.

- Background: This property controls the Brush that is used for the background of the control.

- BorderBrush: This property controls the Brush that is used to paint the outside border of the control.

- BorderThickness: This property controls the thickness of the outside border of the control. When a single value is specified, such as BorderThickness = "5", the specified double is used as the thickness in pixels of all four edges. Alternatively, the syntax BorderThickness = "5, 2, 5, 2" can be used to specify a different value for each edge. These values are evaluated in this order: left, top, right, bottom. If the opposing sides share values as in the previous example, only two values can be provided using the syntax BorderThickness = "5, 2". In this case, the first value is applied to the left and right edges, while the second is applied to the top and bottom.

- CornerRadius: This property controls the degree to which the four corners of the Border are rounded. When a single value is specified, such as CornerRadius = "10", it is used as the radius for each of the four corners. Alternatively, each corner radius can be specified individually using the syntax CornerRadius = "1, 1, 2, 3". When all four values are specified, they are evaluated in this order: top left, top right, bottom right, bottom left.

A Border can be placed on a page using the following XAML:

```
<Border BorderBrush="Black"
        CornerRadius="10" BorderThickness="4"
        Width="100" Height="35">
</Border>
```

This causes a border to be rendered on the page similar to what is shown in Figure 5-8.

Figure 5-8. *A Border without contents*

Put into a more realistic context, the following XAML will be rendered on the page as shown in Figure 5-9:

```
<Border BorderBrush="Black"
        CornerRadius="5" BorderThickness="2"
        Width="100" Height="65">
    <StackPanel>
        <RadioButton Content="Option 1" />
        <RadioButton Content="Option 2" />
        <RadioButton Content="Option 3" />
    </StackPanel>
</Border>
```

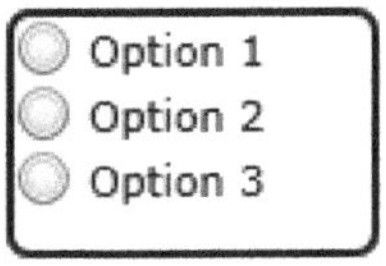

○ Option 1
○ Option 2
○ Option 3

Figure 5-9. *A Border grouping RadioButtons*

TextBlock

The TextBlock control is used to place blocks of read-only text on a page. This could very well be the most commonly used control in the XAML toolbox because whenever you see text on a XAML page, it is most likely contained in a TextBlock.

These are the properties that are most commonly specified for TextBlock:

- FontFamily: This property specifies the font that is to be used to render the text.

- FontSize: This property specifies the font size of the text.

- Foreground: This property specifies the Brush that will be used to paint the text.

The following XAML can be placed on a page to render the TextBlock shown in Figure 5-10:

```
<TextBlock Foreground="Black"
           Text="The quick brown fox..."
           FontFamily="Segoe UI" FontSize="48" />
```

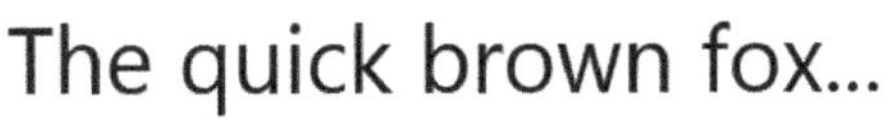

The quick brown fox...

Figure 5-10. *Basic TextBlock*

TextBox

The TextBox control is used to display text that the user can interact with, performing actions such as editing the text or copying it to the clipboard. It is used whenever a free-form response is needed from the user, such as answering the question "What is your name?" In the touch-first world of a Windows app, it is important to realize that the end user may not have a physical keyboard. This means you should expect the user to have to exert greater effort to type an answer than to pick one from a list, and therefore you should not require typing when picking is an option.

These are the properties that you will most commonly use with TextBox:

- FontFamily: This property is used to specify the font that will be used to render the text within the control.

- FontSize: This property is used to specify the size of the text within the control.

- IsEnabled: This property indicates whether the user can interact with the control in any way.

- IsReadOnly: This property indicates whether the contents in the control should be protected from editing.

- IsSpellCheckEnabled: This property indicates whether the text entered into the control should have spell-checking performed upon it.

- IsTextPredictionEnabled: This property indicates whether the user should be presented with autocompletion options for words while they are typing. Using this feature can be a great help to reducing the effort your user has to exert when typing on an on-screen keyboard or with their thumbs.

- MaxLength: This property controls the maximum length of the text that can be typed into the control.

- Text: This property contains the actual text value in the control.

- Width: This property specifies the width of the control. If the length of the text entered causes it to exceed the width of the control, the portion beyond the edge will not be displayed.

The following XAML can be used to display the TextBox shown in Figure 5-11:

```
<TextBox Text="The quick brown fox..."
         FontFamily="Segoe UI" FontSize="48" />
```

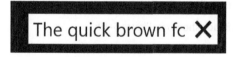

Figure 5-11. *Basic TextBox*

You can prevent the user from interacting with the control in any way by changing the `IsEnabled` property to False. This not only prevents interaction but also changes the way that the control is drawn by giving it a "grayed-out" appearance that users are accustomed to in order to indicate a disabled control. The following XAML produces the disabled `TextBox` shown in Figure 5-12:

```
<TextBox Text="The quick brown fox..." IsEnabled="False"
         FontFamily="Segoe UI" FontSize="48" />
```

Figure 5-12. *Disabled TextBox*

When you want to prevent editing of the text within the control but still want to maintain the look of the enabled control and allow users to copy the contents of the control to their clipboard, setting the `IsReadOnly` to True can be used to achieve that effect.

Because the `TextBox` control also supports interaction with the end user, events become important. These are some of the events you may find yourself responding to for the `TextBox`:

- `GotFocus`: This event fires when the `TextBox` becomes the target of focus on the page. One common use for `GotFocus` with `TextBox` controls is to cause all of the text within the control to be selected. This allows the user to overwrite the current contents just by starting to type. This is less effective in the Windows 8 environment because the touch-optimized `TextBox` in Windows provides a button to clear the text that the user can just tap or click.

- `TextChanged`: This event fires when the `Text` property of the control is updated. It can be used for purposes such as validation and triggering the recalculation of computed fields.

Button

The `Button` control allows the user to invoke an action or submit a command. When the user sees a control on the screen like what is pictured in Figure 5-13, experience tells them that clicking or tapping the button will perform the action described in the text on the button.

Figure 5-13. *Save Button*

A `Button` in Windows 8 has a slightly different appearance that is consistent with the two-tone, high-contrast look and feel but effectively continues to communicate to the user "Click me, and I'll do something," as shown in Figure 5-14.

Figure 5-14. *Windows 8 Save Button*

These are the properties that you will most commonly use for a Button control:

- Command: This property is used to bind the Button to a Command object. Commands are discussed in detail later but will become an important part of your life developing XAML applications.

- CommandParameter: This property is used to specify a parameter to be passed into the bound Command's Execute and CanExecute methods.

- Content: This property specifies the content to be displayed on the Button. This can be simple text, such as is demonstrated in these examples, or other XAML elements.

- FontFamily: This property is used to specify the font that will be used to render the text within the control.

- FontSize: This property is used to specify the size of the text within the control.

- IsEnabled: This property indicates whether the user can interact with the control.

In typical usage, the only event you would find yourself writing code for using a Button would be the Click event. This event fires when the user clicks or taps the control.

To add the Button like the one shown in Figure 5-14 to a page, you would use the following XAML:

```
<Button Content="Save"
        FontFamily="Segoe UI" FontSize="48" />
```

You could also choose to use the alternative syntax, placing the value of the Content property enclosed by opening and closing tags instead. This syntax would be required if the Content property needed to be populated with other controls rather than just a simple string.

```
<Button FontFamily="Segoe UI" FontSize="48">Save</Button>
```

RadioButton

The RadioButton is a control that is familiar to end users for selecting an option among mutually exclusive alternatives. One example might be when making meal reservations; the user could be asked to select for which meal the reservation is being made, as illustrated in Figure 5-15.

Figure 5-15. *RadioButtons for meal selection*

The RadioButton is effective because it allows users to always see all of the possible values for the selection, making them more likely to catch whether a more appropriate selection is available. What is given up in exchange for this transparency is screen real estate, which is often a precious commodity. Displaying too many options will also provide more information than the user can effectively translate and counter the benefit of having them all visible. When deciding whether to use the RadioButton control, a designer should consider the number of available options. That number will determine the amount of space on the screen that would be consumed as well as whether the list will be "glanceable." If there are too many options to fit in the allotted space or the list is not able to be comprehended at a glance, another alternative will need to be selected. As a general rule, I start to question the appropriateness of a list of RadioButton controls once it exceeds four items, so if you were building a reservation system for hobbits, the RadioButton may no longer be the control of choice for selecting a meal.

These are the properties that you will most commonly use for a RadioButton control:

- Content: This property specifies the content to be displayed on the RadioButton. This can be simple text, such as is demonstrated in these examples, or other XAML elements.

- FontFamily: This property is used to specify the font that will be used to render the text within the control.

- FontSize: This property is used to specify the size of the text within the control.

- GroupName: This property is important when you want to have multiple groups of RadioButton controls on the page. Because RadioButton selection is intended to be from among mutually exclusive options, a maximum of one RadioButton from any sharing the same GroupName value will be selected at any given point in time.

- IsChecked: This property indicates whether the RadioButton is currently the selection option.

- IsEnabled: This property indicates whether the user can interact with the control.

The RadioButton control has two events that you will most commonly interact with.

- Checked: This event fires when the value of the IsChecked property changes to True.

- Unchecked: This event fires when the value of the IsCheckedProperty changes to False.

In many cases, you will find that there is code that should be executed whenever the IsCheckedProperty changes at all. In these cases, you may assign the same event handler method to both the Checked and Unchecked events.

A single RadioButton would hardly make sense in most usage scenarios, so to add multiple RadioButton controls to a page as you saw in Figure 5-15, the following XAML would be used:

```
<RadioButton Content="Breakfast" GroupName="MealSelection"
       FontFamily="Segoe UI" FontSize="48" />
<RadioButton Content="Lunch" GroupName="MealSelection"
       FontFamily="Segoe UI" FontSize="48" />
<RadioButton Content="Dinner" GroupName="MealSelection"
       FontFamily="Segoe UI" FontSize="48" />
```

CheckBox

The CheckBox control is similar to the RadioButton in many ways. In fact, they both share the same base class of ToggleButton. The major difference in the purpose of CheckBox and RadioButton is that the CheckBox is used to communicate a Boolean state (yes/no, true/false, on/off) of a single item rather than selecting one item from a list. Figure 5-16 shows one common example of this control, where the user is being asked to affirm that they agree to a set of terms and conditions.

■ I agree to the terms I didn't read

Figure 5-16. CheckBox prompting for agreement

It is not uncommon in developing software applications to find that where you would otherwise have placed a CheckBox to answer a "yes/no" question, the possibility exists for an "I don't know" answer. The CheckBox control meets this need by supplying a mode that is referred to as *tri-state*, in which in addition to storing information about whether it is in a checked state, it can be queried to determine whether its value is indeterminate. This leaves three possible options for the state of the CheckBox, as shown in Figure 5-17.

Figure 5-17. CheckBox states

These are the properties that you will most commonly use for a CheckBox control:

- Content: This property specifies the content to be displayed on the CheckBox. This can be simple text, such as is demonstrated in these examples, or other XAML elements.

- FontFamily: This property is used to specify the font that will be used to render the text within the control.

- FontSize: This property is used to specify the size of the text within the control.

- IsChecked: This property indicates whether the CheckBox is currently checked.

- IsEnabled: This property indicates whether the user can interact with the control.

- IsThreeState: This property indicates whether the CheckBox is being used in tri-state mode and supports an indeterminate state.

The CheckBox control has three events that you will most commonly interact with.

- Checked: This event fires when the value of the IsChecked property changes to True.

- Indeterminate: This event fires when the control is in tri-state mode and the IsChecked property changes to null.

- Unchecked: This event fires when the value of the IsCheckedProperty changes to False.

In many cases, you will find that there is code that should be executed whenever the IsCheckedProperty changes at all. In these cases, you may assign the same event handler method to the Checked, Indeterminate, and Unchecked events.

To add a CheckBox control similar to the one you saw in Figure 5-16 to a page, you would use the following XAML:

```
<CheckBox Content="I agree to the terms I didn't read"
          FontFamily="Segoe UI" FontSize="48" />
```

ComboBox

The ComboBox control is used for scenarios where the user needs to pick from among a list of mutually exclusive options. This control is similar in purpose to RadioButton but can be used when the use of RadioButton is not practical because of space or comprehension constraints or when the designer feels the ComboBox provides a more desirable experience. As shown in Figure 5-18, the control has a similar look in its closed state to a TextBox, with the selected item shown in the viewport and button to toggle the ComboBox into its open state.

Figure 5-18. *Closed ComboBox*

Figure 5-19 shows the ComboBox in its open state. When the ComboBox is open, the user can see the available choices with the currently selected option highlighted. If the list of items is longer than the available space in which to display them, the user can scroll through the list. When the list becomes too long, users will likely be annoyed at the effort that they must exert to find the item they are looking for. Long lists very likely need an alternative to the ComboBox such as switching to another view in which the user can search, sort, and filter the list to narrow it to fewer choices.

Figure 5-19. *Open ComboBox*

When the items contained within a ComboBox are defined in XAML rather than through data binding, the ComboBox is populated by providing a sequence of ComboBoxItem controls. Like most XAML controls, the ComboBoxItem control has a rich set of properties and events that you may want to explore, but to achieve the basic functionality of the ComboBox, the important properties of ComboBoxItem are as follows:

- Content: This property specifies the content to be displayed on the ComboBoxItem. This can be simple text, such as is demonstrated in these examples, or other XAML elements such as Image. You can even place panel controls such as Grid and StackPanel within a ComboBoxItem to come up with quite sophisticated layouts.

- IsSelected: This property indicates whether the ComboBoxItem is the currently selected item within the ComboBox.

These are the properties you will most commonly use with a ComboBox:

- DisplayMember: When used with data binding, this determines which property of the bound item should be displayed in the drop-down list.

- FontFamily: This property is used to specify the font that will be used for the text of the items in the ComboBox.

- FontSize: This property is used to specify the size of font used to display the items in the ComboBox.

- IsEnabled: This property is used to indicate whether the user can interact with the control. It's important to realize that in addition to controlling whether the user can change the selected value, if the ComboBox is disabled, the user will not be able to toggle it into the open state to see the list of available selections.

- Items: This property exposes the collection of contained ComboBoxItem controls.

- ItemsSource: When used with data binding, this property specifies the collection from which the items in the ComboBox should be created.

- SelectedIndex: This property specifies the zero-based index of the item that is currently selected in the ComboBox. If no item is currently selected, the value of this property is -1.

- SelectedItem: This property exposes the actual item that is currently selected. When the items are created by adding ComboBoxItem controls to the ComboBoxItem, as I am doing in this coverage, the SelectedItem will be an instance of a ComboBoxItem. When data binding is being used, the object represented by this property will be of whatever type is in the underlying collection.

- SelectedValue: This property is used in conjunction with the SelectedValuePath property and is used to represent the value of the selected item.

- SelectedValuePath: This property is used with data binding and specifies the property of the bound object that should be considered to be the value for the purposes of setting or retrieving the SelectedValue property.

When writing code to respond to events in the ComboBox, you will most commonly respond to the SelectionChanged event. This event fires whenever the value of the SelectedItem property changes and is useful for performing actions such as filtering the contents of another ComboBox based on the current selection.

To create a ComboBox similar to what was shown in Figure 5-18 and Figure 5-19, you would add the following XAML to your page:

```
<ComboBox>
    <ComboBoxItem Content="Breakfast" />
    <ComboBoxItem Content="Second Breakfast" />
    <ComboBoxItem Content="Elevenses" />
    <ComboBoxItem Content="Luncheon" />
    <ComboBoxItem Content="Afternoon Tea" />
    <ComboBoxItem Content="Dinner" />
    <ComboBoxItem Content="Supper" />
</ComboBox>
```

Image

As its name suggests, the Image control is used to display an image to the user. These images can be in JPEG or PNG and, in keeping with the design goals of a Windows application, should serve to augment your content rather than distract from it.

These are the properties you are most likely to work with when using an Image control:

- Height and Width: These properties specify the height and width of the control.

- Source: This property specifies the image to be displayed.

- Stretch: This property specifies how resizing should be handled if the image dimensions do not match those of the control. Possible values include None, Uniform, Fill, and UniformToFill.

When Height and Width are not specified, the Panel on which the image is placed will determine the dimensions, often defaulting to fill the available space. When the bounds of the image do not match the Height and Width of the control, the Stretch property determines whether the image should be left at its original size or how to resize it. In Figure 5-20, the image used in the sample XAML was resized because the Stretch property was left at its default value of Uniform. To place an image on your page that has been added to the Assets folder in your application, you would use the following XAML:

```
<Image Source="Assets/fairlanes.jpg" />
```

Figure 5-20. *Image expanded to fill its container*

By adding Stretch = "None" to the XAML, as is shown in Figure 5-21, the image itself remains its original size even though the Image control is still expanded to fill its container.

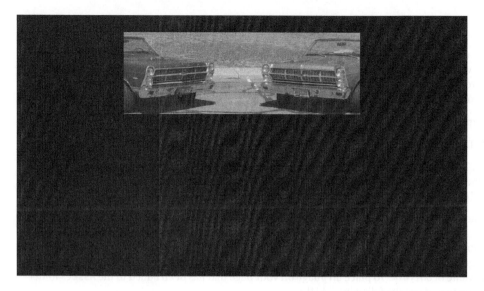

Figure 5-21. *Image with* Stretch *set to None*

FlipView

The FlipView control is a new addition to the Visual Studio Toolbox with Windows 8. This is a list control that displays its contents one at a time, allowing the user to page, or "flip," through the items with only one item in view at a time. Some usage scenarios where you are likely to have seen the FlipView functionality are photo galleries or digital books. The FlipView keeps track of where it is in the content list and displays navigation controls appropriate for the user's position in the list. In Figure 5-22, the user is on the first page of a photo album, and the FlipView allows navigation only to the next item. In Figure 5-23, the user is somewhere in the middle of the list and allowed to move in either direction. Figure 5-24 shows the user on the final item in the list from which the user can only move back.

Figure 5-22. FlipView *first page*

Figure 5-23. `FlipView` *middle page*

Figure 5-24. `FlipView` *last page*

In addition to providing the functionality of being able to flip through pages, the `FlipView` is fully touch-enabled, and users experience functionality that they expect to see in any touch environment such as the pages being animated as the user pulls across to the next page and snapping into place.

Using the `FlipView` is an excellent choice when the content to be displayed is large enough to keep the user fully immersed. It is probably not appropriate for situations when the user would have to exert the effort to move between items and be left staring at a mostly blank screen.

These are some of the properties you will most commonly use as you begin writing applications using the FlipView:

- DisplayMemberPath: When used with data binding, this determines which property of the bound item should be displayed.

- Height: This property specifies the height of the FlipView control.

- Items: This property exposes the collection of contained objects.

- ItemsSource: When used with data binding, this property specifies the collection from which the items in the FlipView should be created.

- SelectedIndex: This property specifies the zero-based index of the item that is currently displayed in the FlipView.

- SelectedItem: This property exposes the actual item that is currently displayed.

- SelectedValue: This property is used in conjunction with the SelectedValuePath property and is used to represent the value of the selected item.

- SelectedValuePath: This property is used with data binding and specifies the property of the bound object that should be considered to be the value for the purposes of setting or retrieving the SelectedValue property.

The event for which you are most likely to write code when getting started with the FlipView control is the SelectionChanged event, which fires whenever the displayed item changes.

To add a FlipView similar to the one shown in Figure 5-20 through Figure 5-22, you would use the following XAML:

```
<FlipView>
    <Image Source="Assets/fairlanes.jpg" Stretch="None" />
    <Image Source="Assets/parthenon.jpg" Stretch="None" />
    <Image Source="Assets/fish.jpg" Stretch="None" />
</FlipView>
```

GridView and ListView

The GridView and ListView controls both fulfill a similar purpose. They share the same base class and can be used interchangeably, so I will discuss them together here. The controls are built for displaying lists of data in a way that is designed for a touch-first environment. A good example of this optimization is the way that the controls use inertia and snap in response to a swipe so that instead of immediately stopping the scroll when the user lifts their finger, it gives the feeling of settling into place.

These controls are intended to be used in scenarios where the list of data is the center of attention, such as an application that displays an album collection. These controls also provide a good solution for applications that drill down from a high-level listing into a detailed view of a single item. In this scenario, the GridView or ListView would be used at the high level, and then when the user selects an item from the list, another page would display the detail view.

The big difference between these two controls is their orientation. The GridView is designed for a horizontal orientation to take advantage of the wide screen, which is normal for desktop computers and tablets. To take advantage of the wide screen, list items are laid out in a grid that is populated from top to bottom and left to right, as shown in Figure 5-25. The ListView, however, is designed for a vertical orientation, with each item arranged beneath the preceding item. This layout is ideal for when the application is snapped to one side of the screen, and many Windows applications will include automatically interchanging the GridView and ListView when the user switches between full-screen and snapped modes.

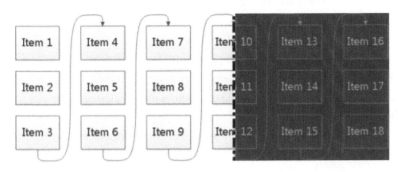

Figure 5-25. GridView item layout

In addition to displaying a continuous list of data, these controls also support displaying groups of items separated by group headers, as shown for the ListView in Figure 5-26.

Figure 5-26. Grouped ListView

GridView and ListView offer a wide range of customization options, but in a basic scenario where you are simply displaying lists of items, these are the properties that will be most often utilized:

- IsItemClickEnabled: This property is used to determine whether the ItemClick event should be raised by the control.

- ItemsSource: When used with data binding, this property specifies the collection from which the items in the control should be created.

- ItemTemplate: This property is used to specify the template that defines the visual layout for each item. These templates will be discussed in greater detail in Chapter 7.

- SelectionMode: This property is used to specify whether the user can select a single item, multiple items, or no items at all. When multiple items are allowed, you can also specify whether those items must be contiguous.

- SelectedIndex: This property specifies the zero-based index of the item that is currently selected in the ComboBox. If no item is currently selected, the value of this property is -1.

- SelectedItem: This property exposes the actual item that is currently selected. If multiple items are currently selected, this property will return the selected item with the lowest index.

- SelectedItems: This property is used to retrieve the list of selected items in the control.

When using the ListView as a drill-down tool, the SelectionMode is typically set to None, and the IsItemClickEnabled property is set to True. In this setup, the most common event that you will use is ItemClick, which is raised when the user taps or clicks an item in the list. When ItemClick is not enabled, the event you will most often use is SelectionChanged, which is fired when the user selects or deselects an item.

GridView and ListView cannot be meaningfully used on a page without using templates and styles, which are both discussed in Chapter 7. Because of this dependency, you will first see GridView and ListView XAML in that chapter as well.

Rectangle

The Rectangle must be the simplest control in the Common controls. The purpose of this control is to draw a rectangle on the page. This might seem like a pretty trivial purpose, but take a look at any Windows application, such as the Start screen shown in Figure 5-27, with rectangles in mind, and you will start to see how pervasive they are.

Figure 5-27. *Rectangles are everywhere*

These are the most common properties of the Rectangle control you will use in developing Windows applications:

- Fill: This property represents the Brush that will be used to paint the body of the Rectangle.

- Height and Width: These properties specify the height and width of the control.

- Stroke: This property specifies the Brush that will be used to paint the outline of the Rectangle.

- StrokeThickness: This property specifies the width of the Brush used to paint the outline of the Rectangle.

The 150 pixel by 300 pixel Rectangle shown in Figure 5-28 can be added to a page using the following XAML:

```
<Rectangle Fill="Yellow" Stroke="White" StrokeThickness="10"
          Height="150" Width="300" />
```

Figure 5-28. Rectangle Stroke and Fill

A Word on Style

Every control covered in this chapter has a very powerful property called Style, which can be used to create predefined collections of property settings and help achieve a consistent look and feel across your applications. I did not discuss styles in this chapter because they will much better fit into the conversation in Chapter 7 when I introduce the sample application and define its user interface.

Conclusion

In this chapter, you learned enough to get started with each of the controls considered pervasive enough to be included on the Common tab of the Visual Studio Toolbox. Just as you did with the Start screen for Rectangle controls, I encourage you to look at different applications with these controls on your mind and see how many you can spot.

■ ■ ■

CHAPTER 6

XAML Controls in the Visual Studio Toolbox: Other Controls

What good is a craftsman without his tools?

—Origin Unknown

Any craftsperson has their "go-to" tools that are used daily within their profession. Additionally, they maintain a toolbox full of additional tools to ensure that when the situation calls for something beyond what is used every day, they will have just what is needed. You have already seen the "daily use" tools, and in this chapter, you will learn about the rest of the controls that come in the Visual Studio Toolbox. The controls you will encounter in this chapter vary widely in use and complexity, so for some I will go deeper than other. For most controls, I will cover the following:

- The purpose of the control
- Common usage scenarios
- Important properties and methods of the control
- The XAML used to add the control to a page

While the common controls were presented grouped by function, the remaining controls will be presented in alphabetical order to allow this chapter to serve as a reference tool.

AppBar

Many applications running on various Windows platforms make use of toolbars and menus to interact with content. A typical example of this is Internet Explorer, which has an address bar for navigation and has multiple menus and toolbars, sometimes providing several ways to perform the same action in order to meet the expectations of every user. For an immersive user experience, the idea of menus and toolbars, which are normally incorporated into the application's window chrome, is counter to the idea that the user should have no distractions from the application's content. In Figure 6-1, you see Internet Explorer launched from the Desktop with toolbars and menus turned on. Notice how much of the screen area is devoted to things other than the content.

Figure 6-1. *Internet Explorer launched from the Desktop with menus and toolbars*

Windows design aims to keep focus on the content, so when launched from the Start screen Internet Explorer does away with toolbars, menus, and status bars, as shown in Figure 6-2.

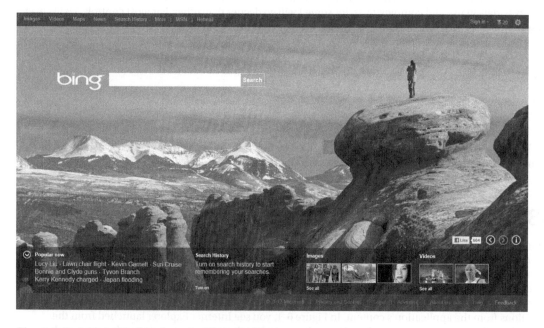

Figure 6-2. *Internet Explorer launched from the Start screen*

The removal of distractions from the content gives a much better overall experience, but there is still the need to perform actions such as entering a new address or switching between active tabs. This is where the AppBar comes into play. The AppBar provides a container designed to house commands that do not have a place on-screen but need to be kept close at hand. Applications can use AppBar controls at the bottom of the page, the top of the page, or both to allow the user to swipe these commands into view. In the case of Internet Explorer (shown in Figure 6-3), a top AppBar allows the user to manage tabs, while the bottom AppBar is more focused on working with the current page and navigation.

Figure 6-3. *Internet Explorer with* AppBars *open*

A key design consideration for incorporating an AppBar into your application is to ensure that it presents commands in an intuitive and familiar manner. One way that this can be accomplished is through looking at the button styles with AppBarButtonStyle in their name from StandardStyles.xaml and using one of these styles if it fits the purpose of your button. I will discuss styles more in Chapter 7.

When using the AppBar, these are the properties with which you normally would interact:

- IsOpen: This property is used to specify whether the AppBar is currently expanded into view. By setting the property to true, the AppBar can be programmatically shown.

- IsSticky: This property controls whether the AppBar will exhibit the default behavior of closing as soon as the user interacts with any other part of the screen or must be explicitly dismissed by the user.

Typical development scenarios will not have the developer responding to AppBar events because the control is fairly autonomous. When events are used, the Opened and Closed events, which are fired when the AppBar is shown and hidden, will be the most typically responded to.

Most of the controls in the Visual Studio Toolbox are either placed directly on the page or placed within a Panel. The AppBar control differs from this model in that it is used to set either the TopAppBar or BottomAppBar property of the Page object. The following XAML will add a bottom AppBar containing a single Save button to a page:

```
<Page.BottomAppBar>
    <AppBar>
        <StackPanel Orientation="Horizontal">
            <Button Style="{StaticResource SaveAppBarButtonStyle}" />
        </StackPanel>
    </AppBar>
</Page.BottomAppBar>
```

Canvas

The Canvas control is the simplest layout control in the XAML toolbox. Its name is very well chosen because it functions as a blank canvas on which you "draw" elements by placing them on the Canvas and specifying their position relative to the top-left corner. Because items are positioned absolutely, the Canvas does not automatically handle things such as resizing and scaling for different screen resolutions. This makes its simplicity somewhat equaled by its inflexibility. The effort required to position each element on the Canvas makes it typically a candidate only for specialized uses requiring granular control such as drawing diagrams.

These are some properties that are commonly specified for a Canvas control:

- Height and Width: These properties control the size of the container. If these properties are not specified by the page author, the control will size itself appropriately to contain all of its content. Unlike other container types, when Height or Width is specified, any content that would push beyond these bounds is drawn outside the bounds of the control.

- Background: This property controls the Brush that is used for the background of the control. Notice that the term Brush is used as opposed to *color*. This is because the Windows Runtime API defines a Brush as an abstract class that defines how a region is to be painted. It need not be a solid color but can also be more complex renderings such as gradients and images.

- DataContext: This property does not impact the way that the Canvas control looks but can be important when used with data binding, which I will discuss in Chapter 8.

Placing a Canvas control on a page without additional contained controls does not provide a result that can be visualized, so the following snippet demonstrates the placement of a Canvas containing a Rectangle on the page:

```
<Canvas>
    <Rectangle Canvas.Left="35" Canvas.Top="50" Height="50" Width="50" Fill="Yellow" />
</Canvas>
```

CaptureElement

The CaptureElement control is used to integrate media captured from devices connected to the Windows 8 PC such as video cameras and microphones. This control requires more manipulation in code than just setting properties in the XAML, and I will cover it in Chapter 19.

ContentControl

The ContentControl control is used as a base class for other controls such as Button and CheckBox and can be used as the basis for your own controls that you want to expose a single Content property. While it is possible to use the ContentControl on a page and it will display the string or element used to populate its Content property, the control does not really have a practical application use. You will most often see ContentControl extended by controls that need to display contents in addition to other functionality. This book will not cover creating and extending controls, so you will not see ContentControl covered in any depth.

ContentPresenter

The ContentPresenter control is used when creating custom control templates and effectively serves as the placeholder for whatever visual content is contained in a ContentControl. Consider the following XAML, which produces the result shown in Figure 6-4:

```
<Button> Save</Button>
```

Figure 6-4. *Save button*

The rectangular border around the button's content was achieved by placing a ContentPresenter control within a Border control in the button's template, demonstrated in a simplified manner with this XAML:

```
<Border>
    <ContentPresenter />
</Border>
```

The building of custom control templates to redefine the visual appearance of existing controls or to create the visual appearance of your own controls is beyond the scope of this book, so I will not cover ContentPresenter in any depth.

Ellipse

The Ellipse control is used to draw elliptical shapes on the page. In a Windows application, this would often be used when drawing a figure using XAML and will not be seen as much as in other environments where developers may be prone to using nonrectangular controls to set their application apart from others.

These are the most common properties of the Ellipse control that you will use in developing Windows applications:

- Fill: This property represents the Brush that will be used to paint the body of the Ellipse.

- Height and Width: These properties specify the height and width of the Ellipse.

- Stroke: This property specifies the Brush that will be used to paint the outline of the Ellipse.

- StrokeThickness: This property specifies the width of the Brush used to paint the outline of the Ellipse.

The 150 pixel by 300 pixel Ellipse shown in Figure 6-5 can be added to a page using the following XAML:

```
<Ellipse Fill="Yellow" Stroke="White" StrokeThickness="10"
         Height="150" Width="300" />
```

Figure 6-5. Ellipse

Frame

The Frame control is the basis for navigation between pages in a Windows application. This control supports displaying and navigating between pages, and any application built to run as a Windows application with more than one page will more than likely make use of a Frame control.

These are the most commonly used properties for the Frame control:

- CanGoBack: This property indicates whether the navigation stack for the Frame contains a "previous page" that the user can navigate to.

- CanGoForward: This property indicates whether the navigation stack for the Frame contains a "next" page that the user can navigate to.

Unlike most controls covered so far, typical use of the Frame control would not have the developer responding to events that are raised by the Frame but would call methods of the control. These are the methods that would typically be invoked:

- GoBack: This method causes the Frame to navigate to the previous entry in the navigation stack.

- GoForward: This method causes the Frame to navigate to the next entry in the navigation stack.

- Navigate: This method causes the Frame to navigate to a specific page. The method will be used with the overload that accepts the Type of the desired page, or an alternate overload also accepts an object that will be passed to the desired page as a parameter.

The Frame will typically be created in code that executes when the application is initialized or launched as opposed to with the XAML that defines a page. The following code is an abbreviated form of the code that is generated by Visual Studio for the OnLaunched method of your application:

```
protected override void OnLaunched(LaunchActivatedEventArgs args)
{
    var rootFrame = new Frame();
    rootFrame.Navigate(typeof(MainPage));
    Window.Current.Content = rootFrame;
    Window.Current.Activate();
}
```

This code creates a new Frame and causes the Frame to navigate to your start-up page. The Frame is then set as the Content for the application's Window, and Activate is called to bring the application to the foreground.

HyperlinkButton

The HyperlinkButton control shares a common parent control as the Button control (ButtonBase) and has many similarities with the Button. The key difference that is apparent to the user is the difference in look. The Button is typically surrounded by a rectangular border, while the default look of the HyperlinkButton does not have this border and responds to MouseOver events by growing brighter or dimmer to signal that interaction is available. Semantically, these two controls are different in that the Button suggests to the user that an action will be performed, and the HyperlinkButton suggests that the user will be taken away from the current page.

These are the properties you will most commonly use for a HyperlinkButton control:

- Command: This property is used to bind the HyperlinkButton to a Command object. Commands are discussed in detail in a later chapter but will become an important part of your life developing XAML applications.

- CommandParameter: This property is used to specify a parameter to be passed into the bound Command's Execute and CanExecute methods.

- Content: This property specifies the content to be displayed on the HyperlinkButton. This can be simple text, such as is demonstrated in these examples, or other XAML elements.

- FontFamily: This property is used to specify the font that will be used to render the text within the control.

- FontSize: This property is used to specify the size of the text within the control.

- IsEnabled: This property indicates whether the user can interact with the control.

- NavigateUri: This property specifies the URI to which navigation should occur when the user taps or clicks the HyperlinkButton.

In typical usage, the developers will not write code to respond to events raised by the HyperlinkButton control because the default behavior of providing navigation to the NavigateUri is what is desired. In some cases, you may find yourself writing code for the Click event. This event fires when the user clicks or taps the control.

To add the HyperlinkButton to a page that would cause Internet Explorer to open to the Bing search engine when clicked, you would use the following XAML:

```
<HyperlinkButton Content="take me away..."
        NavigateUri="http://www.bing.com" />
```

ItemsControl

The ItemsControl control is a control that is not placed on a page on its own but serves as the basis for other controls that are used to allow users to interact with collections of data. It could be said that ItemsControl is to lists what ContentControl is to content. This control serves as the basis for controls such as the ListView, ListBox, and GridView. It is also the control from which you would base your own custom controls designed to expose collections.

ItemsPresenter

The ItemsPresenter goes to the ItemsControl as the ContentPresenter goes to the ContentControl. This control is used within control templates to specify where the list will be rendered. As with ContentControl and ContentPresenter, because I will not be covering more advanced control creation and templating techniques in this book, ItemsControl and ItemsPresenter will not be covered in any depth.

ListBox

The ListBox control has been the "go-to" control for displaying lists of items that allow selection in XAML applications built for WPF and Silverlight, but in the Windows 8 world, many of the cases where a ListBox would be used find the designer choosing a ListView or GridView instead. ListBox may be brought into a design where a selectable list is needed as an element, but the contents of the list should not become the primary focus of the user's attention.

These are the properties that will most often be used with the ListBox:

- ItemsSource: When used with data binding, this property specifies the collection from which the items in the control should be created.

- ItemTemplate: This property is used to specify the template that defines the visual layout for each item. These templates will be discussed in greater detail in Chapter 7.

- SelectionMode: This property is used to specify whether the user can select a single item, multiple items, or no items at all. When multiple items are allowed, you can also specify whether those items must be contiguous.

- SelectedIndex: This property specifies the zero-based index of the item that is currently selected in the ComboBox. If no item is currently selected, the value of this property is –1.

- SelectedItem: This property exposes the actual item that is currently selected. If multiple items are currently selected, this property will return the selected item with the lowest index.

- SelectedItems: This property is used to retrieve the list of selected items in the control.

When working with ListBox events, the event you will most often use is SelectionChanged, which is fired when the user selects or deselects an item.

Although ListBox will typically use data binding rather than having items directly created in XAML, you could add a ListBox such as the one illustrated in Figure 6-6 using the following XAML:

```
<ListBox Height="100" Width="75">
    <ListBoxItem Content="Item 1" />
    <ListBoxItem Content="Item 2" />
    <ListBoxItem Content="Item 3" />
</ListBox>
```

Figure 6-6. `ListBox`

MediaElement

The `MediaElement` control is used to play video and audio in your Windows application. The media may come from a source in the cloud, be stored on the computer's local drive, or be streamed from a device such as a webcam.

These are the properties that will most often be important to developers using the `MediaElement` control:

- `AutoPlay`: This property indicates whether the control should immediately begin playing the source media instead of waiting for playback to be initiated through code.

- `CanPause`: This property indicates whether the control can respond to the `Pause` method.

- `CanSeek`: This property indicates whether the media source of the control supports seek operations.

- `Height`: This property specifies the height of the control.

- `IsMuted`: This property specifies whether the audio is currently muted.

- `Name`: This property specifies a unique name for the control. It is more likely to be used with `MediaElement` than many others because much of the `MediaElement` control's functionality requires manipulation in the code-behind.

- `PosterSource`: This property specifies a static image that is used as a placeholder during media transitions or when no source is loaded.

- `Source`: This property specifies the source of the media to be loaded.

- `Volume`: This property specifies the current volume of the control.

Developers using the `MediaElement` control will most often interact with it through code. These are the methods most relevant to accessing basic media playback functionality with the `MediaElement` control:

- `Pause`: This method is used to pause playback of the media.

- `Play`: This method is used to begin or resume playback of the media.

- `SetSource`: This method is used to specify a stream object, such as captured camera output, which is to be used as the media source.

- `Stop`: This method is used to stop playback of the media.

When responding to events raised by the MediaElement control, the most relevant events provide information about playback state. These events are as follows:

- MediaEnded: This event is raised when the MediaElement is no longer playing.

- MediaFailed: This event is raised when a problem with the media source prevents the MediaElement from being able to play it.

- MediaOpened: This event is raised when the MediaElement has successfully opened a media file and validated the file headers.

To implement a MediaElement in your application using XAML alone would require the AutoPlay property because the MediaElement does not contain its own set of buttons for controlling playback. A pure XAML MediaElement implementation would be achieved as follows:

```
<MediaElement AutoPlay = "True" Source = "Assets/myvideo.wmv" />
```

In a more realistic scenario, you will assign a value to the Name property, and your interface will also contain buttons from whose Click events you will call methods of the MediaElement control to control playback.

PasswordBox

The PasswordBox is essentially a specialized alternative to the TextBox that is used for input of sensitive data. When the user types in the control, rather than displaying the actual text that has been entered, a specified character is repeated once for each character input. This control is essential for collecting passwords and can also be valuable for other types of information such as credit card numbers.

These are the properties that developers are most likely to specify or query when working with PasswordBox:

- IsPasswordRevealButtonEnabled: This property specifies whether a button is displayed that toggles display of the characters entered in the PasswordBox.

- Password: This property specifies the characters entered in the PasswordBox.

- PasswordChar: This property overrides the default character to display in place of password characters. To maintain consistency across applications, the decision to override the default should be well thought out.

- Width: Specifies the width of the PasswordBox.

The most common event that you would respond to of the PasswordBox control is the PasswordChanged event, which fires when a new value is entered in the PasswordBox.

To place a PasswordBox on a page that allows the user to review characters, such as is displayed in Figure 6-7, you would use the following XAML:

```
<PasswordBox Width = "100" IsPasswordRevealButtonEnabled = "True" />
```

Figure 6-7. PasswordBox

Popup

The Popup control is used to hold visual elements that can be opened and closed over the top of other controls. An excellent example of this control in action is the ComboBox, which itself uses a Popup to achieve the drop-down list that is activated by a ToggleButton.

These are the properties that most developers will find useful when using the Popup:

- Child: This property is similar to the Content property of a ContentControl in that the Popup can contain only a single child element. More complex scenarios are possible by using a control that itself can have children as the single child element.

- Height: This property specifies the height of the Popup when open.

- IsLightDismissEnabled: This property specifies whether interacting with other elements on the page should cause the Popup to automatically transition to a closed state.

- IsOpen: This property specifies whether the Popup is currently in an open state.

While typical development scenarios won't require responding to events raised by the Popup control, developers may find occasion to perform work in the Closed and Opened events that fire when the control transitions between open and closed states.

To place a Popup control on a page that is initially open and will automatically transition to closed when the user interacts with other controls on the page, you would use the following XAML:

```
<Popup IsOpen="True" IsLightDismissEnabled="True">
    <TextBlock Text="I am in the popup" />
</Popup>
```

ProgressBar

When building applications that rely on resources outside of the application such as web server response, file downloads, and even accessing files on the local machine, it is inevitable that your end user will eventually be left waiting for the application to deliver on a request. The ProgressBar helps your application maintain a feeling of responsiveness by providing a visual indication that the application is performing work and hasn't "locked up."

The ProgressBar has two main display scenarios. When the work to be performed and current progress toward that goal are able to be calculated, the ProgressBar can give the user an idea of how much longer they will be waiting, such as is displayed in Figure 6-8. When the progress toward the goal cannot be quantified, the ProgressBar can be configured to display an animation instead, communicating "I'm working" to the user. This configuration by default uses a series of dots that move across the screen repeatedly and is shown in Figure 6-9.

Figure 6-8. *Determinate* ProgressBar

Figure 6-9. *Indeterminate* ProgressBar

When using the ProgressBar in applications, these are the properties that will be most important to developers:

- Height and Width: These properties specify the height and width of the control.

- IsIndeterminate: This property specifies whether the control is in indeterminate mode, which uses animation instead of quantified progress.

- Maximum: This property specifies the value at which progress is said to be 100 percent complete. When the ProgressBar is in indeterminate mode, the value of this property is irrelevant.

- Minimum: This property specifies the value at which progress is said to be 0 percent complete. When the ProgressBar is in indeterminate mode, the value of this property is irrelevant.

- Value: This property specifies the current progress as a number somewhere between Minimum and Maximum. When the ProgressBar is in indeterminate mode, the value of this property is irrelevant.

- Visibility: This property specifies whether the control can be viewed on-screen. In many cases, developers will choose to show the ProgressBar only while work is being performed.

In typical usage scenarios, developers will not find themselves writing code to handle ProgressBar events, but occasionally you may find it necessary to respond to the ValueChanged event. This event is raised whenever a new Value is specified.

To add a ProgressBar similar to the one that you saw in Figure 6-8 to your page, you would use the following XAML:

```
<ProgressBar Height="25" Width="200" Minimum="0" Maximum="100" Value="60" />
```

ProgressRing

The ProgressRing fulfills the same function that the ProgressBar does when in indeterminate mode. The difference between using these is that the ProgressBar animates along a horizontal plane while the ProgressRing animates in a circular pattern. Because it is more compact than the ProgressBar, the ProgressRing control is a good choice when multiple independent tasks are occurring that deal with elements on different parts of the screen, such as loading different sections of a dashboard.

These are the most relevant properties to using the ProgressRing:

- Height and Width: These properties specify the height and width of the control. Because the animation in the ProgressRing is circular, if height and width are not equal, the smaller of the two values determines the size of the circle.

- IsActive: This property specifies whether the animation should be actively displayed. When the animation is not active, the control is not visible on the screen by default.

The ProgressRing does not have events that will be responded to in most basic application scenarios. To place a ProgressRing control with animation active on a page, you would use the following XAML:

```
<ProgressRing Height="50" Width="50" IsActive="True" />
```

RepeatButton

The RepeatButton control is a specialized Button that has the added functionality of firing the Click event multiple times at a set interval as the user holds the button pressed. One scenario where this would be useful in a design would be when the button is used to increase or decrease a value. Using the RepeatButton instead of the standard Button in this scenario would save the user effort by not requiring the user to repeatedly click or tap the button.

These are the properties you will most commonly use for a RepeatButton control:

- Command: This property is used to bind the RepeatButton to a Command object. Commands are discussed in detail later but will become an important part of your life developing XAML applications.

- CommandParameter: This property is used to specify a parameter to be passed into the bound Command object's Execute and CanExecute methods.

- Content: This property specifies the content to be displayed on the RepeatButton. This can be simple text, such as is demonstrated in these examples, or other XAML elements.

- Delay: This property specifies that amount of time to delay before raising the first Click event when the RepeatButton is held.

- FontFamily: This property is used to specify the font that will be used to render the text within the control.

- FontSize: This property is used to specify the size of the text within the control.

- Interval: This property specifies the frequency with which the Click event will be raised if the RepeatButton is held down.

- IsEnabled: This property indicates whether the user can interact with the control.

In typical usage, the only event that you would find yourself writing code for using a RepeatButton would be the Click event. This event fires when the user clicks or taps the control and will repeat at the specified interval if held.

To add a RepeatButton to your page that waits 500 milliseconds and then invokes a handler named OnButtonClicked every 250 milliseconds, you would use the following XAML:

```
<RepeatButton Delay="500" Interval="250" Click="OnButtonClicked" Content="Repeat" />
```

RichEditBox

The RichEditBox is very similar to the TextBox in appearance, but while the TextBox deals with a raw string value, the RichEditBox is intended to work with the contents of Rich Text Format (RTF) files. The control exposes a Document property that represents the RTF content of the control and provides methods to load content either from a string or from a file and to save the content to a file. This control meets a fairly specialized need and requires more coordination with other controls and code enabled to add the formatting commands that make it useful as a rich text editor. I will not cover it in depth here.

RichTextBlock and RichTextBlockOverflow

Unlike the `RichEditBox`, *Rich* in the `RichTextBlock` refers to the ability to display richly formatted text as opposed to the RTF file format. This text can include multiple paragraphs and even nontext elements such as images. In addition to displaying rich text, the `RichTextBlock` can be paired with the `RichTextBlockOverflow` control to provide advanced control over the layout of the content. This is often useful in situations where a single logical document must span multiple columns of text and allows the content author to focus on the actual content of the document instead.

Figure 6-10 shows a `RichTextBlock` control containing three paragraphs of text with the first paragraph containing an embedded image. Because the text cannot fit with the bounds of the control and no overflow has been included, the text is cut off in the middle of the first paragraph.

Figure 6-10. *`RichTextBlock` with no overflow*

In Figure 6-11, a `RichTextBlockOverflow` control has been added and configured, and the content now flows into the `RichTextBlockOverflow` control once it reaches the boundary of the `RichTextBlock`.

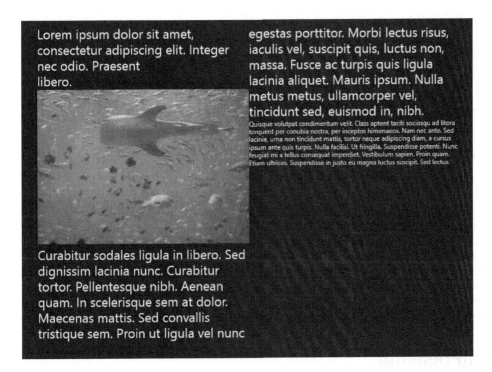

Figure 6-11. `RichTextBlock with RichTextBlockOverflow`

Because the `RichTextOverflow` also supports using another `RichTextBlockOverflow` control to flow content that exceeds its boundaries, the controls can be chained to meet the most sophisticated content layout needs.

These are the most relevant properties of the `RichTextBlock` control:

- `Content`: This property specifies the actual formatted text to be displayed in the control and, if applicable, flowed to the `OverflowContentTarget`. Rather than addressing the property directly, developers will typically specify the value of this property by placing content between the element opening and closing tags in XAML.

- `Height` and `Width`: These properties specify the height and width of the control.

- `OverflowContentTarget`: This property specifies the `RichTextOverflow` control that will display content that exceeds the boundaries set by the height and width of the control.

The `RichTextBlockOverflow` control shares the same relevant properties as `RichTextBlock` with the exception of the `Content` property because `RichTextBlockOverflow` controls by nature do not define their own content. Additionally, because `OverflowContentTarget` is usually specified using binding syntax, the `Name` property of the `RichTextBlockOverflow` control becomes more relevant.

An abbreviated form of the XAML used to create a `RichTextBlock/RichTextBlockOverflow` as shown in Figure 6-11 is as follows:

```
<RichTextBlock Height="600" Width="400"
               OverflowContentTarget="{Binding ElementName=overflow}">
    <Paragraph FontSize="24">
        paragraph 1 text...
```

```
        <InlineUIContainer>
            <Image Source="Assets/fish.jpg" />
        </InlineUIContainer>
        ... more paragraph 1 text
    </Paragraph>
    <Paragraph>
        paragraph 2 text...
    </Paragraph>
</RichTextBlock>
<RichTextBlockOverflow Name="overflow" Height="600" Width="400" />
```

ScrollBar

The concept of a scrollbar has been a fixture of Windows applications for as long as there have been Windows applications. The scrollbar is used when a control or window is designed to contain more content than can be seen in the viewable area of the control. A track containing a button typically referred to as the *thumb* is presented allowing the user to move the thumb's position along the track and control the portion of the content that is currently in the viewable area of the control. In Windows 8 applications, you will use the ScrollBar control when creating your own controls or customizing the appearance of existing controls. Because the control is used in these more advanced scenarios and not as a stand-alone control, I will not cover it in depth here.

ScrollContentPresenter

The ScrollContentPresenter is a specialized version of the ContentPresenter with the additional feature of incorporating a ScrollBar and functionality associated with making content that extends beyond the bounds of the control scrollable. As with ContentPresenter, this control is used in more advanced custom control scenarios and will not be covered in depth here.

ScrollViewer

Unlike the ScrollContentPresenter, the ScrollViewer is intended to be used as a stand-alone control. Content placed on this control is displayed within the visible area of the control, which is known as the *ViewPort* and is illustrated in Figure 6-12. Vertical and/or horizontal ScrollBar controls allow the user to move different portions of the content into the ViewPort.

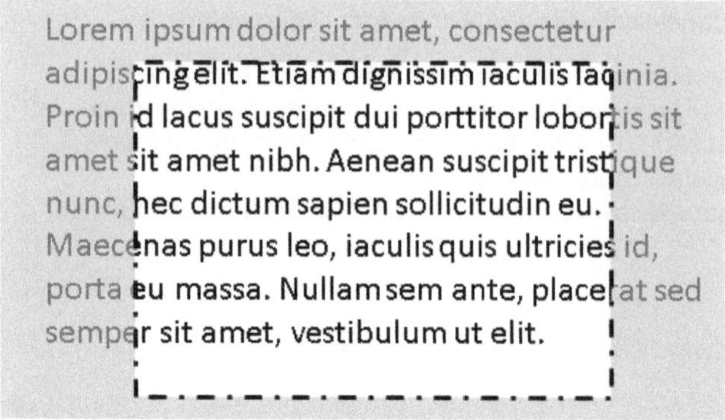

Figure 6-12. *ViewPort*

These are the properties developers will most often specify for the `ScrollViewer` control:

- `Content`: This property specifies the content that will be displayed within the `ScrollViewer`.

- `Height` and `Width`: These properties specify the height and width of the ViewPort. Content extending beyond this bound will be either clipped or available to be viewed by scrolling depending on the value of `VerticalScrollBarVisibility` and `HorizontalScrollBarVisibility`.

- `HorizontalScrollBarVisibility`: This property controls whether the `ScrollViewer` displays a horizontal `ScrollBar`. Possible values include `Disabled`, `Auto`, `Hidden`, or `Visible`.

- `VerticalScrollBarVisibility`: This property controls whether the `ScrollViewer` displays a vertical `ScrollBar`. Possible values include `Disabled`, `Auto`, `Hidden`, or `Visible`.

Because the `ScrollViewer` is used as a layout control, it does not have any events that would be responded to in a typical development scenario.

You would place a `ScrollViewer` with scrollable content as shown in Figure 6-13 on a page using the following XAML:

```
<ScrollViewer VerticalScrollBarVisibility="Auto" HorizontalScrollBarVisibility="Auto"
        Height="200" Width="400">
    <Image Height="259" Width="720" Source="Assets/fairlanes.jpg" />
</ScrollViewer>
```

Figure 6-13. ScrollViewer

SemanticZoom

Most multitouch environments include two very important gestures: pinch and stretch. In applications such as Internet Explorer, the pinch and stretch are used to provide an optical zoom, with the pinch gesture "zooming in" on the content and the stretch "zooming out." Applications that incorporate `SemanticZoom` are able to go beyond this optical zoom and instead allow the user to switch between two levels of detail in order to quickly navigate large lists of grouped data.

Figure 6-14 illustrates an application that displays the products available in a grocery store using `SemanticZoom` at the summary level (or "zoomed out"). In this view, the available aisles are listed in a `GridView`, allowing the user to choose which aisle they would like to display at a more detailed level. Once the user selects the aisle for which they would like more detail, they use the pinch gesture to "zoom in" and receive the more detailed view of the selected aisle, as shown in Figure 6-15.

Figure 6-14. *SemanticZoom zoomed-out view*

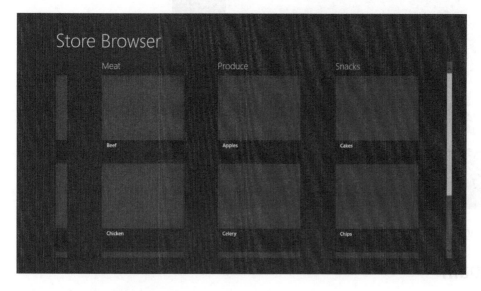

Figure 6-15. *SemanticZoom zoomed-in view*

`SemanticView` works closely with the `ListView` and `GridView` controls you saw in Chapter 5, and you will take a closer look at this control when you visit some more advanced topics in Chapter 7.

Slider

The Slider control is used to allow the user to specify a value within a range using a model similar to a ScrollBar. One example of where this type of control would be effectively used in an application would be an application with audio capabilities where the user is accustomed to a "mixer" metaphor. When using the Slider, it is a good practice to keep in mind that some users may struggle with achieving a fine level of control over the slider and provide an alternative such as a TextBox where the user can directly enter the desired value.

When using the Slider in applications, these are the properties that will be most important to developers:

- Maximum: This property specifies the maximum Value of the Slider.

- Minimum: This property specifies the minimum Value of the Slider.

- Value: This property specifies the current Value and must fall between Minimum and Maximum.

- Width: This property specifies the width of the control.

In typical usage scenarios, developers will not find themselves writing code to handle Slider events because Value will be data bound, but occasionally you may find it necessary to respond to the ValueChanged event. This event is raised whenever a new Value is specified.

The XAML required for adding a Slider to your page as pictured in Figure 6-16 is as follows:

```
<Slider Maximum="100" Minimum="0" Value="25" />
```

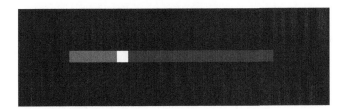

Figure 6-16. *Slider*

ToggleButton

The ToggleButton is a control that is used for on/off values and also supports a third state referred to as *indeterminate*. This should sound much like the CheckBox control to you because the CheckBox and RadioButton controls both share ToggleButton as their base control.

The ToggleButton visually resembles a Button and may be used in situations where the designer prefers the Button look to that of a CheckBox. The decision to use ToggleButton in place of a CheckBox should be considered carefully to make sure the user will not be confused by a control that looks like a Button and behaves like a CheckBox.

These are the properties you will most commonly use for a ToggleButton control:

- Content: This property specifies the content to be displayed on the ToggleButton. This can be simple text, such as is demonstrated in these examples, or other XAML elements.

- IsChecked: This property indicates whether the ToggleButton is currently considered to be in the "on" state.

- IsEnabled: This property indicates whether the user can interact with the control.

- IsThreeState: This property indicates whether the ToggleButton is being used in tri-state mode and supports an indeterminate state.

The ToggleButton control has three events that you will most commonly interact with.

- Checked: This event fires when the value of the IsChecked property changes to True.

- Indeterminate: This event fires when the control is in tri-state mode and the IsChecked property changes to null.

- Unchecked: This event fires when the value of the IsCheckedProperty changes to False.

The XAML required for adding the ToggleButton that is displayed in Figure 6-17 in its "off" state and in Figure 6-18 in its "on" state is as follows:

```
<ToggleButton Content="On/Off" />
```

Figure 6-17. *ToggleButton in off state*

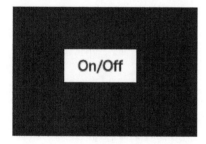

Figure 6-18. *ToggleButton in on state*

ToggleSwitch

The ToggleSwitch is another alternative to the CheckBox that can be used with dealing with information that is "on/off" in nature. This control uses the familiar metaphor of a mechanical switch to illustrate the current state and allows different content to be displayed when in the "on" or "off" state. Unlike the CheckBox and ToggleButton, this control does not provide for an indeterminate state.

These are the properties that you will most commonly use for a ToggleButton control:

- IsEnabled: This property indicates whether the user can interact with the control.

- IsOn: This property indicates whether the ToggleSwitch is currently considered to be in the "on" state.

- OffContent: This property specifies the content to be displayed on the ToggleSwitch when the control is in its "off" state. This can be simple text, such as is demonstrated in these examples, or other XAML elements.

- OnContent: This property specifies the content to be displayed on the ToggleSwitch when the control is in its "on" state. This can be simple text, such as is demonstrated in these examples, or other XAML elements.

The event of the ToggleSwitch control that developers with most often respond to is the Toggled event, which fires when the control switches between states.

The XAML required for adding the ToggleSwitch that is displayed in Figure 6-19 in its "off" state and in Figure 6-20 in its "on" state is as follows:

```
<ToggleSwitch OnContent="Active" OffContent="Inactive" />
```

Figure 6-19. *ToggleSwitch in off state*

Figure 6-20. *ToggleSwitch in on state*

ToolTip

The tooltip is a familiar Windows concept that is used to display content in a popup, usually when a user hovers the mouse pointer over a control, and is intended to provide contextual help by explaining to the user the purpose of or information that should be entered into the control. In the touch-first world of Windows 8, providing contextual help based on a mouse gesture makes less sense, so the concept has been updated to additionally display this information when the user pauses after setting focus to the control.

The ToolTip control is a ContentControl that allows richly formatted information to be presented in the contextual help or even additional controls with which the user can interact but often will just contain text. Developers will normally make use of only the Content property.

The ToolTip control is typically defined connected to another class with assistance of a helper object called ToolTipService. The XAML used to attach a ToolTip control to a TextBox as shown in Figure 6-21 is as follows:

```
<TextBox ToolTipService.ToolTip="Enter phone number formatted (###) ###-####" />
```

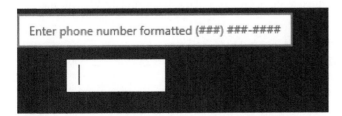

Figure 6-21. *ToolTip*

VariableSizedWrapGrid

The VariableSizedWrapGrid control behaves very much like the StackPanel control in that it lays out child controls sequentially from left to right or top to bottom, one after the other. Where StackPanel and VariableSizedWrapGrid differ in functionality is that the VariableSizedWrapGrid when it reaches the right or bottom bound of the control will begin a new row or column and continue to lay out items. As suggested by its name, the size of each cell within the grid varies by the content with which the cell is filled.

These are some properties that are commonly specified for a VariableSizedWrapGrid control:

- Height and Width: These properties control the size of the container.

- Background: This property controls the Brush that is used for the background of the control.

- Orientation: This property controls whether the VariableSizedWrapGrid expands along a vertical plane, which is its default, or along a horizontal plane.

The XAML used to place a VariableSizedWrapGrid on a page is similar to the StackPanel and looks like the following abbreviated example:

```
<VariableSizedWrapGrid Orientation="Horizontal">
    <TextBlock>Text Block 1</TextBlock>
    <TextBlock>Text Block 2</TextBlock>
    <TextBlock>...</TextBlock>
    <TextBlock>Text Block 100</TextBlock>
</VariableSizedWrapGrid>
```

ViewBox

The ViewBox is a control that displays a single child element stretched or scaled to fit within the ViewBox.

These are the properties you are most likely to work with when using a ViewBox control:

- Child: This property specifies the content to be displayed and is typically populated by adding a child element in XAML rather than specifically referring the property by name.

- Height and Width: These properties specify the height and width of the control.

- Stretch: This property specifies how resizing should be handled if the Child dimensions do not match those of the ViewBox. Possible values include None, Uniform, Fill, and UniformToFill.

- StretchDirection: This property specifies whether the Stretch behavior should apply with scaling the content up, down, or both.

Figure 6-22 illustrates the resizing that is performed by the ViewBox control. Notice in the XAML used to produce the figure that both Ellipse control are defined as the same size, but the one within the ViewBox has been resized by its container:

```
<ViewBox Height="50" Width="50" Stretch="Uniform" StretchDirection="Both">
    <Ellipse Fill="Yellow" Height="100" Width="100" />
</ViewBox>
<Ellipse Fill="Yellow" Height="100" Width="100" />
```

Figure 6-22. `ViewBox`

VirtualizingStackPanel

The `VirtualizingStackPanel` control appears to the user (and to some degree the developer) as a `StackPanel` housed within a `ScrollViewer` to allow for scrolling through a large number of child elements, such as the items in a `ComboBox`, rather than the typical `StackPanel` behavior of clipping the content. What makes the `VirtualizingStackPanel` different from wrapping a `StackPanel` in a `ScrollViewer` is that the `VirtualizingStackPanel` adds intelligence and renders only the content that is within and immediately before and after the ViewPort rather than rendering the entire contents of the control. This provides a significant improvement in memory utilization and performance.

The `VirtualizingStackPanel` is not intended to be a stand-alone control but is used to replace the default `ItemsPanel` used by `ItemsControl`-based controls such as `GridView` and `ListView`. The following XAML replaces the default `ListView` `ItemsPanel` with a `VirtualizingStackPanel`:

```
<ListView>
    <ListView.ItemsPanel>
        <ItemsPanelTemplate>
            <VirtualizingStackPanel Orientation="Vertical" />
        </ItemsPanelTemplate>
    </ListView.ItemsPanel>
</ListView>
```

WebView

The `WebView` control is used to provide an integration point where HTML documents can be presented within a Windows application. One example of this would be the display of a browser-based map application on an application page.

These are the properties you are most likely going to work with when using the `WebView` control:

- `Height` and `Width`: These properties specify the height and width of the control.

- `Source`: This property specifies the URI from which the content of the control should be initially loaded.

In addition to these properties, additional properties exist that are used to specify "safe lists" of URIs that are permitted to interact with the `WebView` by using the JavaScript `window.external.notify()` method within a script in the HTML document. When this JavaScript is called from an allowed URI, the `ScriptNotify` event of the control fires.

While the Source property can specify the initial source of the HTML document hosted within the control, the Navigate and NavigateToString methods can be used to specify new content at runtime. The Navigate method accepts a new URI to which the control should navigate. The NavigateToString method accepts a string containing the actual HTML document, which should be loaded as the new content.

WrapGrid

The WrapGrid control behaves very much like the VirtualizingStackPanel control in that it lays out child controls within an ItemsControl sequentially from left to right or top to bottom, one after the other. When the WrapGrid reaches the right or bottom bound of the control, it will begin a new row or column and continues to lay out items, as illustrated in Figure 6-23.

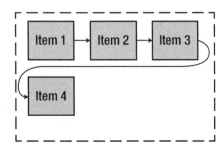

Figure 6-23. *WrapGrid layout*

These are some properties that are commonly specified for a WrapGrid control:

- Height and Width: These properties control the size of the container.

- Orientation: This property controls whether the WrapGrid expands along a vertical plane, which is its default, or along a horizontal plane.

The WrapGrid is not intended to be a stand-alone control but is used to replace the default ItemsPanel used by ItemsControl-based controls such as GridView and ListView. The following XAML replaces the default GridView ItemsPanel with a WrapGrid. This is somewhat redundant in that the WrapGrid is actually the default ItemsPanel used by GridView.

```
<GridView>
    <GridView.ItemsPanel>
        <ItemsPanelTemplate>
            <WrapGrid Orientation="Horizontal" />
        </ItemsPanelTemplate>
    </GridView.ItemsPanel>
</GridView>
```

Conclusion

Between this chapter and the previous, you have now been exposed to all the controls that come in the Visual Studio Toolbox for use in creating Windows applications along with the properties and events that will most commonly be used with each. In the next chapter, you will apply some more advanced concepts, such as styling, and put these pieces together into a usable interface.

CHAPTER 7

■ ■ ■

Building the User Interface

Simplicity is the ultimate sophistication.

—Leonardo da Vinci

In the previous chapters, you learned about touch concepts, Windows design principles, Windows application types, and the many controls that are available to you in the Visual Studio Toolbox. In this chapter, you will learn about XAML styles and data templates, which provide more depth on the `ListView`, `GridView`, `FlipView`, and `SemanticZoom` controls that were introduced in Chapters 5 and 6. Once I have covered these more advanced topics, the foundation will have been laid for me to introduce the sample application that you will build upon through the remainder of the book. You will plan and build the skeleton of the user interface for this sample application.

Introducing Style

When building applications with XAML controls, very often you will find yourself applying custom sets of attributes to controls across the application. For example, you may decide you want all of your `TextBlock` controls to use the Helvetica font. One way to achieve this would be to place `FontFamily = "Helvetica"` in the XAML markup for each `TextBlock` control in the application. This would do the job, but you run the risk of forgetting a `TextBlock` and being left with an inconsistent interface or, even worse, having to go change each `TextBlock` later when you review the design and realize that Segoe UI would have been a more appropriate font. This is where styles come into play.

XAML styles provide a way for developers to create standard sets of property values for UI elements. In many ways, they are similar to the Cascading Style Sheets (CSS) used in HTML development, but because any property of the element being styled can be set within a XAML style, they go far beyond the capabilities of CSS. When creating XAML styles, the following properties, set as attributes within the XAML, are used:

- `TargetType`: This property is required and specifies the element type for which this `Style` will set properties. Only elements of the specified type can reference the `Style`.

- `BasedOn`: This property allows for one `Style` element to inherit the settings of another `Style` element and then provide further customization. The order in which `Style` elements are defined is important, and `Style` elements that are used in the `BasedOn` property of other `Style` elements must first be defined.

- `x:Key`: This property is not technically a property of the `Style` element but of an entry within a `ResourceDictionary`. Because `Style` elements are typically defined as entries in a `ResourceDictionary`, this property is used by elements that reference the `Style`, such as in the `BasedOn` property.

Inside the Style element is a collection of one or more Setter elements. These elements specify the name of the property to be set and the desired value of the property. Often these property values can be expressed using XML attributes, as in Value = "Helvetica", but sometimes the value itself requires additional XML, and in this case the value is specified using element syntax, as in the following:

```
<Setter Property = "Background">
    <Setter.Value>
        <ImageBrush ImageSource = "/Assets/Logo.png" />
    </Setter.Value>
</Setter>
```

Where Styles Are Defined

When adding a Style to your application, the decision should be made whether the Style will be used with only a single page or more globally throughout the application. In this section, you will look at each of these methods.

Page-Level Style Definition

Style elements that will be used only within a single page are typically added to that page's Resources, as in the following example:

```
<Page ...>
    <Page.Resources>
        <Style x:Key = "MyTextBlockStyle" TargetType = "TextBlock">
            <Setter Property = "FontFamily" Value = "Helvetica" />
            <Setter Property = "FontSize" Value = "48" />
        </Style>
    </Page.Resources>
</Page>
```

The preceding sample created a Style that is available throughout the page, and referencing it from any TextBlock will cause the TextBlock to be rendered in 48-point Helvetica font as long as the property has not been overridden by the element itself. This concept of properties being overridden is an important piece of XAML styles. For example, I could define a TextBlock that uses the Helvetica face but an alternative size on the page using the following XAML:

```
<TextBlock Style = "{StaticResource MyTextBlockStyle}" FontSize = "24" Text = "Smaller Text" />
```

I could also create another style based on the first but with a smaller size if I wanted to have multiple TextBlock elements sharing the same attributes. This Style would be defined in the Page.Resources element following the MyTextBlockStyle definition and would look like this:

```
<Style x:Key = "MySmallerTextBlockStyle" TargetType = "TextBlock"
        BasedOn = "{StaticResource MyTextBlockStyle}">
    <Setter Property = "FontSize" Value = "24" />
</Style>
```

EXERCISE: WORKING WITH STYLES

In this exercise, you will use what you have learned about styles to create new styles on a page and reference them from elements within the page. To complete the exercise, you will need Windows 8 and any edition of Visual Studio 2012.

1. To get started, open Visual Studio, and create a new project. The project type should be Blank App (XAML), which can be found in the Windows Store category under Visual C#. Name the project Styles.

2. Double-click MainPage.xaml in the Solution Explorer to open the page you'll be working with.

3. Right-click anywhere on the design surface of the page, and select Change Layout Type ➤ StackPanel.

4. The StackPanel that was just added will, by default, have a self-closing tag. In the XAML editor, change the StackPanel element to include both opening and closing tags. After your edits, the element should appear as follows:

```
<StackPanel Background="{StaticResource ApplicationPageBackgroundThemeBrush}">
</StackPanel>
```

5. Add the following XAML inside the StackPanel to create a TextBlock with no style explicitly specified.

```
<TextBlock Text="No Style Specified" />
```

6. Add the MyTextBlockStyle style to the page by placing the following XAML between the opening Page tag and the StackPanel.

```
<Page.Resources>
    <Style x:Key="MyTextBlockStyle" TargetType="TextBlock">
        <Setter Property="FontFamily" Value="Helvetica" />
        <Setter Property="FontSize" Value="48" />
    </Style>
</Page.Resources>
```

7. Add a new TextBlock referencing the MyTextBlockStyle style. Place the following XAML after the first TextBlock.

```
<TextBlock Style="{StaticResource MyTextBlockStyle}"
           Text="MyTextBlockStyle Specified" />
```

8. Add a second Style based on the first but with smaller text. Place the following XAML immediately following the first style.

```xml
<Style x:Key="MySmallerTextBlockStyle" TargetType="TextBlock"
    BasedOn="{StaticResource MyTextBlockStyle}">
  <Setter Property="FontSize" Value="24" />
</Style>
```

9. Add another `TextBlock` referencing the `MySmallerTextBlockStyle` style. Place the following XAML after the existing `TextBlock` elements:

```xml
<TextBlock Style="{StaticResource MySmallerTextBlockStyle}"
        Text="MySmallerTextBlockStyle Specified" />
```

10. Review the designer window to see the results of having applied—or not applied in the case of the first—styles to your `TextBlock` elements. At this point, the designer window should appear similar to Figure 7-1.

Figure 7-1. TextBlocks with style

11. When examining the properties of the `Style` element, you saw that `x:Key` was an optional property. Not setting the property value specifies that the style will by default be applied to any instance of `TargetType` that does not specify a `Style`. Let's see this in action by adding a default style for `TextBlock` elements. Add the following XAML in the `Page.Resources` element following the `Style` elements that you added earlier:

```xml
<Style TargetType="TextBlock">
  <Setter Property="FontFamily" Value="Cambria" />
  <Setter Property="FontSize" Value="72" />
</Style>
```

12. Review the designer window to see the result of this change. In Figure 7-2, you can see that even though your most recent change did not include changing anything on the `TextBlock` elements themselves, your first `TextBlock` is now displayed in a 72-point Cambria font. The other `TextBlock` elements are unaffected by the change because they explicitly reference other `Style` elements and do not have the new implicit style applied.

Figure 7-2. *TextBlock with implicit style*

In this exercise, you have created Style elements used both explicitly and implicitly on the page where they are defined. For further practice, make additional updates to the styles to see the effect on the elements, or try creating styles applied to different XAML elements.

Application-Level Style Definition

Windows applications and other XAML-based environments such as WPF and Silverlight share the concept of having a central XAML file named App.xaml provide resources that can be globally accessed across the application. It is within this file that you can create, or reference via MergedDictionaries, Style elements that can be applied in all areas of the application.

When creating Style elements that can be applied throughout the application within the App.xaml file, a similar path is taken as you saw when placing Style elements on a page. Within the App.xaml file is an element called Application.Resources. The Application.Resources element will typically contain a single ResourceDictionary element, and this is where you can add Style elements. When the Style elements are added with x:Key specified, the Style can be referenced in the same way you referenced the on-page Style elements from any page in the application. When the x:Key attribute is omitted, the Style is considered an implicit style and is applied to any instance of TargetType to which a style has not already been applied.

■ **Note**   It is important to remember that Style settings are applied in the closest scope possible to the element. If the element contains an explicit Style attribute, then that is used. Otherwise, the scope is walked upward, such as to the page level and then the application level, until an implicit style is found. This means if you are using implicit styles on a page, the elements will not be affected by implicit styles defined in App.xaml.

The ResourceDictionary-default App.xaml created with a new Visual Studio project also includes MergedDictionaries, which references additional ResourceDictionary files either defined in the project or imported from other assemblies. This merged dictionary includes a reference to a ResourceDictionary provided by Visual Studio called StandardStyles.xaml, which is used heavily by many controls in the Visual Studio Toolbox. To help keep your application well organized and maintainable, it is recommended that you follow this pattern and create your own dictionaries to import into the MergedDictionaries. You will have the opportunity to do this in the following exercise.

EXERCISE: APPLICATION STYLES

In this exercise, you will build upon the previous exercise and add styles at the application level. To complete the exercise, you will need Windows 8 and any edition of Visual Studio 2012. You should also have completed the previous exercise and have created the Styles project.

1. Open the Styles project created in the previous exercise.

2. Open `MainPage.xaml`, and verify that the designer appears as shown in Figure 7-2 from the previous exercise.

3. Double-click `App.xaml`, and observe the current contents of the file. The file should contain a single `ResourceDictionary` element that contains a reference to `Common/StandardStyles.xaml` within its `MergedDictionaries`.

4. Add an application-level `Style` that implicitly sets the `Foreground` property of `TextBlock` elements to `Yellow`. Place the following XAML in `App.xaml` after the closing tag of `ResourceDictionary.MergedDictionaries` and before the closing tag of the outermost `ResourceDictionary`:

```
<Style TargetType="TextBlock">
    <Setter Property="Foreground" Value="Yellow" />
</Style>
```

5. What do you expect to have happened to the `TextBlock` on `MainPage.xaml` that has no `Style` property set? Open `MainPage.xaml` to see whether your expectation is met. A reasonable expectation would have been that the two implicit styles—one from the page and one from the application—would have merged and the text contained in the `TextBlock` would have turned yellow. Because of the way implicit styles work, this is not the case, and the `TextBlock` remained unchanged from what you saw in Figure 7-2.

6. In `MainPage.xaml`, comment out the implicit style by adding `<!--` before the element and `-->` after, as shown in the following XAML:

```
<!--
<Style TargetType="TextBlock">
    <Setter Property="FontFamily" Value="Cambria" />
    <Setter Property="FontFace" Value="72" />
</Setter>
-->
```

7. Examine the page in the designer. Note that the size and font of the text has returned to what you saw in Figure 7-1, and the color is now yellow. The `TextBlock` is now having its `Style` implicitly defined as set in `App.xaml`.

8. At this point, you have created a `Style` that can be applied across all pages in the application, but you are not following the best practice of keeping the `App.xaml` as clean as possible. You'll correct this by moving the style into its own `ResourceDictionary`. Right-click the `Common` folder, and select Add ➤ New Item.

In the Add New Item dialog, select Resource Dictionary as the item type, and name the file `MyStyles.xaml`.

9. Cut the XAML `Style` that you added in step 4 out of `App.xaml` and paste it into `MyStyles.xaml`. The `MyStyles.xaml` file should now appear as follows:

```
<ResourceDictionary
    xmlns="http://schemas.microsoft.com/winfx/2006/xaml/presentation"
    xmlns:x="http://schemas.microsoft.com/winfx/2006/xaml"
    xmlns:local="using:Styles.Common">
    <Style TargetType="TextBlock">
        <Setter Property="Foreground" Value="Yellow" />
    </Style>
</ResourceDictionary>
```

10. Examine `MainPage.xaml` in the designer again. Note that the text in the `TextBlock` with no `Style` specified has returned to its original value of White.

11. Add the `MyStyles.xaml` file `ResourceDictionary` to the `MergedDictionaries` in `App.xaml`. Place the following XAML before the closing `ResourceDictionary`. `MergedDictionaries` tag in `App.xaml`:

```
<ResourceDictionary Source="Common/MyStyles.xaml" />
```

12. Return to `MainPage.xaml`, and observe that the color of the text in the `TextBlock` with no `Style` specified has now returned to Yellow.

In this exercise, you have learned to create `Style` elements that are accessible throughout the application using `App.xaml` and resource dictionaries. These will help ensure you can create applications that have a consistent look and feel throughout the application and that are easier to maintain than setting properties on each control.

StandardStyles.xaml

In the previous section, you saw that Visual Studio creates a ResourceDictionary called StandardStyles.xaml, which is imported into App.xaml as a MergedDictionary and available throughout the application. The styles defined in this dictionary not only are used by many of the Visual Studio templates but can serve as a valuable resource in helping you create applications with a look and feel that is consistent with other Windows applications. When defining the look of controls on a page, the styles in this dictionary should be examined to see whether there is one that already meets your needs. For example, the TextBlock at the top of the page holding a page title should most likely be assigned the PageHeaderTextStyle style. If no style within StandardStyles.xaml meets your needs and you need a variation, it is important to heed the advice of the ReadMe.txt file that is created alongside StandardStyles.xaml and directs the developer to create their own styles in another ResourceDictionary rather than making any changes at all to StandardStyles.xaml.

DataTemplates

The DataTemplate is used to define the layout for each repeating item in an ItemsControl such as ListView, GridView, or FlipView. This allows you to support more complex layouts than the simple lists of strings you saw in Chapters 5 and 6.

■ **Note** By necessity, some of the examples in this section make reference to data binding features, which are introduced in the next chapter. Don't dwell on it too much yet; you'll get there soon.

Where DataTemplates Are Defined

As with Style elements, the DataTemplate can be defined in a ResourceDictionary. This means it can be found anywhere you find a Style such as in Page.Resources on a page, within App.xaml, or in your own imported ResourceDictionary. Additionally, DataTemplates that are not intended to be reused within multiple controls can be defined inline with its containing control.

ResourceDictionary

The most common place to find a DataTemplate defined is within a ResourceDictionary. The StandardStyles.xaml dictionary you learned about earlier in this chapter contains several DataTemplate definitions that are referenced from some of the default page templates and serve as an example of how to build your own DataTemplate definitions. One of the simplest of these is the template named Standard250x250ItemTemplate. It is intended for use within a GridView and is defined with the following XAML:

```
<DataTemplate x:Key="Standard250x250ItemTemplate">
    <Grid HorizontalAlignment="Left" Width="250" Height="250">
        <Border Background="{StaticResource ListViewItemPlaceholderBackgroundThemeBrush}">
            <Image Source="{Binding Image}" Stretch="UniformToFill " />
        </Border>
        <StackPanel VerticalAlignment="Bottom"
                    Background="{ListViewItemOverlayBackgroundThemeBrush}">
            <TextBlock Text="{Binding Title}"
                       Foreground="{ListViewItemOverlayForegroundThemeBrush}"
                       Style="{StaticResource TitleTextStyle}"
                       Height="60" Margin="15,0,15,0" />
            <TextBlock Text="{Binding Subtitle}"
                       Foreground="{ListViewItemOverlaySecondaryForegroundThemeBrush}"
                       Style="{StaticResource CaptionTextStyle}"
                       TextWrapping="NoWrap" Margin="15,0,15,0" />
        </StackPanel>
    </Grid>
</DataTemplate>
```

The DataTemplate requires that exactly one element be a direct child of the DataTemplate element. This means that individual controls can be used for simple layouts, but more often the DataTemplate will contain a Panel of some sort, which, in turn, contains additional controls used to achieve the desired layout.

■ **Note** An interesting thing to note about the DataTemplate used in the previous example is the "stacking" technique used to layer the UI elements. Notice that a Grid has been used as the layout container for the rest of the controls but that Grid does not define any rows or columns. This leaves the Grid with a single cell at row 0, column 0. Items placed within the same cell in a Grid will stack from bottom up in the order they are defined within the XAML, which creates some interesting design possibilities.

When the DataTemplate has been defined within a ResourceDictionary, its Key is used to reference it from controls that will use it. The following XAML illustrates the Standard250x250ItemTemplate DataTemplate being applied to a GridView:

```
<GridView ItemTemplate="{StaticResource Standard250x250ItemTemplate}">
</GridView>
```

Inline

For simple "one-off" DataTemplate instances that apply to a single control, the ItemTemplate can be defined inline with the control itself. When choosing to create DataTemplate definitions inline, it is important to decide whether it will make your XAML easier to read and understand or more difficult. There is no hard and fast rule for this, but consider the following two GridView instances:

```
<GridView x:Name="GridView1">
    <GridView.ItemTemplate>
        <DataTemplate>
            <TextBlock Text="{Binding Title}" />
        </DataTemplate>
    </GridView.ItemTemplate>
</GridView>

<GridView x:Name="GridView2">
    <GridView.ItemTemplate>
        <DataTemplate x:Key="Standard250x250ItemTemplate">
            <Grid HorizontalAlignment="Left" Width="250" Height="250">
                <Border
                    Background="{StaticResource ListViewItemPlaceholderBackgroundThemeBrush}">
                    <Image Source="{Binding Image}" Stretch="UniformToFill" />
                </Border>
                <StackPanel VerticalAlignment="Bottom"
                            Background="{ListViewItemOverlayBackgroundThemeBrush}">
                    <TextBlock Text="{Binding Title}"
                               Foreground="{ListViewItemOverlayForegroundThemeBrush}"
                               Style="{StaticResource TitleTextStyle}"
                               Height="60" Margin="15,0,15,0" />
                    <TextBlock Text="{Binding Subtitle}"
                               Foreground="{ListViewItemOverlaySecondaryForegroundThemeBrush}"
                               Style="{StaticResource CaptionTextStyle}"
                               TextWrapping="NoWrap" Margin="15,0,15,0" />
                </StackPanel>
            </Grid>
        </DataTemplate>
    </GridView.ItemTemplate>
</GridView>
```

In the example GridView elements, the one named GridView1 was easily read and understood and is a good candidate for inline definition. GridView2 was a different story. This is much more complicated and can't easily be taken in at a glance, leaving the developer trying to understand the code by going back and forth between opening and closing tags and visualizing the control. In this case, the DataTemplate is much better defined within a named resource.

■ **Note**   Like with any code, breaking the XAML used to build your user interfaces into smaller, well-organized chunks can make it easier to manage in the long run.

The MovieBrowser Sample Application

Throughout the next several chapters, you will be working on a fully functional application used to access data from the cloud and display it in a compelling Windows style user interface. You'll call the application MovieBrowser, and, as the name implies, it will be used to view information about movies stored in an online catalog. In this chapter, you will begin work on the user interface, establishing the layout and navigation pattern. After you've had the opportunity to learn about the rich data binding features of XAML and the Model-View-ViewModel design pattern, you'll return to this application and build upon it using these concepts. The downloadable code for each chapter in which you build upon the application will include a solution including the application as it stands at the end of that chapter.

Applications designed to browse information are ideal for Windows styling, especially for the three containers that will be used heavily in this application: GridView, ListView, and FlipView. The application will include a primary view (illustrated in Figure 7-3) in which movie genres contained in the catalog are listed along with a sampling of the movies that appear within each genre. Additionally, there will be a view that lists the titles within a genre (shown in Figure 7-4), as well as a view that shows a detailed view of a single title within a genre (Figure 7-5). Figure 7-6 uses a diagram known as a *navigation diagram* to capture the interactions that will cause the user to move between views within the application.

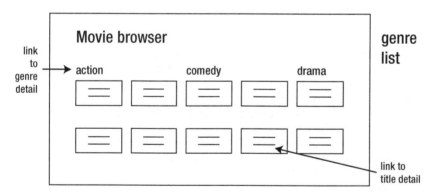

Figure 7-3. *Genre list*

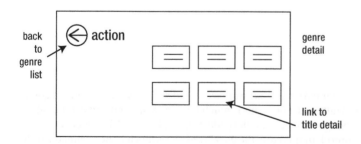

Figure 7-4. *Genre detail*

100

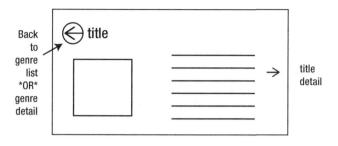

Figure 7-5. *Title detail*

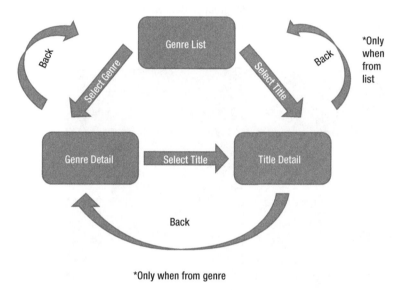

Figure 7-6. *Navigation diagram*

■ **Note** The initial pass at determining the screens within the application and how they relate to one another is intentionally very rough in these figures. I recommend using hand-drawn sketches when deciding the general layout of the application screens and functionality. Too many critical design sessions have been derailed before knowing *what* the application should do because of a screen mock-up using the wrong shade of blue.

EXERCISE: STARTING THE MOVIEBROWSER UI

In this exercise, you will start building the MovieBrowser application. You will see how the templates that ship with Visual Studio 2012 enable you to rapidly get started with Windows applications that have a consistent look and feel with other applications. To complete the exercise, you will need Windows 8 and any version of Visual Studio 2012.

1. To get started, open Visual Studio, and create a new project. The project type should be Grid App (XAML), which can be found in the Windows Store category under Visual C#. Name the project MovieBrowser.

2. Examine the application that was created from the template. The application consists of three pages: GroupedItemsPage.xaml, GroupDetailPage.xaml, and ItemDetailPage.xaml. These pages correspond to the Genre List, Genre Details, and Item Details views that you need for the application.

3. Run the application by pressing F5 on the keyboard.

4. The initial screen that displays is GroupedItemsPage, as shown in Figure 7-7. It is making use of a GridView control that is configured for grouped data with a header defined for each group. Scroll back and forth to view the data on the screen.

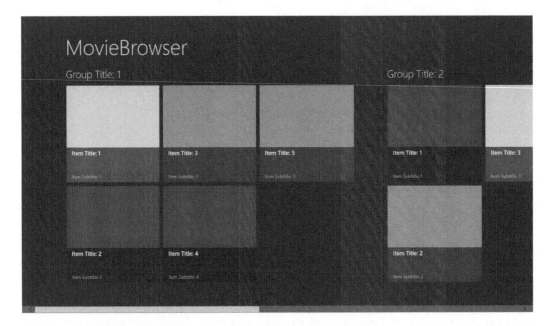

Figure 7-7. GroupedItemsPage

5. The group header within the GridView control is a styled Button. Hover over the text Group Title: 1, and see the text go from dim to light, indicating that it can be tapped to activate.

6. Each item within the GridView's groups can be clicked or tapped. Using the mouse, hover over several items to see how they advertise that they can be clicked.

7. Click the group header labeled Group Title: 1. You are navigated to the GroupDetailPage page (shown in Figure 7-8). This page lists information about the group itself and provides a listing of the titles within the group. A `GridView` is used for this functionality.

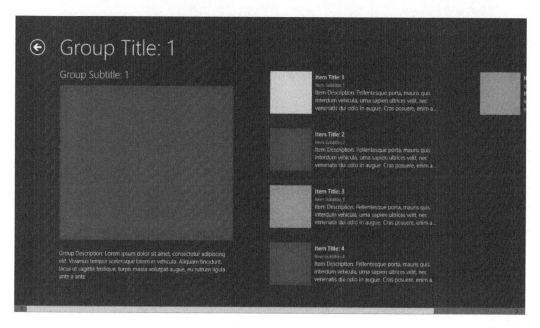

Figure 7-8. *GroupDetailPage*

8. Click the item labeled Item Title: 1. You are navigated to the ItemDetailPage page (shown in Figure 7-9). This page displays a large image and text containing details from the item. The left and right edges near the center of the screens have arrows allowing you to navigate between items within the item's group. This functionality is achieved using a `FlipView` control. Additionally, an arrow at the top-left corner of the screen can be clicked or tapped to navigate back to the group detail page. Click the arrow.

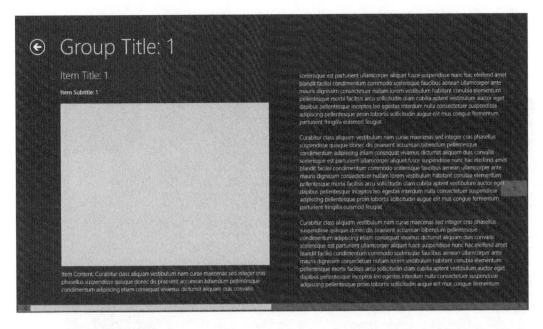

Figure 7-9. ItemDetailPage

9. Back on the GroupDetailPage page, click the arrow at the top-left corner to navigate back to the initial GroupedItemsPage page.

10. Click the item labeled Item Title: 1. You're taken to the ItemDetailPage page as before.

11. Click the arrow at the top-left corner of the page, and note that you are taken back to the GroupedItemPage page because that was the previous page in your navigation.

12. Return to Visual Studio, and press Shift + F5 to stop debugging.

Without writing any code, Visual Studio has provided the structure of an application that comes very close to what you need for the MovieBrowser application. You will return to this application and start customizing it for your needs in Chapter 10.

Conclusion

In this chapter, you learned about using Style elements to achieve a consistent look and feel throughout your application and about the DataTemplate elements that are used to lay out items within controls such as ListView, GridView, FlipView, and SemanticZoom. Finally, I introduced the MovieBrowser application you will be building over the next several chapters and used the Grid App template to have Visual Studio build the foundation of your application's user interface. In Chapters 8 and 9, you will learn some key concepts that will help you customize the application to meet your needs. For further study, examine StandardStyles.xaml to learn more about the Style and DataTemplate elements that it contains.

■ ■ ■

CHAPTER 8

Data Binding

Because if you have a strong foundation like we have, then you can build or rebuild anything on it. But if you've got a weak foundation, you can't build anything.

—Jack Scalia

You've learned about the application types available in Windows 8, the controls in the Visual Studio Toolbox, and how to put these elements together to "draw your screen," but now you have a screen (perhaps even a pretty one, depending on your design skills) that is just an empty shell that does nothing of value. In the next couple of chapters, you will learn how to use one of the most popular features of XAML—its rich binding functionality—to fill that screen with data from your application and add interactive functionality to connect your user with the application. This chapter sets the groundwork by providing an in-depth look at binding. I will cover dependency objects, dependency properties, and value converters. Once you've learned what is happening under the covers, you will see how these elements are brought together to tie the application's data and behavior to the user interface.

Observer Pattern

Before diving into the objects used to bind data in Windows applications, it will be helpful to spend some time learning about the Observer pattern. The Observer pattern is one of the patterns cataloged by the "Gang of Four" in the book *Design Patterns: Elements of Reusable Object-Oriented Software* and describes a scenario that has been central to data binding strategies since the Model-View-Controller paradigm was first used in Smalltalk applications. In the Observer pattern, an object that may have state changes of interest, known as the *subject*, provides a mechanism to publish these state changes, and a class that is interested in these state changes, known as an *observer*, uses this mechanism to register interest in the subject's state changes. Figure 8-1 shows the relationship between subject and observer in a common scenario.

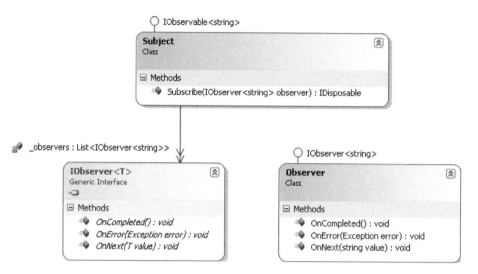

Figure 8-1. *Observer-subject class relationship*

In this sample implementation, which is based on interfaces designed for this purpose in the .NET Framework, the Subject class maintains a list of IObserver <string> objects that are interested in state changes. The IObservable <string> interface defines the Subscribe method, which communicates to the subject that a specific observer should receive notifications. Figure 8-2 illustrates the subscription mechanism.

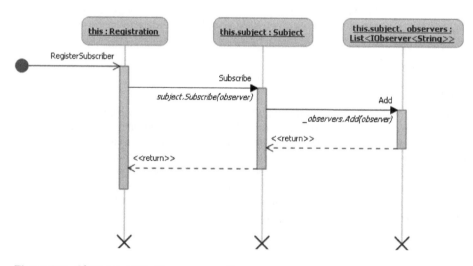

Figure 8-2. *Observer registration sequence diagram*

Once registration has been completed, the subject maintains its list of subscribers and, when state changes of interest occur, calls the OnNext method of each observer, passing the new value. Figure 8-3 illustrates the subject notifying observers when the state of interest changes.

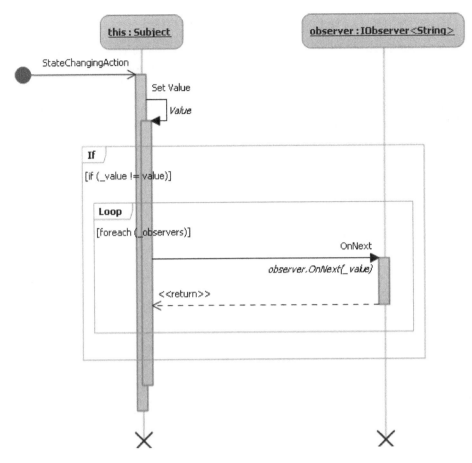

Figure 8-3. *Observable state change notification*

I will not be using the IObserver <T> and IObservable <T> interfaces in this chapter other than to explain the concepts behind the Observer pattern, so the additional methods in the IObserver <T> class will not be discussed. The objects I will be using instead share the characteristics discussed here but also add other functionality more useful to building applications in XAML. At this point, you should have enough understanding of what the Observer pattern is and the role that it fills to make the rest of this chapter make more sense.

Managing and Synchronizing Application Data with the User Interface

In many applications and examples, application data is managed within the controls in the user interface, and it is the responsibility of the developer writing the application to keep track of the semantic meaning of the data held by the control, the relationship of the data to data contained by other controls, and whether to enable or disable controls based on the state of other controls in the application. In all but the simplest of applications, this can often lead to a jumble of syntax in the source file that holds the user interface code that not only is hard to read but is error prone and difficult to test and maintain. Microsoft addressed this difficulty by building a system into the XAML-based development platforms Windows Presentation Foundation and Silverlight, bringing this system forward into the Windows Runtime.

Dependency Objects and Dependency Properties

At the core of data binding for applications written on the Windows Runtime is a system of classes that the runtime knows how to bind to, collectively referred to as the *dependency property system*. Simply put, the dependency property system is a way to express that the value of a property of an object is dependent upon or computed from the value of some other property or properties. In the Windows Runtime, the management of these properties is represented using the Windows.UI.Xaml.DependencyProperty object applied to objects deriving from Windows.UI.Xaml.DependencyObject.

Windows.UI.Xaml.PropertyMetadata

The PropertyMetadata class in the dependency property system contains the information regarding the data to be bound, the type to which properties should be registered, and behaviors such as value coercion and property change notification. This class is used both when creating a new DependencyProperty and when retrieving information about an existing DependencyProperty.

Constructors

The PropertyMetadata object has no default constructor without arguments. To create an instance of this object, one of two constructors must be selected.

- The first overload accepts a single parameter that is of type object and represents the default value that should be applied for the property.

- An additional constructor accepts, in addition to the default value, a callback method that is invoked by the dependency property system whenever the value of the dependency property changes. This property change callback method will be discussed in greater detail later in this chapter and accepts metadata describing the property and object that has changed.

Create Method

In addition to the constructors, PropertyMetadata defines several overloads of a static method called Create. This is used to instantiate and initialize a new instance of the PropertyMetadata class.

- The first of these overloads accepts a callback method that is invoked to return the default value for the property. This method of establishing the default value for the property value allows for the default to be set at runtime instead of when the code is compiled and can be especially useful in situations when the application needs to support internationalization or drive default values from configuration.

- The second overload accepts, in addition to the default value callback, a property change callback, as described in the previous section of constructors.

- The remaining two Create overloads accept the same arguments and exhibit the same behavior as the two constructors.

CreateDefaultValueCallback Property

The CreateDefaultValueCallback property is a read-only property. It is used to retrieve the method that will be invoked to obtain or create the default value to be used for this property. In cases where a fixed default value was provided through either the constructor or the Create method that accepts a fixed default value, the property returns a null value.

DefaultValue Property

The DefaultValue property is a read-only property. It is used to retrieve the value supplied as the default value when the PropertyMetadata object was constructed using either the constructor or one of the Create overloads. This property returns only the fixed value supplied, so if the PropertyMetadata object was constructed using a CreateDefaultValueCallback instead of a fixed value, the property returns a null value.

Windows.UI.Xaml.DependencyProperty

The DependencyProperty class is used to represent a "catalog entry" of a property that is registered on a dependency object. While this class is of vital importance, it has surprisingly few methods and properties.

Register Method

The Register method is the primary method for connecting a DependencyProperty to a DependencyObject in the dependency property system. This method accepts the following:

- A string to represent the name of the DependencyProperty being registered

- A Type representing the data type of the property's value

- A Type representing the type of the DependencyObject to which the DependencyProperty is being registered (or the "owner type")

- An instance of the PropertyMetadata class describing any default value and property change notification behavior

When called, this method handles registration of the DependencyProperty and returns the registered property. As I'll demonstrate later, this method should be used to populate static, read-only variables.

RegisterAttached Method

The RegisterAttached method is used to create a special kind of DependencyProperty known as an *attached property*, which I will not discuss in this chapter. As with the Register method, this method accepts the following:

- A string representing the name of the DependencyProperty being registered

- A Type representing the data type of the property's value

- A Type representing the type of the DependencyObject to which the DependencyProperty is being registered (or the "owner type")

- An instance of the PropertyMetadata class describing any default value and property change notification behavior

When called, this method handles registration of the DependencyProperty and returns the registered property.

GetMetadata Method

The GetMetadata method is used to retrieve the metadata from the dependency property system that is defined for the DependencyProperty on a specific type. The method accepts a single parameter, which is the type for which the property metadata should be retrieved and returns an object of type PropertyMetadata.

UnsetValue Property

DependencyProperty contains a single property called UnsetValue. This is a read-only property and is used instead of null or a default to indicate that the property is registered but that the property system has not yet assigned a value to the property.

Windows.UI.Xaml.DependencyObject

The objects you've learned about so far have all been about defining and creating properties, but you can't have properties without some container to bring these properties together into something meaningful. Just as System.Object is the base container for holding together CLR properties, the Windows.UI.Xaml.DependencyObject class serves as the base for objects that expose data using the dependency property system. This object defines several methods used to manage dependency properties and a single property.

SetValue Method

The SetValue method is used to assign a value to the dependency property. Semantically, this is similar to using a property setter using CLR properties. As you will see in the code samples later in this chapter, it is recommended when you create objects using the dependency property system that CLR properties be used to "wrap" dependency properties, allowing developers to write code using your object with familiar property syntax. The method accepts a parameter for the dependency property to be set and a parameter of type object that represents the value to be set.

GetValue Method

Just as SetValue correlates to a CLR property setter, the GetValue method is used to provide the dependency property system's equivalent of the CLR property getter. The method accepts a single parameter that is the dependency property storing the value to be retrieved and returns an object representing the stored value.

■ **Note** Notice that both SetValue and ClearValue use the object type for the property value. Internally, the dependency object system stores all dependency properties as objects; when retrieving values to be used in your application, they must be cast to the appropriate type. Besides the familiar syntax, this is another good reason to wrap dependency property access in CLR properties and centralize the data conversion.

ReadLocalValue Method

In the previous section, you learned that GetValue is equivalent to a CLR property getter, but it's a little more complicated than that with the dependency property system. One of the things that makes this system powerful is that the effective value, which is the value return by the GetValue method at any point in time, of a dependency property can come from many places, so the value set to the property may be different from the value returned by the GetValue method. The ReadLocal method is used to obtain the actual value set to the property or the UnsetValue property value if no local value has been assigned. This method accepts a single argument representing the property for which the value should be retrieved and returns an object representing the stored property value.

ClearValue Method

As its name implies, the ClearValue method removes the value that has been set for a dependency property, making it as if the value had never been set. This is different from setting the value to its default value because there are times when the binding system will treat a property that has not been set very differently from a property that has had its value set even if set to the default value, as you will see later in this chapter. This method accepts a single parameter representing the dependency property whose value should be reset and a void return.

GetAnimationBaseValue Method

XAML features the ability to apply animations to objects and relies heavily on the dependency property system. At any given point in time, a dependency object's value may be impacted by one or more active animations. When you need to retrieve what the value of a property would be if unaffected by any active animation, the GetAnimationBaseValue will do the job for you. This method accepts a single parameter representing the dependency property for which the base value should be retrieved and returns an object with the value of the property.

Dispatcher Property

Windows applications have a Dispatcher, which is the object responsible for receiving messages from the operating system; these messages are known as *window messages* and send relevant events to the client application. This dispatcher is extremely important when it comes to managing the way that your application behaves with threads, and each dependency object has a reference to it through the Dispatcher property.

EXERCISE: PUTTING DEPENDENCY PROPERTIES TOGETHER

In this exercise, you'll take what you've learned so far in this chapter and create your first objects using the dependency property system. To complete this exercise, you will need any version of Microsoft Visual Studio 2012.

1. To get started, open Visual Studio and create a new project. The project type should be Blank App (XAML), which can be found in the Windows Store category under Visual C#. Name this project DependencyObjectSampleCs.

2. Right-click the project in the Solution Explorer window, and select Add ➤ New Folder. Name the folder Entities. This folder will be used to hold the objects you create.

3. Now you're ready to add your dependency objects. You're going to create a Person object that could be used in a number of application scenarios. Right-click the Entities folder you created in the previous step and select Add ➤ Class. Name the new class Person.cs. The generated class produced by Visual Studio should look like this (namespace and using statements omitted):

```
class Person
{
}
```

4. At this point, Person is a normal CLR object. To make it an object that participates in the dependency property system, you need to make it a dependency object. To do this, add using Windows.UI.Xaml to the using statements at the top of the code file, and modify the class declaration as follows:

```
public class Person : DependencyObject
{
}
```

5. Now you'll add the LastName property. You do this by creating and registering with the dependency property system a dependency property. As a requirement of the dependency property system, this property is defined as a static property, so it is owned by the class itself rather than each instance. You use the DependencyProperty. Register method to handle the creation and registration for you, specifying that the property type should be a string and should be owned by the Person class. Additionally, you'll provide a default value of an empty string in the PropertyMetadata. By convention, the name of the variable holding the DependencyProperty should be the name of the property followed by Property, in this case LastNameProperty. When you create the property, your resulting code should look like this:

```
public class Person : DependencyObject
{
  public static readonly DependencyProperty LastNameProperty
  = DependencyProperty.Register("LastName"
  , typeof(string)
  , typeof(Person)
  , new PropertyMetadata(string.Empty));
}
```

6. Using the previous step as a guide, create a FirstName property, which should also have a string value and default to an empty string.

7. At this point, you have a fully functional object that participates in the dependency property system. The following code could be used to interact with your object's data:

```
Person p=new Person();
p.SetValue(Person.LastNameProperty, "Jones");
p.SetValue(Person.FirstNameProperty, "Sam");
string fullName=(string) p.GetValue(Person.LastNameProperty)
+ " "+(string) p.GetValue(Person.FirstNameProperty);
```

8. For anyone used to using CLR properties, the previous sample should look like a pretty long-winded way just to get at stored property values. Let's make the object easier to interact with from .NET code by adding standard CLR property accessors that will handle interacting with the dependency property system for you. In the Person class, add the following code to create a standard CLR property for LastName:

```
public string LastName
{
 get
 {
 return (string) GetValue(LastNameProperty);
 }
 set
 {
 SetValue(LastNameProperty, value);
 }
}
```

9. Using the previous step as a guide, create a `FirstName` CLR property to wrap the
    `FirstNameProperty` dependency property.

Now you have completed your first object using the dependency object system and exposing properties in
a way that is friendly for other .NET developers. You can see the much more natural manner with which you
can interact with the object in the following code, which does the same thing as the example in step 7:

```
Person p = new Person();
p.LastName = "Jones";
p. FirstName = "Sam";
string fullName = p.LastName + " " + p.FirstName;
```

XAML Binding

You've just taken an in-depth look at the dependency property system, and in this section you will learn how
the XAML binding system is built around the dependency property system. You'll learn how the Binding object,
which is itself a descendant of DependencyObject, can be used to bind data from nearly any source to any
dependency object as well as how you can use value converters to help translate data from how it is stored in its
source into something that can be used in the user interface of your application.

Why Is Binding Important?

Before jumping into the gritty details of binding, let's consider what life would be like without binding. Assume
you have requirements to build a simple application in which the user can enter criteria and perform a search
for products. When the search results come back, the product title will be shown in a list, and when an item is
selected from the list, its summary description should be displayed. For laying out a very rudimentary form of the
user interface, you might come up with something like the following XAML:

```
<StackPanel Background="{StaticResource ApplicationPageBackgroundBrush}">
    <TextBlock Style="{StaticResource PageHeaderTextStyle}" Text="Product Search" />
    <TextBox Name="criteriaTextBox" />
    <Button Name="searchButton" Content="Search" />
    <ListBox Height="100" Name="resultList" />
    <TextBlock Style="{StaticResource ItemTextStyle}" Name="summaryTextBlock" />
</StackPanel>
```

This sets up the look of the application, so now you just need to make it do something. As a preparatory step for this example, I created a simple class called SearchResultItem to represent items being returned from a search and defined it as follows:

```
public class SearchResultItem
{
    public string Title { get; set; }
    public string Summary {get; set; }
}
```

Next you need some code to perform the search (or, in this case, pretend a search is performed). The code-behind of the page contains the following method:

```
private IEnumerable<SearchResult> DoSearch(string criteria)
{
    return new[]
    {
        new SearchResultItem
            {
                Title = "Bread",
                Summary = "Good for sandwiches"
            },
        new SearchResultItem
            {
                Title = "Milk",
                Summary = "Healthy, but tastes better flavored"
            }
    };
}
```

Now that you have search results and code to find them, it's time to invoke the search from your page and display results. Double-clicking the search button in the designer brings up the code editor with the searchButton_Click method stubbed out and ready to fill out with the following code:

```
private void searchButton_Click(object sender, RoutedEventArgs e)
{
    var results = DoSearch(criteriaTextBox.Text);
    // empty out what was there before
    resultList.Items.Clear();

    // now fill it with the new results
    foreach(SearchResultItem result in results)
    {
        ListBoxItem listItem = new ListBoxItem
        {
            Content = result.Title,
            Tag = result
        };

        resultList.Items.Add(listItem);
    }
}
```

When you run the application and click Search, the list is filled, and you see the result shown in Figure 8-4.

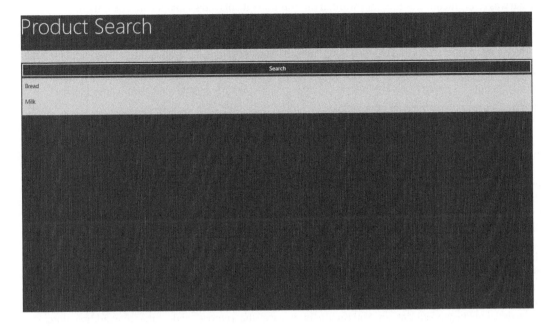

Figure 8-4. *Product search result*

So far, you've implemented part of the requirement, but you still need to build the summary display when items are selected in the ListBox control. To implement this feature, go back to the XAML page's designer, select the resultList ListBox control, and type resultList_SelectionChange into the SelectionChanged event in the Properties window. This will cause Visual Studio to stub out the event handler for you and open the code window where the following code can be added:

Note Notice the number of assumptions being made in this code. This is acceptable for a quick sample, but for an application that would see production use, this is just asking for a midnight support call.

```
private void resultList_SelectionChanged(object sender, SelectionChangedEventArgs e)
{
    // go ahead and clear the summary box in case nothing is selected
    summaryTextBlock.Text = string.Empty;
    if(resultList.SelectedItem != null)
    {
        var selection = (ListBoxItem) resultList.SelectedItem;
        summaryTextBlock.Text = ((SearchResultItem) selection.Tag).Summary;
    }
}
```

Now you can run the application and see that the summary for the selected item displays as the requirements dictate. You had a couple of minor hurdles to deal with as the data was being interacted with on-screen, but nothing major, and this looks like it could be a workable programming model. That is, you thought you were done. You see, when the user said that they wanted the summary to be displayed when they selected an item in the ListBox, what was really meant was that they wanted the summary displayed so that it could be edited.

■ **Note** There's an old folk story called "Stone Soup," which I think everyone involved in the software requirements process should read; the story, in which a traveler (or in some versions a group of travelers) convinces villagers that he can make soup out of a single stone but tricks them into adding other ingredients a piece at a time, closely parallels the way software requirements often unfold.

Without too much effort, you can change summaryTextBlock to instead be summaryTextBox by updating its XAML tag and name. This will make the content editable, but very quickly you see that as you switch back and forth between the items in the list, the updates you make in the TextBox have no impact on the value displayed for each list item.

Your first impulse based on the code you've been writing might be to put code in the TextChanged event of the TextBox and in this code use the reverse of the code you used in the SelectionChanged event of the ListBox to update the Summary property for the search result represented by the SelectedItem of the ListBox with the new value of the TextBox. This type of approach has been taken for years both in Windows applications written in various languages/platforms and in rich web applications written in HTML and JavaScript; this of course can be done in XAML applications as well, but even the simplest application quickly becomes very complicated and brittle using this style of connecting data to the screen, as you can see by the amount of code needed to make this little application do what is needed. Let's instead look at how you can do this in a way that removes code rather than adding more.

Windows.UI.Xaml.Data.Binding Object

The Binding object (and its associated XAML element) is used as the glue to tie data both to elements that you see on the screen and to nonvisual components that derive from FrameworkElement and have dependency properties. I will talk about some of the properties of the Binding object now and expand your knowledge when I discuss value converters later in this chapter.

ElementName Property

The ElementName property is used when binding to a data contained within another XAML element. The property value should match the Name property of the element whose data you want to bind. In the case of the previous example, the ElementName would be set to resultList. This property is optional and will be omitted when the binding source is not an element on the page.

Source Property

The Source property is used when binding to data other than elements on the page. Often you will see this used when binding to application or page resources. I will revisit this when discussing the Model-View-ViewModel pattern later in this book.

RelativeSource Property

In many advanced binding scenarios, you may not know the name of the element that should serve as the source of the data to which you are binding. The primary scenario in which this is seen is when you are building reusable controls that can have templates applied. The RelativeSource property allows you to reference this parent element by using RelativeSource of TemplatedParent. RelativeSource can also be used as a way to bind related properties of the same control by using RelativeSource of Self. A simple example of how this could be used would be to place a Rectangle control on the page and ensure that it remains a square by binding the Height property to the Width property.

```
<Rectangle Width="100" Fill="Blue">
    <Rectangle.Height>
        <Binding RelativeSource="{RelativeSource}" Path="Width" />
    </Rectangle.Height>
</Rectangle>
```

■ **Note**   The Binding properties discussed provide different ways to set the object that will serve as the source for data binding. It's important to remember that for any given Binding, you can set only one of these properties because they are mutually exclusive.

Path Property

The Path property is either the name of the property on the binding source (whether that source is resolved through ElementName, Source, or RelativeSource) or a navigation starting with a property and using dot notation to work through subproperties until the desired data is reached. In the case of the earlier search example, the Binding used for the summary TextBox would have to navigate an object hierarchy and would have a Path value of SelectedItem.Tag.Summary when binding with an ElementName of resultList.

Mode Property

The Mode property is used to control how (or even if) the Binding is to keep data synchronized between the binding's source and target. The possible values are OneTime, OneWay, and TwoWay.

- With OneTime binding, the target is updated with the value retrieved from the source at the time of binding, but no further synchronization takes place. OneTime binding is good for data such as static lists of values that are not going to be updated during the execution of the application because this type of binding does not incur the additional overhead required to monitor for change events and keep values synchronized.

- OneWay binding is used when the target needs to be kept updated with changes that may occur at the source, but no attempt will be made to update the source if the target causes the value to change. This binding mode is useful for labels or other read-only controls because, while it has more overhead than OneTime binding, it has less overhead than TwoWay binding.

- TwoWay binding establishes a bidirectional synchronization between the source and target. When either causes the value to change, the other is updated. This binding mode is useful when multiple controls need to make writes that are propagated to the others or when, like in the search example, you have some sort of master-detail relationship.

EXERCISE: USING THE BINDING ELEMENT

Now that you've had a chance to see the product search example written the hard way, let's make it a little easier to manage by taking advantage of what you've learned about the Binding object. To work through the exercise, you will need Windows 8 and any edition of Visual Studio 2012. You'll implement the same user interface for the search and start with the same requirements you started with in the example.

1. To get started, open Visual Studio and create a new project. The project type should be Blank App (XAML), which can be found in the Windows Store category under Visual C#. Name the project SimpleBindingCs.

2. Create the folder in which you'll define your search result object by right-clicking the project in the Solution Explorer window and selecting Add ➤ New Folder. Use Entities for the folder name.

3. Add the search result object by right-clicking the Entities folder you created in the previous step and clicking Add ➤ Class. In the dialog that displays, ensure Class is selected and change the name to SearchResultItem.cs before clicking Add.

4. Once Visual Studio displays the generated code file, edit it so that the class looks like this:

```
public class SearchResultItem
{
 public string Title { get; set; }
 public string Summary { get; set; }
}
```

5. Double-click MainPage.xaml to open the page designer.

6. Instead of a Grid, you're going to use a StackPanel for the simple layout, so right-click the page in Design view and select Change Layout Type ➤ StackPanel in the menu. If the Change Layout Type option is not available, you do not have the root container selected and need to click anywhere in the black rectangle that should be filling most of the designer in order to select the container before right-clicking.

7. Add the TextBlock for the page header. This can be done either by editing the XAML directly or by using the control Toolbox. To help become accustomed to the using the designer, you'll use the control Toolbox this time.

   a. In the Toolbox, select TextBlock from the Common XAML Controls category and drag it onto the page designer.

   b. With the TextBlock selected, find the Text property in the Properties window (it may help to select Arrange By: ➤ Name in this window when you are looking for a property by its name) and update the property to the value Product Search.

   c. For the Style property, click the square next to the property value and select Local Resource ➤ PageHeaderTextStyle.

8. Drag a TextBox control from the Toolbox onto the designer. In the Properties window, update Name to criteriaTextBox, and clear the Text property.

9. Drag a Button object from the Toolbox onto the designer, and update its Name to searchButton and its Content to Search.

10. Drag a ListView control from the Toolbox to the designer. Update its Name to resultList.

11. Drag a TextBlock to the design surface. Clear the Text property, and for the Style property, click the square and select Local Resource ➤ ItemTextStyle.

12. At this point, you've drawn the user interface for your binding application, and it's time to get some data showing. Double-click the Search button, and Visual Studio will generate the method stub of a handler. Before you fill in the handler code, write the following method in the same code file to simulate a search:

```
private IEnumerable<Entities.SearchResultItem> DoSearch(string criteria)
{
return new[]
{
new Entities.SearchResultItem
{
Title = "Bread",
Summary = "Good for sandwiches"
},
new Entities.SearchResultItem
{
Title = "Peanut Butter",
Summary = "Goes on the sandwiches"
}
};
}
```

13. Now that you can simulate a search, let's add code to the Search button's click handler to invoke the search and populate the results list with the data returned. Put the following code in the empty searchButton_Click method:

```
private void searchButton_Click(object sender, RoutedEventArgs e)
{
var results = DoSearch(criteriaTextBox.Text);
// remove anything that's already in the list
resultList.Items.Clear();

foreach(var result in results)
{
var listItem = new ListBoxItem();
listItem.Content = result.Title;
listItem.Tag = result;

resultList.Items.Add(listItem);
}
}
```

■ **Note** A ListBoxItem would not normally be used in this manner, but I'm using it here to avoid having to create a template for the ListView.

---

14. Run the application. If you've followed all the steps, after clicking Search and selecting the first item in the list, your screen should look similar to Figure 8-5.

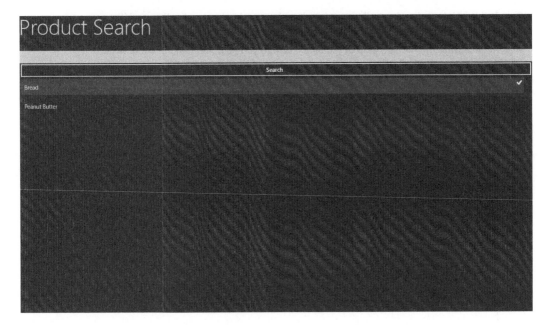

Figure 8-5. *Search result before binding applied*

15. You haven't written the code yet to display the summary for the selected item, and the really cool thing about XAML binding is that you're already done writing code for this exercise; everything else you do will be in the markup. To start wiring up the summary, find the TextBlock tag in BlankPage.xaml. If there's a Text attribute on the element, remove it.

16. The TextBlock element is most likely using the shorthand syntax that doesn't use closing tags. You need to add nested tags inside it, so add the closing tag so that it looks something like this:

```
<TextBlock Style="{StaticResource ItemTextStyle}" >
</TextBlock>
```

17. Now it's time to bind the Text property. To do this, you'll add a nested element for the Text dependency property and use a Binding element to establish a connection between the Text property of the TextBlock and the Summary property of the selected SearchResultItem. You'll have to use element binding because another control holds the data you're interested in the our Path will have to navigate down a couple levels in order to get to the data you want. Modify the TextBlock element to look like this:

```
<TextBlock Style="{StaticResource ItemTextStyle}">
 <TextBlock.Text>
 <Binding ElementName="resultList" Path="SelectedItem.Tag.Summary" />
 </TextBlock.Text>
</TextBlock>
```

18. Run the application again, and you should now see the summary change as you select different items from the results, as shown in Figure 8-6.

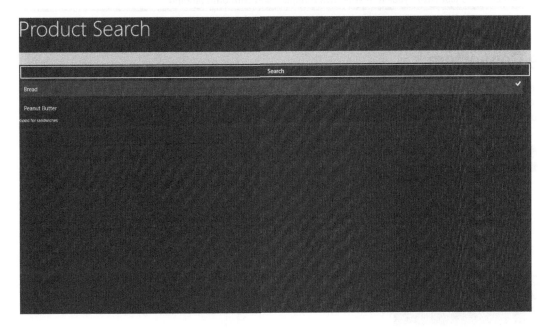

Figure 8-6. Search result after binding applied

19. All that's left for you now is to respond to that last-minute requirements change and make the summary updateable. Since you're using a XAML binding, the hardest part will be changing the TextBlock to a TextBox. You'll have to change the element name in the opening and closing tags as well as the TextBlock.Text element to TextBox.Text. Additionally, the Style attribute must be removed because it references a style resource that is for use with TextBlock elements. The updated TextBox XAML should look like this:

```
<TextBox>
 <TextBox.Text>
 <Binding ElementName="resultList" Path="SelectedItem.Tag.Summary" />
 </TextBox.Text>
</TextBox>
```

20. At this point, running the code would display the summary for the selected item in an editable TextBox, but just as before, changing the item selection back and forth shows the editing doesn't actually update the source. To make editing the TextBox

update the source in the `ListView`, add a `Mode` attribute to the `Binding` element with a value of `TwoWay` so that it looks like this:

```
<Binding ElementName="resultList" Path="SelectedItem.Tag.Summary"
Mode="TwoWay" />
```

21. Run the application and admire your handiwork!

Congratulations! You just wrote your first Windows 8 application with data binding.

Value Converters

In the previous section, you saw that UI elements can be bound to each other in a very powerful way. What you didn't see was that fairly frequently you find that the data as stored on the source is not in a format that can be directly used by the target. Think about the binding story implied by Figure 8-7.

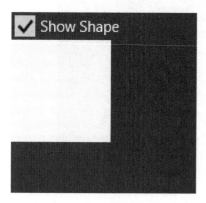

Figure 8-7. *Show/hide binding screen*

The screen suggests that when the user unchecks the check box, the rectangle is no longer visible. When the user checks the box, the rectangle should once again be visible. "That's easy," you say. "I'll just use my new binding skills and won't even have to write any code." If you jumped ahead of me when you saw the figure, you may have already discovered the problem. When you try to bind the `Visibility` property of the `Rectangle` to the `IsChecked` property of the `CheckBox`, you'll find that changing the checked state of the `CheckBox` has no apparent effect on the visibility of the `Rectangle`. This is because the `IsChecked` property of the `CheckBox` has a bool type, and the `Visibility` property on the `UIElement` class is an enumerated value with either `Visibility.Visible` or `Visibility.Collapsed` as the valid values; therefore, we need to bridge `True`/`False` to `Visible`/`Collapsed`. This is where value converters come into play.

Windows.UI.Xaml.Data.IValueConverter

The `IValueConverter` interface is a very simple interface with an important task. It defines a `Convert` method, which is used to change a value that is stored in the source into a format usable by the target. In two-way binding scenarios, the ConvertBack method is used to change the value that was updated on the target into a form suitable for storage at the source. When you create a new Windows application in Visual Studio 2012, a BooleanToVisibilityConverter, which can be used to solve the problem of mapping the CheckBox's checked property to the Rectangle's Visibility property, is created for you in the Common folder of the project. Let's look at that converter to discuss the methods on the interface.

Convert Method

The Convert method receives the value as stored on the source as its first parameter. Additionally, it receives a targetType parameter indicating the Type to which the conversion is requested, an object representing any parameter that may have been specified on the binding, and the current UI language. The convert method uses the value along with any of the other parameters that may be relevant to the specific conversion and returns an object representing the converted value. In the case of the BooleanToVisibilityConverter, the value parameter is the only parameter of interest, so the method ignores the rest and contains just a single line of code.

```
public object Convert(object value, Type targetType, object parameter, string language)
{
    return (value is bool && (bool)value) ? Visibility.Visible : Visibility.Collapsed;
}
```

The method says that if given a value that can be cast into a bool and that bool has a value of True, the converted value should be Visible. If given a value that cannot be cast into a bool or one that is a bool but evaluates to False, the converted value is Collapsed.

ConvertBack Method

The ConvertBack method does the opposite of the Convert method. When the target of a two-way binding is updated, the value is passed to the ConvertBack method to produce a converted value that is used to update the source. In addition to the value parameter, the ConvertBack method also includes the same parameters as the Convert method, and these serve the same purpose. In the case of the BooleanToVisibilityConverter, the value parameter is the only parameter of interest, so the method ignores the rest and contains just a single line of code.

```
public object ConvertBack(object value, Type targetType, object parameter, string language)
{
    return value is Visibility && (Visibility)value == Visibility.Visible;
}
```

This ConvertBack implementation is pretty simple to follow. If passed a Visibility object with a value of Visible, True is returned. Otherwise, False is returned.

Binding and the Value Converter

Value converters don't do anything on their own but are used in conjunction with bindings, as shown in Figure 8-8.

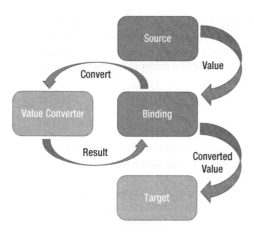

Figure 8-8. *Binding with value converter*

When I covered the properties of the Binding object, there were some properties I skipped. The skipped properties are related to value converters, and it is now time to look at them.

Converter Property

The Converter property specifies an object that implements IValueConverter and should be used to modify data going in each direction during binding.

ConverterParameter Property

The ConverterParameter property is used to supply a value to be used by the logic inside Convert and ConvertBack for making the appropriate conversion. One example would be a format string used when the method converts the value using String.Format.

ConverterLanguage Property

The ConverterLanguage property is used to specify the value that will be passed to conversion methods for use when the language/culture should be taken into account during the conversion process, such as for currency formatting. If the property is not specified, the current application context is used to determine the value that should be passed to the converter methods.

EXERCISE: USING THE BOOLTOVISIBILITYCONVERTER

In this exercise, you'll use the BoolToVisibilityConverter class that is provided by Visual Studio to create a working implementation of the application shown in Figure 8-7. Besides the converter, which has been written for you, you will not write any application code to make the application work—relying only on XAML markup and binding. To complete this exercise, you will need Windows 8 and any edition of Visual Studio 2012.

1. To get started, open Visual Studio and create a new project. The project type should be Blank App (XAML), which can be found in the Windows Store category under Visual C#. Name the project ValueConverterCs.

---

2. Right-click `MainPage.xaml` in the Solution Explorer, and select Delete.

3. Right-click the project in the Solution Explorer window, and select Add ➤ New Item. From the Windows Store category, select Basic Page. Name the page `MainPage.xaml`, and click Add.

4. Build the project.

5. Double-click `MainPage.xaml` to open the page designer.

6. In XAML view, replace the `Grid` element and any contents with the following markup:

```
<StackPanel Background="{StaticResource ApplicationPageBackgroundThemeBrush}">
<CheckBox Name="showCheckBox" Content="Show Shape" HorizontalAlignment="Left" />
<Rectangle HorizontalAlignment="Left" Fill="Yellow" Height="100" Width="100" />
</StackPanel>
```

7. Set up the data binding.

    a. Select the `Rectangle` in the designer and find its `Visibility` property in the Properties window.

    b. Click the square next to the property value and select Create Data Binding....

    c. In the "Binding type" drop-down of the dialog that is shown, select ElementName, and then use the ElementName and Path lists to navigate to the `IsChecked` property of the `showCheckBox` element.

    d. In the Converter drop-down, select Add Value Converter, and select the BooleanToVisibilityConverter box that displays.

    e. Click OK in each open dialog until they are all closed.

8. At this point, you should notice that the `Rectangle` is no longer visible in the designer. Changing the value of `showCheckBox`'s `IsChecked` property through either the XAML or the Properties window will toggle the visibility of the `Rectangle`.

9. Run the application to see the converter at work.

Conclusion

In this chapter, you learned about dependency objects, bindings, and value converters, which work together to form the backbone of the data binding support that is one of the features that makes XAML stand out as an outstanding development platform. The knowledge you have gained of data binding will serve as a solid foundation as you learn about the Model-View-ViewModel pattern in the next chapter.

■ ■ ■

CHAPTER 9

Introducing MVVM

It's not about what you know, it's about what you can prove.

—Denzel Washington (as Alonzo Harris)

By this time, it should be clear to you that the designers and developers of Visual Studio have done a great job of creating an environment where it is a simple undertaking to drag a few controls onto a form, double-click them in the designer, and start writing your application logic. They have been doing this very well since long before the .NET languages. Now I'm going to tell you that taking advantage of this great functionality is probably one of the last things you want to do if you're developing anything but the most trivial of applications. (By the way, a trivial application that does its job and is well used rarely becomes trivial.)

In this chapter, I will introduce the popular Model-View-ViewModel (MVVM) design pattern that is used to develop maintainable and testable applications with XAML-based tools such as Windows Presentation Foundation, Silverlight, and now Windows 8. I will also discuss some related patterns and unit testing to help frame up the conversation about the need for separation and patterns. These subjects truly do deserve a book of their own, but I will cover them with only enough depth to give a general understanding of the pattern, its advantages, and how you can start building on it today.

The Problem When Code Is Too Close to the User

Before diving in, let's take a look at Figure 9-1. I'll base the discussion on the application that it represents.

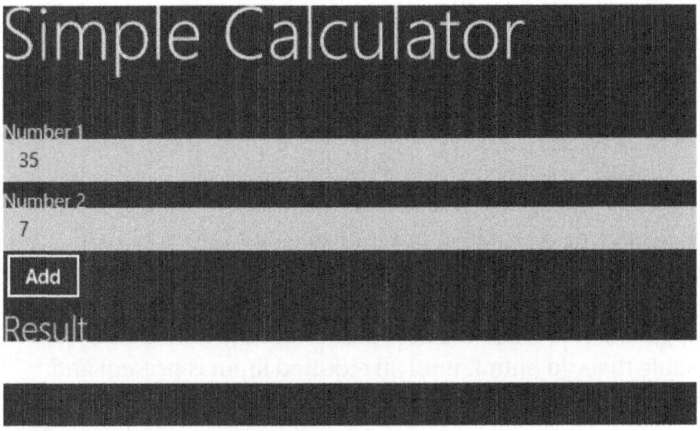

Figure 9-1. Simple calculator

Looking at Figure 9-1, it's pretty easy to imagine the application that this image represents. The user expects to enter values into the Number 1 and Number 2 fields and click Add, causing the sum of the numbers to be displayed in the Result field. Let's take a look at how this might be built without applying design patterns. You start with the following XAML:

```
<StackPanel Background="{StaticResource ApplicationPageBackgroundBrush}">
    <TextBlock Style="{StaticResource PageHeaderTextStyle}">Simple Calculator</TextBlock>
    <TextBlock Style="{StaticResource ItemTextStyle}">Number 1</TextBlock>
    <TextBox Name="number1TextBox" />
    <TextBlock Style="{StaticResource ItemTextStyle}">Number 2</TextBlock>
    <TextBox Name="number2TextBox" />
    <Button Name="addButton">Add</Button>
    <TextBlock Style="{StaticResource SubheaderTextStyle}">Result</TextBlock>
    <TextBox IsReadOnly="True" Name="resultTextBox" />
</StackPanel>
```

Once you have the screen "drawn" with the XAML, you double-click the Add button and fill in code similar to the following:

```
private void addButton_Click(object sender, RoutedEventArgs e)
{
    int number1 = Int32.Parse(number1TextBox.Text);
    int number2 = Int32.Parse(number2TextBox.Text);
    resultTextBox.Text = (number1+number2).ToString();
}
```

You're done, right? No. Now is when all the "what ifs" come into play. What if the user left one of the fields blank? What if the user enters a value that's not numeric or even just not a 32-bit integer value? You're going to need more rules and, with them, more code.

Let's start the rules by making sure the application doesn't blow up with a bad entry. You'll make the method a little more defensive by processing only valid input.

```
private void addButton_Click(object sender, RoutedEventArgs e)
{
    int number1;
    int number2;

    if(Int32.TryParse(number1TextBox.Text, out number1)
      && Int32.TryParse(number2TextBox.Text, out number2))
    {
        resultTextBox.Text = (number1 + number2).ToString();
    }
}
```

At this point, the code is protected from throwing an error when the input is invalid, but the user is left wondering why nothing happened. One solution would be to put an else statement in the method and display a message either in a dialog or in the result text box, indicating that the request could not be processed because of bad input, but a nicer solution would be for the application to guide the user to submit only valid input. A common approach to this guidance would be to disable the Add button until all required input is present and passes validation. You can centralize this logic by creating the following method in the page:

```
private void EnableDisableAdd()
{
    int number;
    if(Int32.TryParse(number1TextBox.Text, out number)
      && Int32.TryParse(number2TextBox.Text, out number))
    {
        addButton.IsEnabled = true;
    }
    else
    {
        addButton.IsEnabled = false;
    }
}
```

This code can be called from the TextChanged event of each of the operands' text boxes, and you can even share the code by pointing to the same event handler for both. The event handler would simply look like this:

```
private void OnOperandChanged(object sender, TextChangedEventArgs e)
{
    EnableDisableAdd();
}
```

You now have a simple calculator that adds two numbers together and prevents the user from creating the most common error scenarios by cutting off access to the Add button when clicking it would cause these errors. You can even add a Clear button that you're told you "forgot" (all too often developers are expected to "just know" about uncommunicated requirements), which sets the Text property of all the text boxes to string.Empty; this action will fire the TextChanged events, ensuring that the Add button isn't left enabled. You add the button to the page and add the following code to its Click event:

```
private void clearButton_Click(object sender, RoutedEventArgs e)
{
    number1TextBox.Text = string.Empty;
    number2TextBox.Text = string.Empty;
    resultTextBox.Text = string.Empty;
}
```

So, if the app works and meets the requirement, what's the problem with this solution? In the case of this application, where only a single function is performed on a very limited set of inputs, the answer is "probably nothing," but look at the code required to validate and control input even in this limited scenario and project the amount of code required to build a resilient scientific calculator application. The complexity and its associated code have to go somewhere, but the code behind the XAML file isn't the place to put it. Code placed directly in the code behind the XAML file is considered to be "close" to the user because it lives interspersed with the user interface code, which requires the application to actually be displayed on-screen to run and test the code. In the following sections, you'll see the motivation behind moving the code further from the user and learn some techniques to help you do this.

Automated Testing

When you walked through the creation of the simple calculator application, you used a set of tools to verify that the application was working correctly—your own eyes and hands. You ran the application, watched it display (paying attention to whether the Add button was enabled or disabled), put values (I hope both valid and invalid) into the operand fields to observe whether the Add button becomes enabled, and eventually clicked Add with valid values entered to make sure that the correct answer was displayed in the result field.

When you added the Clear button, you may have just thrown valid values into the operand fields, clicked Add, and then clicked the Clear button to observe that it did indeed remove values from all the fields. You may or may not have thought to reexecute all the original tests to make sure you didn't introduce any unintended side effects when you changed code to add the new feature. The more complicated the application becomes, the greater the risk is that you will, in the process of adding a new feature or applying a fix to an existing one that does not work correctly, affect some dependent code in a way that wasn't anticipated. Executing a complete test of the application's functionality is the only effective way to mitigate this risk, but time is precious, and it's easy for a person to leave out a test, so the only realistic way to make sure that all the tests are performed every time you make a change is to have the tests be executed by a computer.

A unit test is a specific kind of test that focuses on verifying that each piece of the application functions correctly, the idea being that if each piece is tested at the most granular level possible (or practical), it will be very easy to determine and correct the cause of any breakage. *Unit testing* is often used as a generic term for any automated testing, but it is very different from other tests such as integration tests in that a unit test leaves you pointing at a line of code saying, "There's the problem," while an integration test leaves you saying, "The problem is somewhere between here and there."

Visual Studio provides a set of tools to create and execute automated tests of your code. These tests are referred to by Visual Studio as *unit tests*, but in practical application, I find that whenever I can, I will use Visual Studio test projects to create a set of unit tests to ensure that every piece works as well as integration tests, which can show me that the pieces are working together the way they should.

Unit testing involves following a series of steps referred to as "Arrange, Act, Assert":

- In the Arrange step, you create or obtain an instance of the object that is the subject of the test and set the object's properties or other environmental characteristics that should lead to the behavior being tested.

- In the Act step, you actually invoke the behavior you're testing, whether that is by calling a method or setting some property.

- In the Assert step, you look for evidence that the subject behaved as expected. This could include steps such as examining properties of the object, making sure that it called a specific method of another method, or ensuring that a certain exception was thrown.

One of the places where many developers can go wrong in unit testing is that they leave out the Assert step, assuming that if they call a method on the subject and it doesn't throw an exception, then the method must have worked. Every test should be written with complete knowledge of what constitutes proof of success, and the Assert step should require this proof to be present or consider the test to be a failure. Leaving a test that assumes success with no proof just creates a sense of false security and will allow errors to creep in unnoticed.

So, how does the value of automated testing relate to the need to get the application logic further from the user? Simply put, testing code in the user interface itself is hard to do in an automated manner, and testing code that has reasonable structure and is not directly embedded in the user interface is relatively easier given the tools available both "out of the box" and freely available such as nUnit, mbUnit, and others. Whether it's a character flaw or an admirable trait, given the choice between hard and easy with the same outcome, I'll freely admit that I will always weigh in on the side of easy.

Moving the Code Away from the User

In a 2006 paper, Martin Fowler discussed a pattern descended from the Model-View-Controller design pattern that was popularized with Smalltalk and again emerged with server-based web applications. His pattern was called PresentationModel and focused on separating the state and behavior needed by views from the view code. A variation of this pattern emerged when the rich binding support was introduced when Windows Presentation

Foundation was released as the first XAML-based platform in the Microsoft .NET Framework 3.0. The XAML-flavored variation of the pattern was called Model-View-ViewModel. The pattern aims to separate the behavior and data of the View from the View itself by creating a class referred to as the ViewModel. This ViewModel class knows nothing about the View , and, in theory, you could have multiple versions of the View for different presentation needs (think: having the same data and behavior laid out differently on mobile device, desktop PC, and big screen via Xbox). Figure 9-2 illustrates the key players in this pattern and the way they interact.

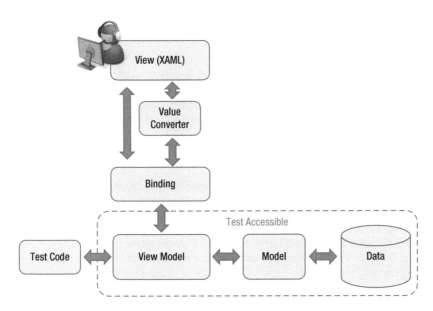

Figure 9-2. *MVVM at a high level*

Model

The Model is sometimes referred to as the Domain Model and represents the business logic and data related to the management and retrieval for entities in the application. The implementation can vary by the type of data and how it is stored, but the Model should contain everything necessary to ensure that the data remains consistent. When you return to the simple calculator example, you will actually be blurring the line between ViewModel and Model because there is no persistent data, and you will not be defining a Model.

View

Some opinions may vary, but I consider the View to be comprised of the XAML that draws the screen, code-behind that is directly related to drawing the screen or producing its effects (this is where "spinning button" code would go), and value converters necessary to adapt the UI-agnostic data stored in the ViewModel into a form necessary to draw the specific UI needed. Some developers take a very strict stance that absolutely no code should go into the code-behind, but I feel a more pragmatic approach is to adhere to a policy of having absolutely no business in logic in the view code, but beyond that, to get the job done without introducing more complexity than necessary, favoring whenever practical to keep code out of the code-behind. In the case of the simple calculator sample, you will be able to get away without having to place code in the code-behind.

ViewModel

The ViewModel can be thought of as the View's Model. That is, it has all of the data and business logic required to service the View. The data may be a direct representation of the data contained by the model, but often it is reshaped into a form more appropriate to how the View will display it. Data is made available to the View via properties, and behavior is exposed through commands, which will be discussed later in this chapter. Because the ViewModel is fairly specific to a View (other than possibly having multiple versions of the same View for different formats), the data and behavior that it exposes should also be very specific to the View. In other words, don't try to create a ViewModel with a thought toward being able to reuse it for some other View.

Important Interfaces to MVVM

Before you start to put together the simple calculator using MVVM, you need to learn about some .NET interfaces that are critical to making MVVM work with XAML data binding. These interfaces are INotifyPropertyChanged, INotifyDataErrorInfo, and ICommand. These interfaces are well-known to the binding system and are used in different ways to communicate information about data and behavior between the View and its associated ViewModel.

INotifyPropertyChanged

Like most interfaces, the INotifyPropertyChanged interface advertises a capability. The capability advertised in this case is to provide a notification when any of the object's properties change in value. This notification is used by the binding system as an indication that any control bound to the changed property should have its data refreshed. The INotifyPropertyChanged event consists of a single event, PropertyChanged, which provides the object that is providing notification in the sender argument and an instance of PropertyChangedEventArgs. PropertyChangedEventArgs accepts the name of the changed property in its constructor and provides access to that value as a read-only property named PropertyName. Here's an example of a class implementing the INotifyPropertyChanged interface:

```
public class Notifier : INotifyPropertyChanged
{
    public event PropertyChangedEventHandler PropertyChanged;
    private string _myProperty;
    public string MyProperty
    {
        get
        {
            return _myProperty;
        }
        set
        {
            if(_myProperty != value)
            {
                _myProperty = value;
                if(PropertyChanged != null)
                {
                    PropertyChanged(this, new PropertyChangedEventArgs("MyProperty"));
                }
            }
        }
    }
}
```

Some of the key things to note about this sample are in the property set accessor.

- Unlike most .NET property set accessors, this one contains a check to make sure that the new value being passed to the setter is actually different from the property value already held by the object. The main purpose of this is to avoid a situation where an infinite loop is triggered by code that calls the property set accessor within a PropertyChanged event handler. Without the safety provided here, that would definitely be crossing the streams, Ray.

- Like with any event, you have to ensure that PropertyChanged is not null prior to invoking it because if there are no subscribers to the event, it will be null.

- The last notable thing here is that because the PropertyName property of PropertyChangedEventArgs is a string, it is very easy for a misspelling to cause you to send the wrong property name or to rename the property during refactoring and forget to update the string in the argument.

As you can see, building your own implementation of INotifyPropertyChanged can add its own set of complexity to what would have been a simple container of data, but Microsoft provides a nice alternative toward building your own implementation by generating a helper class designed specifically to remove some of this complexity. The class is BindableBase and is in the Common folder when you create a new Windows application. The class provides a method that wraps up the property change detection and event invocation and allows your code to be freer from infrastructure clutter. Revised to benefit from BindableBase, the Notifier class looks like this:

```
public class Notifier : BindableBase
{
    private string _myProperty;
    public string MyProperty
    {
        get
        {
            return _myProperty;
        }
        set
        {
            SetProperty(ref _myProperty, value);
        }
    }
}
```

INotifyPropertyChanged is critical to building objects that will be bound in a XAML document because the binding framework hooks into the PropertyChanged event and updates all bound controls whenever a property changes.

INotifyDataErrorInfo

Many applications share the need to communicate to the user that a problem exists with the data entered in a field or fields. By implementing the INotifyDataErrorInfo interface, you can advertise to the binding framework that you are capable of providing this type of notification to the user interface. Slightly more complex than the INotifyPropertyChanged interface, the INotifyDataErrorInfo interface includes an ErrorsChanged event that indicates there has been a change in the error state for a given property, a GetErrors method that returns an IEnumerable that the subscriber can use to iterate the list of errors for a property, and a HasErrors read-only property to query the existence of errors.

A typical implementation of this interface will store error information in a dictionary using the string property name as Key and a list of strings representing the error messages as the Value. The following code example will give a good idea of what an implementation looks like:

■ **Note**   To be a completely functioning example, this would also have to include functionality to remove errors that would also need to raise ErrorsChanged, but this has been omitted from the example.

```
public class DeepThought : BindableBase, INotifyDataErrorInfo
{
    private string _theAnswer;
    public string TheAnswer
    {
        get
        {
            return _theAnswer;
        }
        set
        {
            if (IsValidAnswer(value))
            {
                SetProperty(ref _theAnswer, value);
            }
            else
            {
                AddError("TheAnswer", "You don't know where your towel is");
            }
        }
    }

    private bool IsValidAnswer(string answer)
    {
        return answer == "42";
    }

    private Dictionary<string, List<string>> errors = new Dictionary<string, List<string>>();
    private void AddError(string propertyName, string error)
    {
        if (!errors.ContainsKey(propertyName))
        {
            errors[propertyName] = new List<string>();
        }

        if (!errors[propertyName].Contains(error))
        {
            errors[propertyName].Add(error);
            if (ErrorsChanged != null)
```

```
        {
            ErrorsChanged(this, new DataErrorsChangedEventArgs(propertyName));
        }
    }
}

public event EventHandler<DataErrorsChangedEventArgs> ErrorsChanged;
public System.Collections.IEnumerable GetErrors(string propertyName)
{
    if (errors.ContainsKey(propertyName))
    {
        return errors[propertyName];
    }

    return null;
}

public bool HasErrors
{
    get { return errors.Count > 0; }
}
}
```

As is evident from the code sample, a fair amount of code needs to be added to your class to support this error reporting, but the benefit is that the user interface responds to the presence of this contract by providing rich feedback to the user that you do not have to write, so it is a pretty fair trade. One way to reduce the additional noise generated in your code would be to follow the pattern set with `BindableBase` and provide yourself with a base class that encapsulates this work and simply exposes methods that your derived classes can call to signal that errors are to be added or removed.

ICommand

The `ICommand` interface provides for objects that can be bound and used to invoke an action. The interface includes a `CanExecute` method that accepts an object parameter and returns a Boolean value indicating whether it is valid to execute the command with the given parameter, an `Execute` method that accepts an object parameter and performs its action, and a `CanExecuteChanged` event that signals to any subscriber that it should requery the `CanExecute` method.

The power of this interface is that the `ButtonBase` class contains the `Command` and `CommandParameter` properties, and when these properties are used, the button will use `CanExecute` to determine the appropriate state for the `IsEnabled` property of the button and will invoke `Execute` with the bound `CommandParameter` property when the `Click` event is fired. This means you can effectively bind to behavior in addition to data.

The .NET Framework libraries provide just the interface, so you have to supply your own implementation, but many good examples of ICommand interface implementations are available because the same need exists for Silverlight. You may want to take a look at the `DelegateCommand` implementation provided by the Microsoft Patterns and Practices team in its Prism library available on CodePlex. For the calculator, you'll use a simpler version but will go ahead and give it the `DelegateCommand` name.

EXERCISE: BUILDING THE CALCULATOR VIEWMODEL

In this exercise, you'll use what you've learned in this chapter about the Model-View-ViewModel pattern and associated interfaces to build the simple calculator application shown earlier using MVVM. To work through the example, you will need Windows 8, any edition of Visual Studio 2012, and an active Internet connection.

1. To get started, open Visual Studio and create a new project. The project type should be Blank App (XAML), which can be found in the Windows Store category under Visual C#. Name the project MvvmCalculatorCs.

2. Right-click the project in the Solution Explorer window, and select Add ➤ New Folder. Use ViewModels for the folder name.

3. Right-click the ViewModels folder you created in the previous step, and select Add ➤ Class. Name the new class DelegateCommand.cs.

4. Update the DelegateCommand class to provide a simple ICommand implementation using the following code (you'll need to ensure you have a using statement referencing System.Windows.Input):

```
public class DelegateCommand : ICommand
    {
    public event EventHandler CanExecuteChanged;
    private readonly Action<object> _executeAction;
    private readonly Func<object, bool> _canExecutePredicate;

    public DelegateCommand(Action<object> execute, Func<object, bool> canExecute)
    {
        _executeAction = execute;
        _canExecutePredicate = canExecute;
    }

    public bool CanExecute(object parameter)
    {
        return _canExecutePredicate(parameter);
    }

    public void Execute(object parameter)
    {
        if(!CanExecute(parameter))
        {
            throw new InvalidOperationException("Cannot execute now");
        }
        _executeAction(parameter);
    }
```

```
    public void RaiseCanExecuteChanged()
    {
        if(CanExecuteChanged != null)
        {
            CanExecuteChanged(this, EventArgs.Empty);
        }
    }
}
```

■ **Note** The next two steps are a little bit counterintuitive, but their purpose is to ensure that Visual Studio creates the helper classes needed for the rest of the exercise. Visual Studio creates these classes the first time that a page requiring them is created and the functionality present when the Blank App (XAML) project template is used doesn't require them. The MainPage page created with the project template is based on the Blank Page template, which does not require the helper classes. By deleting this page and replacing it with one based on the Basic Page template, you will force the creation of the helper classes.

---

5. Right-click MainPage.xaml in the Solution Explorer, and select Delete.

6. Right-click the project in the Solution Explorer, and select Add ➤ New Item. In the Add New Item dialog, select Basic Page under Windows Store. Name the item `MainPage.xaml`. Add the item and select Yes if Visual Studio prompts you to add missing files.

7. Build the project by pressing F6.

8. At this point, you have a simple, but functional, implementation of `ICommand`. You're ready to define the ViewModel. To meet the needs of the View you're going to build, the ViewModel needs a property for each of the operands, one for the result, and an `ICommand` implementation each for the Add and Clear actions. Right-click the `ViewModels` folder, and select Add ➤ Class. Name the class `CalculatorViewModel`. Add using `System.Windows.Input;` and using `MvvmCalculatorCs.Common;` to the `using` statements, and update the class with the following code:

```
public class CalculatorViewModel : BindableBase
{
    public CalculatorViewModel()
    {
        // we'll come back to this
    }

    private int? _operand1;
    public int? Operand1
    {
        get { return _operand1; }
        set { SetProperty(ref _operand1, value); }
    }
```

```
        private int? _operand2;
        public int? Operand2
        {
            get { return _operand2; }
            set { SetProperty(ref _operand2, value); }
        }

        private int? _result;
        public int? Result
        {
            get { return _result; }
            set { SetProperty(ref _result, value); }
        }

        public ICommand AddCommand
        {
            get;
            private set;
        }

        public ICommand ClearCommand
        {
            get;
            private set;
        }
    }
```

■ **Note**   Notice that although you have built a DelegateCommand implementation, the AddCommand and ClearCommand properties are exposed as ICommand. This is to ensure that binding will work correctly.

9. The ViewModel is almost done. The work that's left to do is in the constructor. You need to add the functionality to the two commands and provide the logic for the CanExecute functionality of the AddCommand. Since ClearCommand should always be accessible, you will simply return true from its CanExecute. Additionally, you need to ensure that every time one of the properties changes, the AddCommand signals that the UI should query whether this command can execute. Update the CalculatorViewModel constructor to read as follows:

```
public CalculatorViewModel()
{
    AddCommand = new DelegateCommand(
        o =>{
            Result = Operand1.Value + Operand2.Value;
        }
        , o => {
            return Operand1.HasValue && Operand2.HasValue;
        });
```

```
    ClearCommand = new DelegateCommand(
        o =>{
            Operand1 = null;
            Operand2 = null;
            Result = null;
        }
        , o => { return true; });

    PropertyChanged += (sender, args) =>
        ((DelegateCommand) AddCommand).RaiseCanExecuteChanged();
}
```

10. The ViewModel is complete, but you have one more step before you can move
    on to the user interface. The nullable int properties on the ViewModel will
    not directly work well with a string entered in a bound TextBox, so you need
    to use an implementation of IValueConverter to bridge this gap. Right-click
    the Common folder in your project and select Add ➤ Class. Name your class
    StringToNullableIntConverter and add the following code (you'll need to add
    Windows.UI.Xaml.Data to your using statements):

```
public class StringToNullableIntConverter : IValueConverter
{
    public object Convert(object value, Type targetType,
        object parameter, string language)
    {
        if(value == null) return string.Empty;
        return value.ToString();
    }

    public object ConvertBack(object value, Type targetType,
        object parameter, string language)
    {
        if(value == null || string.IsNullOrEmpty(value.ToString())) return
null;
        int valueInt;
        if(Int32.TryParse(value.ToString(), out valueInt))
        {
            return valueInt;
        }

        return null;
    }
}
```

11. At this point, you've written all of the C# code that will be required for this exercise.
    Go ahead and build the project to ensure that the binaries are available to the XAML
    designer as you move to the next step.

12. Now it's time to draw the user interface. You're going to add a couple of namespace
    declarations to the opening Page tag to ensure that the CalculatorViewModel
    and the custom ValueConverter are available to the page, create a

CalculatorViewModel and StringToNullableIntConverter in the resources section, and then draw the screen using these resources in the bindings. Open MainPage.xaml, and replace the XAML in the file with the following markup:

```xml
<common:LayoutAwarePage
x:Class="MvvmCalculatorCs.MainPage"
xmlns="http://schemas.microsoft.com/winfx/2006/xaml/presentation"
xmlns:x="http://schemas.microsoft.com/winfx/2006/xaml"
xmlns:local="using:MvvmCalculatorCs"
xmlns:d="http://schemas.microsoft.com/expression/blend/2008"
xmlns:mc="http://schemas.openxmlformats.org/markup-compatibility/2006"
xmlns:vm="using:MvvmCalculatorCs.ViewModels"
xmlns:common="using:MvvmCalculatorCs.Common"
mc:Ignorable="d">
    <Page.Resources>
        <vm:CalculatorViewModel x:Name="CalculatorVm" />
        <common:StringToNullableIntConverter x:Name="stringToIntConverter" />
    </Page.Resources>
    <StackPanel Background="{StaticResource ApplicationPageBackgroundThemeBrush}"
                DataContext="{Binding Source={StaticResource CalculatorVm}}">
        <TextBlock Style="{StaticResource PageHeaderTextStyle}">Simple
Calculator</TextBlock>
        <TextBlock Style="{StaticResource ItemTextStyle}">Number 1</TextBlock>
        <TextBox Text="{Binding Operand1, Mode=TwoWay, Converter={StaticResource
stringToIntConverter}}" />
        <TextBlock Style="{StaticResource ItemTextStyle}">Number 2</TextBlock>
        <TextBox Text="{Binding Operand2, Mode=TwoWay, Converter={StaticResource
stringToIntConverter}}" />
        <StackPanel Orientation="Horizontal">
            <Button Command="{Binding AddCommand, Mode=TwoWay}">Add</Button>
            <Button Command="{Binding ClearCommand, Mode=TwoWay}">Clear</Button>
        </StackPanel>
        <TextBlock Style="{StaticResource SubheaderTextStyle}">Result</TextBlock>
        <TextBox IsReadOnly="True" Text="{Binding Result, Converter={StaticResource
stringToIntConverter}}" />
    </StackPanel>
</common:LayoutAwarePage>
```

13. If you have successfully completed all the previous steps, you should now be able to run your first MVVM application and see your calculator function and interact with the user with no code in the code-behind.

Conclusion

In this chapter, you learned about the motivation behind separating the user interface code from application logic and how the Model-View-ViewModel pattern can be used to leverage the binding support given to you by XAML in Windows applications to eliminate or significantly decrease the need to place code where it cannot be tested. You also learned about additional interfaces that help you build applications using this pattern. You will see this pattern and these interfaces throughout the rest of the book as you use them to build up to your finished application.

■ ■ ■

CHAPTER 10

Starting the ViewModel

In union there is strength.

—Aesop

In the previous two chapters, you learned about the interrelated concepts of XAML data binding and the Model-View-ViewModel design pattern. This chapter builds upon this progression by guiding you through the creation of the Model and ViewModel classes and updating the user interface to bind to the ViewModel and the data it exposes. Because of its focus on the practical application of concepts that have already been covered, much of this chapter will consist of exercises that build upon each other, so it is important to complete the exercises in order.

The MovieBrowser Model

The MovieBrowser application that you began working on in Chapter 7 is a simple read-only application that will eventually display catalog information retrieved from an OData web service published by the popular DVD rental and streaming video provider Netflix. The application is concerned only with a subset of the data available from the service, so the Model of MovieBrowser will be based on this subset.

In this section, I will discuss the objects in this Model, moving from the greatest level of detail to the least. Notice that each class inherits from the `BindableBase` object that was created in the MovieBrowser project by Visual Studio, which ensures the necessary change notifications are available to keep the user interface synchronized with the bound Model.

Title

The `Title` object represents a single item within the catalog and is shown as a class diagram in Figure 10-1. The object is named `Title` as opposed to `Movie` because the data model supports media types other than movies, such as television episodes or even audio recordings. The properties of the `Title` object include the following:

- `Name`: This property represents the title of the movie.

- `ShortName`: This property provides a shortened form of the title.

- `Synopsis`: This property provides a summary of the movie's plot.

- `ShortSynopsis`: This property provides a shortened form of the movie's synopsis.

- `BoxArt`: This property provides URIs at which cover art for the movie is available.

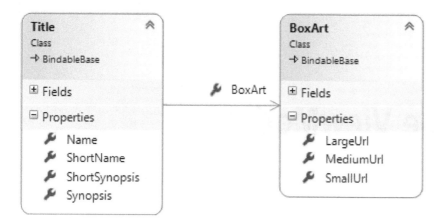

Figure 10-1. *Title class diagram*

The BoxArt class contains the following properties, each providing the URL at which the corresponding sized cover art image is located:

- SmallUrl

- MediumUrl

- LargeUrl

EXERCISE: BUILDING THE TITLE AND BOXART CLASSES

In this exercise, you will build the Title and BoxArt classes used in the Model for the MovieBrowser application. To complete the exercise, you will need any edition of Visual Studio 2012. Additionally, you will either need to have completed the MovieBrowser exercise in Chapter 7 or use the MovieBrowser solution from the Ch07 folder in the downloadable source code as a starter.

1. Open the MovieBrowser solution created in Chapter 7.

2. Right-click the DataModel folder in the Solution Explorer, and select Add ➤ Class. Name the class BoxArt.cs.

3. Update the using statements at the top of BoxArt.cs to ensure the following statements are included:

    ```
    using System;
    using MovieBrowser.Common;
    ```

4. Update the class definition of BoxArt to make the class public and inherit from BindableBase. The updated definition should look appear as follows:

    ```
    public class BoxArt : BindableBase
    ```

5. Add a backing field and property statements for the SmallUrl property. In the property setter, use the SetProperty method of the base class to ensure property change notification is handled correctly. The field and property should appear as follows:

```
private Uri _smallUrl;
public Uri SmallUrl
{
    get
    {
        return _smallUrl;
    }
    set
    {
        SetProperty(ref _smallUrl, value);
    }
}
```

6. Using the field and property statements for SmallUrl as a template, create the backing field and property statements for the MediumUrl and LargeUrl properties. This completes the BoxArt class.

7. Right-click the DataModel folder in the Solution Explorer, and select Add ➤ Class. Name the class Title.cs.

8. Update the using statements at the top of Title.cs to include the following statement:

```
using MovieBrowser.Common;
```

9. Update the class definition of Title to make the class public and inherit from BindableBase. The updated definition should look appear as follows:

```
public class Title : BindableBase
```

10. Add a backing field and property statements for the Name property. In the property setter, use the SetProperty method of the base class to ensure property change notification is handled correctly. The field and property should appear as follows:

```
private string _name;
public string Name
{
    get
    {
        return _name;
    }
    set
    {
        SetProperty(ref _name, value);
    }
}
```

11. Using the field and property statements for Name as a template, create the backing field and property statements for the ShortName, Synopsis, and ShortSynopsis properties. Each of these properties should use the string data type.

12. Create the backing field and property statements for the `BoxArt` property. The field and property should appear as follows:

```
private BoxArt _boxArt;
public BoxArt BoxArt
{
    get
    {
        return _boxArt;
    }
    set
    {
        SetProperty(ref _boxArt, value);
    }
}
```

13. Save and build the solution.

At this point, you have completed writing the code for the `Title` and `BoxArt` classes. These classes will be used later in the chapter.

Genre

The Genre object, shown with its relationship to `Title` in the class diagram in Figure 10-2, represents a categorical grouping for `Title` objects. It has the following properties:

- Name: This property represents the name of the Genre.

- Titles: This property represents a collection of `Title` objects categorized within the Genre.

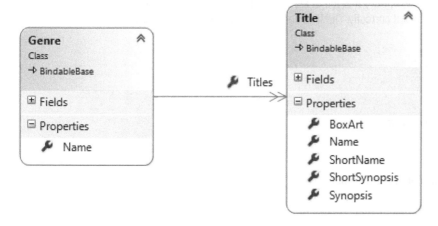

Figure 10-2. *Genre class diagram*

EXERCISE: BUILDING THE GENRE CLASS

In this exercise, you will build the Genre class used in the Model for the MovieBrowser application. To complete the exercise, you will need any edition of Visual Studio 2012.

1. Open the MovieBrowser solution if it is not already open.

2. Right-click the DataModel folder in the Solution Explorer, and select Add ➤ Class. Name the class Genre.cs.

3. Update the using statements at the top of Genre.cs to include the following statements:

    ```
    using System.Collections.ObjectModel;
    using MovieBrowser.Common;
    ```

4. Update the class definition of Genre to make the class public and inherit from BindableBase. The updated definition should look appear as follows:

    ```
    public class Genre : BindableBase
    ```

5. Create the backing fields and property statements for the Name and Titles properties. Use the following code:

    ```
    private string _name;
    public string Name
    {
        get
        {
            return _name;
        }
        set
        {
            SetProperty(ref _name, value);
        }
    }

    private ObservableCollection<Title> _titles;
    public ObservableCollection<Title> Titles
    {
        get
        {
            return _titles;
        }
        set
        {
            SetProperty(ref _titles, value);
        }
    }
    ```

6.   Save and build the solution.

At this point you have completed the implementation of the Genre class. This class will be used later in the chapter.

Data Templates

In Chapter 7 you learned about data templates and in Chapter 8, data binding. In this section, you will combine the two in order to define templates appropriate to display the data exposed by the Model objects. As in the Model section, I will cover the template from the greatest level of detail to the lowest.

■ **Note**   As you complete the data template exercises, data will stop being visible on the pages. This is because you still have work to do on the ViewModel and design-time data source that will be completed following the data templates.

Title

The Title object contains the richest set of data to display in the application, with long and short versions of the Name and Synopsis and three different sizes of BoxArt images to display. In this section, you will receive an introduction to the data templates that will be used to display the Title object in different formats and complete the implementation of these data templates as exercises.

ItemDetailPage

ItemDetailPage displays a single Title within a FlipView. Because the whole screen is available to dedicate to this display, you can use the large image and full version of the Name and Synopsis properties rather than any abbreviation.

EXERCISE: CREATING THE ITEM DETAIL TEMPLATE

In this exercise, you will create the data template that will be used to display a detailed view of the Title object with its Name, Synopsis, and large image. To complete the exercise, you will need any edition of Visual Studio 2012.

1.   Open the MovieBrowser solution if it is not already open.

2.   Right-click the Common folder in the Solution Explorer, and select Add ➤ New Item. Select the Resource Dictionary item type under Windows Store, and name the new item MovieBrowserStyles.xaml.

3.   Open App.xaml, and add the following XAML after the entry importing StandardStyles.xaml:

```
<ResourceDictionary Source="Common/MovieBrowserStyles.xaml" />
```

▪ **Note** Remember that order matters in XAML. You will be using resources defined in the StandardStyles.xaml dictionary from your templates, so StandardStyles.xaml must be defined before MovieBrowserStyles.xaml or you will get an error parsing at runtime.

---

4. Open MovieBrowserStyles.xaml, and add the following data template inside the ResourceDictionary element:

```
<DataTemplate x:Key="TitleDetailTemplate">
    <StackPanel Orientation="Vertical">
        <TextBlock Style="{StaticResource HeaderTextStyle}"
                Text="{Binding Name}" />
        <Image Height="150" Width="110"
            Stretch="UniformToFill"
            Source="{Binding BoxArt.LargeUrl}" />
        <TextBlock Text="{Binding Synopsis}" />
    </StackPanel>
</DataTemplate>
```

5. Build the project. This ensures the new template is available to be referenced.

6. Open ItemDetailPage.xaml. Find the FlipView.ItemTemplate element in the XAML, and delete this element with its contents.

7. Assign the TitleDetailTemplate as the ItemTemplate for the FlipView named flipView. The updated XAML element should read as follows:

```
<FlipView x:Name="flipView"
        AutomationProperties.AutomationId="ItemsFlipView"
        AutomationProperties.Name="Item Details" TabIndex="1"
        Grid.Row="1" Margin="0,-3,0,0"
        ItemsSource="{Binding Source={StaticResource itemsViewSource}}"
        ItemTemplate="{StaticResource TitleDetailTemplate}">
</FlipView>
```

You have now created the data template for displaying the detailed view of a Title and associated it to the FlipView, which displays the Titles.

GroupDetailPage

GroupDetailPage displays all of the Title instances within the selected Genre. Because more items must be displayed on the page, a more compact rendering of each item is needed. For this rendering, the medium-sized box art, the full title, and the shortened version of the synopsis will be used. GroupDetailPage displays either the horizontally oriented GridView or the vertically oriented ListView depending on whether the page is snapped, so a template will be created for each.

EXERCISE: CREATING THE GROUPDETAIL TITLE TEMPLATES

In this exercise, you will create the data templates that will be used to display a view of the Title object with its Name, ShortSynopsis, and medium image. To complete the exercise, you will need any edition of Visual Studio 2012.

1. Open the MovieBrowser solution if it is not already open.

2. Open MovieBrowserStyles.xaml in the Common folder.

3. Create the data template for use in the GridView. Use the following XAML:

```xml
<DataTemplate x:Key="TitleGenreGridViewTemplate">
    <Grid Width="195">
        <Grid.ColumnDefinitions>
            <ColumnDefinition Width="65" />
            <ColumnDefinition Width="*" />
        </Grid.ColumnDefinitions>
        <Border Background="{StaticResource
ListViewItemPlaceholderBackgroundThemeBrush}">
            <Image Height="90" Width="65" Stretch="UniformToFill"
                    Source="{Binding BoxArt.MediumUrl}" />
        </Border>
        <StackPanel Grid.Column="1" Orientation="Vertical">
            <TextBlock Style="{StaticResource TitleTextStyle}"
                    Text="{Binding Name}" />
            <TextBlock Text="{Binding ShortSynopsis}" />
        </StackPanel>
    </Grid>
</DataTemplate>
```

4. Within the same file, create the data template for use in the ListView. Use the following XAML:

```xml
<DataTemplate x:Key="TitleGenreListViewTemplate">
    <StackPanel Orientation="Vertical">
        <TextBlock Style="{StaticResource TitleTextStyle}"
                    Text="{Binding Name}" />
        <Border
          Background="{StaticResource
ListViewItemPlaceholderBackgroundThemeBrush}">
            <Image Height="90" Width="65" Stretch="UniformToFill"
                    Source="{Binding BoxArt.MediumUrl}" />
        </Border>
        <TextBlock Text="{Binding ShortSynopsis}" />
    </StackPanel>
</DataTemplate>
```

5. Build the project.

6. Open GroupDetailPage.xaml.

7. Update the `ItemTemplate` property of the `GridView` named `itemGridView` to read as follows:

```
ItemTemplate="{StaticResource TitleGenreGridViewTemplate}"
```

8. Update the `ItemTemplate` property of the `ListView` named `itemListView` to read as follows:

```
ItemTemplate="{StaticResource TitleGenreListViewTemplate}"
```

You have now created the data templates used to display `Title` objects on `GroupDetailPage` and assigned those templates to the appropriate controls on the page.

GroupedItemsPage

GroupedItemsPage displays multiple Genres with their Titles and has the least room to give to each individual Title. For this page, a view of Title will be given that includes only the shortened name and the small image. GroupedItemsPage, like GroupDetailPage, displays either the horizontally oriented GridView or the vertically oriented ListView depending on whether the page is snapped. Unlike GroupDetailPage, a different rendering of the Title is not necessary because it is already a compact view. Only one data template will be created.

EXERCISE: CREATING THE GROUPEDITEMS TITLE TEMPLATE

In this exercise, you will create the data template that will be used to display a view of the `Title` object with its `ShortName` and small image. To complete the exercise, you will need any edition of Visual Studio 2012.

1. Open the MovieBrowser solution if it is not already open.

2. Open `MovieBrowserStyles.xaml` in the `Common` folder.

3. Create the data template for use in both the `GridView` and `ListView`. Use the following XAML:

```xml
<DataTemplate x:Key="TitleGroupedItemsTemplate">
    <StackPanel Orientation="Vertical">
        <TextBlock Style="{StaticResource TitleTextStyle}"
                    Text="{Binding ShortName}" />
        <Border
          Background="{StaticResource
ListViewItemPlaceholderBackgroundThemeBrush}">
            <Image Height="53" Width="38" Stretch="UniformToFill"
                    Source="{Binding BoxArt.SmallUrl}" />
        </Border>
    </StackPanel>
</DataTemplate>
```

4. Build the project.

5. Open `GroupedItemsPage.xaml`.

6. Update the `ItemTemplate` property of the `GridView` named `itemGridView` to read as follows:

    ```
    ItemTemplate="{StaticResource TitleGroupedItemsTemplate}"
    ```

7. Update the `ItemTemplate` property of the `ListView` named `itemListView` to read as follows:

    ```
    ItemTemplate="{StaticResource TitleGroupedItemsTemplate}"
    ```

You have now created the data template used to display `Title` objects on `GroupedItemsPage` and assigned the template to the appropriate controls on the page.

Genre

Besides its contained `Titles` that have already been accounted for, the only other property of `Genre` that is displayed is the `Name` property. Because of its simplicity and slight differences in how it is displayed in different situations, the display of `Genre` information will be handled in the XAML on the page rather than creating templates in a resource dictionary. In this section, you will see the pages on which `Genre` is displayed and complete exercises to bind `Genre` data to the user interface in these pages.

ItemDetailPage

`ItemDetailPage` contains a `TextBlock` with the `Name` of the selected `Genre`.

EXERCISE: UPDATE ITEMDETAILPAGE FOR GENRE DISPLAY

In this exercise, you will update `ItemDetailPage` to display the `Name` of the selected `Genre`. To complete the exercise, you will need any edition of Visual Studio 2012.

1. Open the MovieBrowser solution if it is not already open.

2. Open `ItemDetailPage.xaml`.

3. Find the `TextBlock` named `pageTitle`. Update the binding for the `Text` property of the `TextBlock` to reference the `Name` property of the `Genre`. The updated XAML should read as follows:

    ```
    <TextBlock x:Name="pageTitle" Text="{Binding Name}"
               Style="{StaticResource PageHeaderTextStyle}" Grid.Column="1" />
    ```

You have now updated `ItemDetailPage` to display `Genre.Name` as the page title. Don't worry that the page now appears blank; I'll get to that.

GroupDetailPage

Like ItemDetailPage, GroupDetailPage features the Name of the Genre as the page title. Additionally, it provides screen space for attributes of the sample data's group that are not present in the Genre object. In addition to changing the page title, the display elements related to this additional data will be removed.

EXERCISE: UPDATE GROUPDETAILPAGE FOR GENRE DISPLAY

In this exercise, you will update GroupDetailPage to display the Name of the selected Genre and remove the display of additional Genre attributes. To complete the exercise, you will need any edition of Visual Studio 2012.

1. Open the MovieBrowser solution if it is not already open.

2. Open GroupDetailPage.xaml.

3. Find the TextBlock named pageTitle. Update the binding for the Text property of the TextBlock to reference the Name property of the Genre. The updated XAML should read as follows:

    ```
    <TextBlock x:Name="pageTitle" Text="{Binding Name}"
                Style="{StaticResource PageHeaderTextStyle}" Grid.Column="1" />
    ```

4. Find the GridView named itemGridView. Remove the GridView.Header element and its content.

5. Find the ListView named itemListView. Remove the ListView.Header element and its content.

You have now updated GroupDetailPage to display the Genre.Name as the page title and removed the display of additional data that does not apply to Genre.

GroupedItemsPage

GroupedItemPage displays the Name of each Genre as a group header in a button that, when clicked, takes the user to GroupDetailPage.

EXERCISE: UPDATE GROUPEDITEMSPAGE FOR GENRE DISPLAY

In this exercise, you will update GroupedItemsPage to display the Name of each Genre as the header for each group of Titles. To complete the exercise, you will need any edition of Visual Studio 2012.

1. Open the MovieBrowser solution if it is not already open.

2. Open GroupedItemsPage.xaml.

3. Find the GridView named itemGridView. Within the GroupStyle element of this GridView, find the Button element under the GroupStyle.HeaderTemplate. Update the binding for the Content property of the Button to reference the Name property of the Genre. The updated XAML should read as follows:

```
<Button AutomationProperties.Name="Group Title" Content="{Binding Name}"
        Click="Header_Click"
        Style="{StaticResource TextButtonStyle}" />
```

4. Find the ListView named itemListView. Within the GroupStyle element of this ListView, find the Button element under the GroupStyle.HeaderTemplate. Update the binding for the Content property of the Button to reference the Name property of the Genre. The updated XAML should read as follows:

```
<Button AutomationProperties.Name="Group Title" Content="{Binding Name}"
        Click="Header_Click"
        Style="{StaticResource TextButtonStyle}" />
```

You have now updated GroupedItemsPage to display Genre.Name as the header for each group of Title instances.

Sample Data

As you completed each of the exercises in the previous section, you should have noticed that the designer was showing less data than when the exercise began. This is because the elements on the page are using a design-time binding to a sample data source that exposes data that has different properties than this model. In this section, you will create a new sample data source that exposes the MovieBrowser Model objects. In addition to serving as the design-time data source, this sample data will also serve as a placeholder for data retrieved from the cloud until you are ready to add the functionality of interaction with the Netflix API. After creating the new sample data source, additional changes will be made on each page to bind to this design-time data.

EXERCISE: CREATING SAMPLEMOVIEDATASOURCE

In this exercise, you will create a sample data source that can be used to display design-time data in Visual Studio. To complete the exercise, you will need any edition of Visual Studio 2012.

1. Open the MovieBrowser solution if it is not already open.

2. Right-click the DataModel folder in the Solution Explorer, and select Add ➤ Class. Name the class SampleMovieDataSource.cs.

3. The pages are set up with the expectation that the sample data source will be contained in the MovieBrowser.Data namespace, so change the namespace declaration in SampleMovieDataSource.cs to meet this expectation. Modify the file to read as follows:

```
namespace MovieBrowser.Data
{
    public class SampleMovieDataSource
    {
    }
}
```

4. Add the following using statements to the top of `SampleMovieDataSource.cs`:

    ```
    using System;
    using System.Collections.ObjectModel;
    using MovieBrowser.DataModel;
    ```

5. Create a variable to hold the sample data. Add the following code inside the
    `SampleMovieDataSource` class:

    ```csharp
    private static readonly ObservableCollection<Genre> _genres
        = new ObservableCollection<Genre>
        {
            new Genre
            {
                Name="Action",
                Titles = new ObservableCollection<Title>
                {
                    new Title
                    {
                        Name = "Action Movie 1",
                        ShortName = "AM1",
                        Synopsis = "This is the longer bit of text...",
                        ShortSynopsis = "Short synopsis",
                        BoxArt = new BoxArt
                        {
                            SmallUrl = new Uri("ms-appx:Assets/SmallBoxArt.png"),
                            MediumUrl = new Uri("ms-appx:Assets/MediumBoxArt.png"),
                            LargeUrl = new Uri("ms-appx:Assets/LargeBoxArt.png")
                        }
                    },
                    new Title
                    {
                        Name = "Action Movie 2",
                        ShortName = "AM2",
                        Synopsis = "This is the longer bit of text...",
                        ShortSynopsis = "Short synopsis",
                        BoxArt = new BoxArt
                        {
                            SmallUrl = new Uri("ms-appx:Assets/SmallBoxArt.png"),
                            MediumUrl = new Uri("ms-appx:Assets/MediumBoxArt.png"),
                            LargeUrl = new Uri("ms-appx:Assets/LargeBoxArt.png")
                        }
                    }
                }
            }
        };
    ```

■ **Note** To keep you from having to read and type pages of repetitive code, this step is shown with only a single
Genre and two Title instances, enough to see how the controls work. The downloadable source code with the book
is populated with additional data, and you can copy from there if you want to see more data on your screen.

6. Add a Genres property through which this data can be accessed. Use the following code:

```
public ObservableCollection<Genre> Genres
{
    get
    {
        return _genres;
    }
}
```

7. Build the application.

You have now added a class that can be used to provide design-time data with which to view your pages.

EXERCISE: UPDATE PAGES TO USE SAMPLEMOVIEDATASOURCE

In this exercise, you will update the pages in the MovieBrowser application to use the sample data source that you created in the previous exercise for design-time data. You will not yet make this data available to the pages at runtime. To complete the exercise, you will need any edition of Visual Studio 2012.

1. Open the MovieBrowser solution if it is not already open.

2. Open ItemDetailPage.xaml.

3. Within the Page.Resources element, locate the CollectionViewSource named itemsViewSource. Update the XAML to read as follows:

```
<CollectionViewSource x:Name="itemsViewSource" Source="{Binding SelectedGenre.
Titles}"
    d:Source="{Binding Genres[0].Titles, Source={d:DesignInstance
    Type=data:SampleMovieDataSource, IsDesignTimeCreatable=True}}" />
```

4. Save and build your application. You should see data for the Title named Action Movie 1 appear in the designer.

5. Find the Grid that immediately follows the comment containing "Back button and page title." Update the XAML to read as follows:

```
<Grid DataContext="SelectedGenre"
    d:DataContext="{Binding Genres[0], Source={d:DesignInstance
      Type=data:SampleMovieDataSource, IsDesignTimeCreatable=True}}">
```

6. Save and build your application. At this point, you should see the page title populated with "Action."

7. Open GroupDetailPage.xaml.

8. Within the Page.Resources element, locate the CollectionViewSource named itemsViewSource. Update the XAML to read as follows:

```
<CollectionViewSource x:Name="itemsViewSource"
  Source="{Binding SelectedGenre.Titles}"
  d:Source="{Binding Genres[0].Titles, Source={d:DesignInstance
  Type=data:SampleMovieDataSource, IsDesignTimeCreatable=True}}" />
```

9. Save and build your application. You should see the `GridView` in the designer populated with `Title` data.

10. Find the `Grid` immediately following the comment that reads "Back button and Page title." Update the XAML to read as follows:

```
<Grid DataContext="{Binding SelectedGenre}"
    d:DataContext="{Binding Genres[0], Source={d:DesignInstance
      Type=data:SampleMovieDataSource, IsDesignTimeCreatable=True}}">
```

11. Save and build your application. At this point, you should see the page title populated with "Action."

12. Open `GroupedItemsPage.xaml`.

13. Within the `Page.Resources` element, locate the `CollectionViewSource` named `groupedItemsViewSource`. Update the XAML to read as follows:

```
<CollectionViewSource x:Name="groupedItemsViewSource"
  Source="{Binding Genres}" IsSourceGrouped="true"
  d:Source="{Binding Genres, Source={d:DesignInstance
  Type=data:SampleMovieDataSource, IsDesignTimeCreatable=True}}" />
```

14. Save and build your application. You should see the `GridView` in the designer populated with `Title` data grouped by `Genre`.

At this point, you have successfully updated the user interface for the MovieBrowser application to make use of the sample data source.

ViewModel

As you learned in Chapter 9, the job of the ViewModel is to present Model data in a way that is usable to the page and provide separation between the View and code that executes as a result of the user interacting with the View. In this section, you will create the ViewModel that will be used with the MovieBrowser application along with its associated helper objects and tie the ViewModel to the sample data source created in the previous section.

`MovieBrowserViewModel` (shown in Figure 10-3) has the following properties:

- `Genres`: This property exposes the available `Genres` in the catalog.

- `SelectedGenre`: This property represents the `Genre`, if any, which is currently selected.

- `SelectedTitle`: This property represents the `Title`, if any, which is currently selected.

- `SelectGenreCommand`: This property exposes the `ICommand` that is invoked by the UI to select a `Genre`.

- `SelectTitleCommand`: This property exposes the `ICommand` that is invoked by the UI to select a `Title`.

Figure 10-3. MovieBrowserViewModel class diagram

There are many ways available to keep navigation code out of the ViewModel, and frameworks are available that handle this task in sophisticated manners. You will keep this application simple, however, by raising events from the ViewModel, which can be handled in the UI code of the application to perform navigation. The following are the two events for this purpose:

- ViewGenre: This event is raised by the ViewModel to indicate that a Genre has been selected and the UI should transition to GroupDetailPage.

- ViewTitle: This event is raised by the ViewModel to indicate that a Title has been selected and the UI should transition to ItemDetailPage.

EXERCISE: CREATING THE VIEWMODEL'S HELPER OBJECTS

Before creating the ViewModel itself, helper objects must be created to provide an ICommand implementation and to serve as arguments for the events raised by the ViewModel. In this exercise, you will create these helper objects. To complete this exercise, you need any edition of Visual Studio 2012.

1. Open the MovieBrowser solution if it is not already open.

2. Right-click the Common folder in the Solution Explorer, and select Add ➤ Class. Name the new class DelegateCommand.cs.

■ **Note**   If you completed the exercises in Chapter 9, you can save some typing in step 3 by copying and pasting the DelegateCommand code you typed for that exercise.

---

3. Update the DelegateCommand class to provide a simple ICommand implementation using the following code (you'll need to ensure you have a using statement referencing System.Windows.Input):

```csharp
public class DelegateCommand : ICommand
{
    public event EventHandler CanExecuteChanged;
    private readonly Action<object> _executeAction;
    private readonly Func<object, bool> _canExecutePredicate;

    public DelegateCommand(Action<object> execute, Func<object, bool> canExecute)
    {
        _executeAction = execute;
        _canExecutePredicate = canExecute;
    }

    public bool CanExecute(object parameter)
    {
        return _canExecutePredicate(parameter);
    }

    public void Execute(object parameter)
    {
        if(!CanExecute(parameter))
        {
            throw new InvalidOperationException("Cannot execute now");
        }
        _executeAction(parameter);
    }

    public void RaiseCanExecuteChanged()
    {
        if(CanExecuteChanged != null)
        {
            CanExecuteChanged(this, EventArgs.Empty);
        }
    }
}
```

4. Right-click the `DataModel` folder in the Solution Explorer, and select Add ➤ Class. Name the new class `ViewGenreEventArgs.cs`.

5. Update the `ViewGenreEventArgs` class with the following code:

```csharp
public class ViewGenreEventArgs : EventArgs
{
    public ViewGenreEventArgs(Genre genre)
    {
        Genre = genre;
    }

    public Genre Genre
    {
        get;
        private set;
    }
}
```

6. Right-click the DataModel folder in the Solution Explorer, and select Add ➤ Class. Name the new class ViewTitleEventArgs.cs.

7. Update the ViewTitleEventArgs class with the following code:

```
public class ViewTitleEventArgs : EventArgs
{
    public ViewTitleEventArgs(Title title)
    {
        Title = title;
    }

    public Title Title
    {
        get;
        private set;
    }
}
```

8. Save and build the application.

You have completed creating the helper objects that will be used to support the ViewModel in your application.

EXERCISE: CREATING THE MOVIEBROWSERVIEWMODEL

In this exercise, you will create the MovieBrowserViewModel class. To complete this exercise, you need any edition of Visual Studio 2012.

1. Open the MovieBrowser solution if it is not already open.

2. Right-click the DataModel folder in the Solution Explorer, and select Add ➤ Class. Name the new class MovieBrowserViewModel.cs.

3. Update the MovieBrowserViewModel.cs file to include the following using statements at the top of the file:

```
using System;
using System.Collections.ObjectModel;
using System.Linq;
using System.Windows.Input;
using MovieBrowser.Common;
using MovieBrowser.Data;
```

4. Update the MovieBrowserViewModel class to include the events and properties shown previously in Figure 10-3. When finished, your code should read as follows:

```
public class MovieBrowserViewModel : BindableBase
{
    public event EventHandler<ViewTitleEventArgs> ViewTitle;
    public event EventHandler<ViewGenreEventArgs> ViewGenre;
```

```
public MovieBrowserViewModel()
{
}
private readonly SampleMovieDataSource _catalog = new
SampleMovieDataSource();
public ObservableCollection<Genre> Genres
{
    get { return _catalog.Genres; }
}

private Genre _selectedGenre;
public Genre SelectedGenre
{
    get { return _selectedGenre; }
    set
    {
        SetProperty(ref _selectedGenre, value);
    }
}

private Title _selectedTitle;
public Title SelectedTitle
{
    get { return _selectedTitle; }
    set
    {
        SetProperty(ref _selectedTitle, value);
    }
}

public ICommand SelectTitleCommand
{
    get;
    private set;
}

public ICommand SelectGenreCommand
{
    get;
    private set;
}
}
```

5. Add helper methods to the `MovieBrowserViewModel` that will raise the navigation events only if there are any subscribers to the events. The code for the methods should read as follows:

```
private void RaiseViewTitle(Title title)
{
    if(ViewTitle != null)
    {
        ViewTitle(this, new ViewTitleEventArgs(title));
```

```
        }
    }

    private void RaiseViewGenre(Genre genre)
    {
        if(ViewGenre != null)
        {
            ViewGenre(this, new ViewGenreEventArgs(genre));
        }
    }
```

6. Implement `SelectGenreCommand`. When executed, the `Command` should set the `SelectedGenre` property to the specified `Genre` and then raise the `ViewGenre` event, which will trigger the user interface to navigate to `GroupDetailPage`. Add the following code to the constructor of `MovieBrowserViewModel`:

```
SelectGenreCommand = new DelegateCommand(
    arg =>
    {
        var genre = (Genre)arg;
        SelectedGenre = genre;
        RaiseViewGenre(genre);
    },
    arg =>
    {
        return arg is Genre;
    });
```

7. Implement `SelectTitleCommand`. This `Command` functions similarly to `SelectGenreCommand` except that in addition to setting the `SelectedTitle` property it also ensures that the `SelectedGenre` property is set to the `Genre`, which contains the selected `Title`. This is to ensure that `ItemDetailPage`, which expects a selected `Genre`, works appropriately. Add the following code to the constructor of `MovieBrowserViewModel`:

```
SelectTitleCommand = new DelegateCommand(
    arg =>
    {
        var title = (Title)arg;
        SelectedTitle = title;
        SelectedGenre = Genres.Where(g => g.Titles.Contains(title)).
FirstOrDefault();
        RaiseViewTitle(title);
    },
    arg =>
    {
        return arg is Title;
    });
```

8. Save and build your solution.

You have finished creating the `MovieBrowserViewModel`.

Integrating the ViewModel

Now that you have created the ViewModel for your application, you need to make it available to bind to the user interface controls. As with many other tasks, there are many correct ways to complete this task, and the only truly incorrect way is the way that doesn't work. In the MovieBrowser application, the `MovieBrowserViewModel` will have a single instance that is shared across multiple pages, so this instance will be created as an entry in the `App.xaml` resource dictionary. In addition to creating `MovieBrowserViewModel` instance, the navigation events raised by the ViewModel must be responded to appropriately, and some adjustment to the code for each page is necessary. In this section, a series of exercises will walk you through completing each of these tasks.

EXERCISE: ADDING MOVIEBROWSERVIEWMODEL TO THE APPLICATION

In this exercise, you will add `MovieBrowserViewModel` as an application-wide resource and update the application start-up code to subscribe to navigation events and respond appropriately. To complete this exercise, you will need any edition of Visual Studio 2012.

1. Open the MovieBrowser solution if it is not already open.

2. Open `App.xaml`.

3. On the `Application` element, add the following attribute:

   ```
   xmlns:model="using:MovieBrowser.DataModel"
   ```

4. Find the section of `App.xaml` that includes the comment "Application-specific resources." Add the following element:

   ```
   <model:MovieBrowserViewModel x:Key="MovieBrowserViewModel" />
   ```

5. Save and build the solution.

6. Open `App.xaml.cs`.

7. Ensure that the `using` statements at the top of `App.xaml.cs` include the following statement:

   ```
   using MovieBrowser.DataModel;
   ```

8. Add the event handler code to the `App` class to handle navigation in response to events raised by `MovieBrowserViewModel`. The completed code should read as follows:

   ```
   private void OnGenreView(object sender, ViewGenreEventArgs e)
   {
       var rootFrame = Window.Current.Content as Frame;
       if(rootFrame != null)
       {
           rootFrame.Navigate(typeof(GroupDetailPage));
       }
   }
   ```

161

```
private void OnTitleView(object sender, ViewTitleEventArgs e)
{
    var rootFrame = Window.Current.Content as Frame;
    if(rootFrame != null)
    {
        rootFrame.Navigate(typeof(ItemDetailPage));
    }
}
```

9. Use the event handlers created in the previous step to subscribe to the events of the application-wide `MovieBrowserViewModel` instance. Find the `OnLaunched` method of the `App` class. After the initial `if` block that checks `args.PreviousExecutionState`, add the following code:

```
var viewModel = this.Resources["MovieBrowserViewModel"] as MovieBrowserViewModel;
viewModel.ViewTitle += OnTitleView;
viewModel.ViewGenre += OnGenreView;
```

10. Save and build the solution.

You have completed adding the `MovieBrowserViewModel` as an application-wide resource and updated the application to navigate to the appropriate page when navigation events are raised by the ViewModel.

EXERCISE: UPDATING MOVIEBROWSER PAGES TO BIND TO VIEWMODEL

Now that you have created the ViewModel and made it available throughout your application, the application's pages need some adjustments to utilize the ViewModel. This task involves some changes in the XAML and some in the code file that sits behind the XAML file (or *code-behind*). In this exercise, you will finish integrating `MovieBrowserViewModel`. To complete this exercise, you will need any edition of Visual Studio 2012.

1. Open the MovieBrowser solution if it is not already open.

2. Open `ItemDetailPage.xaml`.

3. In the `common:LayoutAwarePage` element, find the `DataContext` attribute and update it to read as follows:

```
DataContext="{StaticResource MovieBrowserViewModel}"
```

4. In the `FlipView` element named `flipView`, add the following attribute:

```
SelectedItem="{Binding SelectedTitle}"
```

5. Save and build the solution.

6. Open `ItemDetailPage.xaml.cs`.

7. Delete the `LoadState` method.

8. Delete the `SaveState` method.

9. Save and build the solution.

10. Open `GroupDetailPage.xaml`.

11. In the `common:LayoutAwarePage` element, find the `DataContext` attribute and update it to read as follows:

    ```
    DataContext="{StaticResource MovieBrowserViewModel}"
    ```

12. Save and build the solution.

13. Open `GroupDetailPage.xaml.cs`.

14. Add the following `using` statement to the top of `GroupDetailPage.xaml.cs`.

    ```
    using MovieBrowser.DataModel;
    ```

15. Delete the `LoadState` method.

16. Replace the body of the `ItemView_ItemClick` method with the following code:

    ```
    var vm = DataContext as MovieBrowserViewModel;
    var title = e.ClickedItem as Title;
    vm.SelectTitleCommand.Execute(title);
    ```

17. Save and build the solution.

18. Open `GroupedItemsPage.xaml`.

19. In the `common:LayoutAwarePage` element, find the `DataContext` attribute and update it to read as follows:

    ```
    DataContext="{StaticResource MovieBrowserViewModel}"
    ```

20. Save and build the solution.

21. Open `GroupedItemsPage.xaml.cs`.

22. Add the following `using` statement to the top of `GroupedItemsPage.xaml.cs`:

    ```
    using MovieBrowser.DataModel;
    ```

23. Delete the `LoadState` method.

24. Replace the body of the `Header_Click` method with the following code:

    ```
    var vm = DataContext as MovieBrowserViewModel;
    var genre = (sender as FrameworkElement).DataContext as Genre;
    vm.SelectGenreCommand.Execute(genre);
    ```

25. Replace the body of the `ItemView_ItemClick` method with the following code:

    ```
    var vm = DataContext as MovieBrowserViewModel;
    var title = e.ClickedItem as Title;
    vm.SelectTitleCommand.Execute(title);
    ```

26. Save and build the solution.

You have now successfully integrated `MovieBrowserViewModel` with your application. As a finishing touch, you can choose to add the image files from the `Sample BoxArt` folder in the downloadable code for this chapter to the `Assets` folder in the project.

Conclusion

You have done a lot of work in this chapter. You have mocked data to be used both at design time and at runtime, built your application's ViewModel, and integrated the ViewModel into your application's user interface. You should now feel familiar with the way that pieces of the Model-View-ViewModel fit together. Be sure to explore the application and admire your work.

■ ■ ■

CHAPTER 11

Inversion of Control

Our intellect is not the most subtle, the most powerful, the most appropriate, instrument for revealing the truth. It is life that, little by little, example by example, permits us to see that what is most important to our heart, or to our mind, is learned not by reasoning but through other agencies. Then it is that the intellect, observing their superiority, abdicates its control to them upon reasoned grounds and agrees to become their collaborator and lackey.

—Marcel Proust

Along with MVVM, Inversion of Control (IoC) plays a huge part in building solid Windows applications that are easy to test and maintain. In this chapter, you'll take a quick look at IoC and the two primary patterns used to achieve IoC: Dependency Injection and Service Location. While I will barely scratch the surface of these topics, you will build a strong enough understanding to make clear their use in building the behavioral aspects of the sample application.

Interfaces and Abstract Classes

Before diving too deeply into Inversion of Control, let's take a little bit of time to consider the role of an interface or an abstract class. In the world of application development, the term *interface* refers to a contract through which components can interact with each other. It describes a set of known properties and methods that are exposed by an object. The classic "real-world" example of the usage of interfaces is the automobile. If you are going to test-drive a new car, you will typically sit in the driver's seat, glance around to ensure yourself of the location of all the controls, start the car, and start driving. How did you know that big round thing in front of you is used to steer? How do you know how to start and stop? The interface between driver and machine is so commonly understood that these seem like silly questions. The answer is that auto makers have adhered to a common contract for so long that it would probably be dangerous for them to stray too far from the pattern because people would not know how to drive the car and would crash.

When you build an application using C#, you can choose in many cases to write code that depends on a specific implementation class, or you can look at the interfaces exposed by that class and write instead to one or more of the interfaces. Writing to the interface allows your code to become more flexible, leading both to an easier time testing the code and to a high probability that the code will be able to be reused directly without the copy-paste-tweak cycle, commonly referred to as *keyboard inheritance*. Let's look at a real-world problem and its solution to demonstrate the point.

Examining an Inflexible Solution

One of the common problems that I have been asked to solve over the years has been to get data from somewhere (usually a database of some sort) into a Microsoft Excel spreadsheet. Sometimes this has been done in an environment where I can depend on Excel to be installed, but in most cases it has been in a server environment where automating Excel is simply not an option. The earliest solution to this problem had programmers without the budget for specialized components, writing the data out to a series of comma-separated value (CSV) files, which was a simple task. The files could be opened in Excel but had very limited formatting options and did not leave users feeling like they were getting a "real" Excel export. Later versions of Microsoft Office replaced the very complicated binary format (called BIFF) of Excel workbooks with a documented XML format that, while not uncomplicated, can be understood and can produce a full-featured workbook using plain text.

In my earliest solutions using the Office spreadsheet format, I would create a worksheet in Excel with my headers and a couple rows of data, save the file as XML, and then open it in Notepad to determine the XML that I needed to generate. I would then write a method similar to the following to create the spreadsheet:

```
public void GenerateContactSpreadSheet(List<Contact> contacts, string filePath)
{
    XDocument doc;
    // create XML document
    // create header row with contact attribute names
    // for each contact create data row with attribute values
    doc.Save(filePath);
}
```

This approach works, but it falls short on a couple of points. The first point where it could use some improvement is that this works only to output data representing my custom Contact class. If I want to output data produced from some other type, I have to create another similar copy of the procedure. As you will see when you look at the final result, producing the right XML may not be hard, but it is also not a trivial task, and it would be best to do it only once if at all possible. The other way that this solution falls short is that the method is required to create a file in order to write its output. This means that if I want to write a unit test for the method, I have to read and write files on disk, which makes testing a bit more brittle, but it also limits the usage of the method to a runtime execution environment where the code is allowed to create a file at the specified path. If security restrictions placed on the execution of code require the use of a dialog that interacts with the user to create its file and then gives access to a stream (such as is the case in many sandboxed environments), this code simply cannot work as is.

To solve the problems with this less flexible solution, let's consider the job of the method shown previously. The job of this method is to create XML in a very specific format. The data it uses to do its job includes column headers and row data, and the current implementation creates a file, but you don't necessarily have to keep it knowing about the source of its data, and it is the XML within the file that is important and not the file itself.

Defining the Structure of Data

Let's address the data first. The earlier example was in control of the column headers, and in order to exert this control, it "knew" the names of all the attributes that would be column headers. A more generic approach would be to remove this control from the method by passing the values that are to be used in the header into the method. Since I know that I'm going to have to enumerate the values in some way to create my column headers, I want to use a data type that can be easily enumerated. A collection of values that is going to be considered fixed is often represented as an array, but I want to create a solution that does not lock calling code into the use of an array. Therefore, I can look at the interfaces implemented by Array, and I find that the ICollection <T> interface offers the iteration that I'll need, so I'll use ICollection <string> as the data type for the column headers. The row data itself could pretty much be anything and I need to generically represent rows and columns, so for this example I've chosen again to use ICollection <T> to represent the rows, but the columns themselves I'll represent as an array of object. Having removed the responsibility of knowing about its data, so far the method is evolving to look like this:

■ **Note** I could have just as easily assumed that the first row represents the column headers, but I preferred to list them separately, and it *is* my program after all.

```
public void GenerateExcelSpreadSheetXml(ICollection<string> columnHeaders
    , ICollection<object[]> rowData
    , string filePath)
{
    XDocument doc;
    // create XML document
    // loop through columnHeaders to create header row
    // loop through rowData to create rows
    doc.Save(filePath);
}
```

Removing Dependencies

Now that I've addressed the method being required to know the structure of the data that it is to output, let's turn our attention to removing its dependence on being able to write a file. Assuming you want to preserve the ability to save the XML document to something, you can start by looking at the overloads available on the XDocument.Save method to see whether a suitable alternative is presented that doesn't require file I/O.

Looking at the different overloads defined for the Save method shows you that you can pass the method either a string that represents the file to which the document should be written, an XmlWriter object, a Stream object, or a TextWriter object. Besides the string filePath, the other objects are all abstract classes. Abstract classes are very similar to interfaces in that they cannot be directly created and define a contract to which derived classes will adhere, but they also provide some sort of behavior that will be inherited by derived classes. Through a series of decisions about how generic each of the choices would be and the complexity of writing client code to implement each, I chose TextWriter as the best option for the example application.

The refactored method, which now is free from the responsibility of writing files or understanding the structure of the data types to be output (now in its entirety), looks like this:

```
public void GenerateExcelSpreadSheetXml(ICollection<string> columnHeaders
    , ICollection<object[]> rowData
    , TextWriter output)
{
    string worksheetName = "Sheet1";
    XNamespace spreadsheetNamespace = "urn:schemas-microsoft-com:office:spreadsheet";
    var doc = new XDocument(new XDeclaration("1.0", "UTF-8", "true")
        , new XProcessingInstruction("mso-application", "progid=\"Excel.Sheet\"")
        , new XElement(
            spreadsheetNamespace + "Workbook"
            , new XAttribute(XNamespace.Xmlns + "ss", spreadsheetNamespace.NamespaceName)
            , new XElement(spreadsheetNamespace + "Styles"
            , new XElement(spreadsheetNamespace + "Style"
                , new XAttribute(spreadsheetNamespace + "ID", "Default")
                , new XAttribute(spreadsheetNamespace + "Name", "Normal")
```

```
                    , new XElement(spreadsheetNamespace+"Alignment"
                        , new XAttribute(spreadsheetNamespace+"Vertical", "Bottom"))
                    , new XElement(spreadsheetNamespace+"Borders")
                    , new XElement(spreadsheetNamespace+"Font"
                        , new XAttribute(spreadsheetNamespace+"FontName", "Calibri")
                        , new XAttribute(spreadsheetNamespace+"Size", "11")
                        , new XAttribute(spreadsheetNamespace+"Color", "#000000"))
                    , new XElement(spreadsheetNamespace+"Interior")
                    , new XElement(spreadsheetNamespace+"NumberFormat")
                    , new XElement(spreadsheetNamespace+"Protection")
                    )
            , new XElement(spreadsheetNamespace+"Style"
                , new XAttribute(spreadsheetNamespace+"ID", "HeaderStyle")
                , new XElement(spreadsheetNamespace+"Font"
                    , new XAttribute(spreadsheetNamespace+"FontName", "Calibri")
                    , new XAttribute(spreadsheetNamespace+"Size", "11")
                    , new XAttribute(spreadsheetNamespace+"Color", "#000000")
                    , new XAttribute(spreadsheetNamespace+"Bold", "1"))
                )
            )
        , new XElement(spreadsheetNamespace+"Worksheet"
            , new XAttribute(spreadsheetNamespace+"Name", worksheetName)
            , new XElement(spreadsheetNamespace+"Table"
                , new XAttribute(spreadsheetNamespace+"ExpandedColumnCount"
                    , columnHeaders.Count)
                , new XAttribute(spreadsheetNamespace+"FullColumns", 1)
                , new XAttribute(spreadsheetNamespace+"ExpandedRowCount"
                    , rowData.Count+1)
                , new XAttribute(spreadsheetNamespace+"FullRows", 1)
                , new XElement(spreadsheetNamespace+"Row"
                    , from header in columnHeaders
                        select new XElement(spreadsheetNamespace+"Cell"
                            , new XAttribute(spreadsheetNamespace+"StyleID"
                                , "HeaderStyle")
                            , new XElement(spreadsheetNamespace+"Data"
                                , new XAttribute(spreadsheetNamespace+"Type", "String")
                                    , header)))
                , from row in rowData
                    select new XElement(spreadsheetNamespace+"Row"
                        , from value in row
                                select new XElement(spreadsheetNamespace+"Cell"
                                    , new XElement(spreadsheetNamespace+"Data"
                                        , new XAttribute(spreadsheetNamespace+"Type",
"String"), value))
                    )
                )
            )
        )
    );

    doc.Save(output);
}
```

■ **Note**   If you are interested in learning more about Microsoft's XML Formats for Office documents, the schema references can be found on Microsoft's web site. Go to www.microsoft.com/download and search for *office schema*.

Back to Inversion of Control

In the previous section, I discussed how the use of interfaces and abstract classes can help you remove responsibilities from a piece of code and make the code control only that which directly relates to the job of fulfilling its responsibilities. This is the essence of Inversion of Control.

One of the simplest forms of Inversion of Control that you may not realize you use is event delegates in any development environment that supports them. A button, for example, is a fairly simple thing. It has a defined look for its different states (Enabled, Disabled, Focused, Pressed) and is responsible to "know" that if it is enabled, it should raise its Click event (or in other words "call the delegate methods associated with its click event") when the user activates the button. This is where the magic happens; as the developer of the application, you get to inject your own logic into this scenario by creating the delegate that will be called from the button's Click handler code. The author of the button's code had no idea what kind of logic would be executed in your application to respond to the button click, but by using a defined contract and providing an injection point, the button's behavior can be reused for your scenario.

Inversion of Control is achieved in many different forms and through many patterns. In this chapter, I will focus on two of the patterns: Dependency Injection and Service Locator. These are the two most commonly used patterns today when Inversion of Control is intentional and many of the other patterns that exist can relate back to one or the other.

Dependency Injection

One of the simpler ways to achieve Inversion of Control is through Dependency Injection. With Dependency Injection, classes that are needed to fulfill a responsibility (called *collaborators*) are created outside of the component and passed into the component, usually either via a constructor that accepts these collaborators or by setting properties. Typically the class written to take advantage of Dependency Injection will not know the specific type that will be injected at runtime, instead knowing only the interface or abstract base class that advertises capabilities needed. As a contrived example that is simple enough to follow easily but complex enough to rely on outside services, let's consider a class used by a fictitious online ordering system to place an order for a product. When placing orders, the class needs to interact with the inventory system to check inventory, the shipping system to schedule delivery, and a credit card processing system to process the payment. The process flow may look something like Figure 11-1.

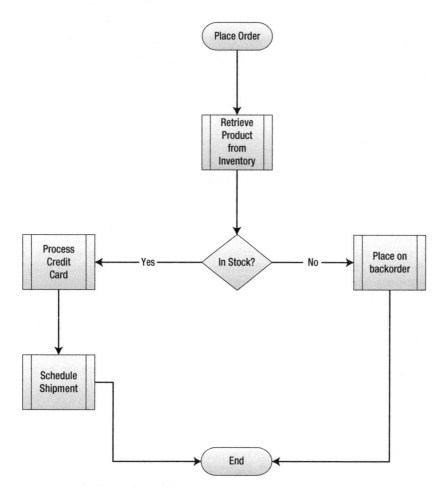

Figure 11-1. *Order product flow*

Without using Inversion of Control, the code to implement this flow would be similar to the following:

```
public class OrderProcessor
{
    public void OrderProduct(int productId, string creditCardNumber, Customer customer)
    {
        IInventorySystem inventory = new InventorySystem();
        ICreditCardProcessor cardProcessor = new CreditCardProcessor();
        IShippingSystem shipping = new ShippingSystem();
        ProductInventoryInfo product = inventory.GetProduct(productId);
        if(product.IsAvailable == true)
        {
            cardProcessor.ProcessPayment(creditCardNumber, product.Price);
            shipping.ScheduleShipment(productId, customer);
        }
```

```
        else
        {
            inventory.Backorder(productId, customer.CustomerId);
        }
    }
}
```

Ignoring for a moment the complete lack of error handling and somewhat naïve view of how processing an order would flow, the most significant problem with this code is that by creating the collaborators within the code, a dependency on a specific implementation of each collaborator is required, and the order method cannot be tested without the rest of the services in place and ready to process requests. You can rewrite the order processor to remove this dependency by requiring an instance of each needed interface to be provided to the class's constructor. The order processor updated to allow for Inversion of Control through Dependency Injection would read as follows:

```
public class OrderProcessor
{
    private IInventorySystem _inventory;
    private ICreditCardProcessor _cardProcessor;
    private IShippingSystem _shipping;

    public OrderProcessor(IInventorySystem inventory, ICreditCardProcessor cardProcessor
                          , IShippingSystem shipping)
    {
        _inventory = inventory;
        _cardProcessor = _cardProcessor;
        _shipping = shipping;
    }

    public void OrderProduct(int productId, string creditCardNumber, Customer customer)
    {
        ProductInventoryInfo product = _inventory.GetProduct(productId);
        if(product.IsAvailable == true)
        {
            _cardProcessor.ProcessPayment(creditCardNumber, product.Price);
            _shipping.ScheduleShipment(productId, customer);
        }
        else
        {
            _inventory.Backorder(productId, customer.CustomerId);
        }
    }
}
```

Removing the capability (and with it the responsibility) of creating the collaborator objects now allows you to create alternate implementations of the collaborating interfaces and will enable very focused and isolated testing. Very often, applications that make use of either Dependency Injection or Service Locator, which is discussed in the next section, use specialized libraries that are responsible for creating objects and ensuring that their dependencies are resolved. These libraries are often referred to as IoC *containers*.

Service Locator

An alternative to Dependency Injection is the Service Locator pattern; classes using the Service Locator pattern differ from those using Dependency Injection in that instead of having the collaborators passed into the class from outside via constructor or property injection, the class instead calls upon the functionality of a Service Locator class, asking that class to provide an appropriate implementation of the collaborator. Many early implementations of the Service Locator pattern built for use with the .NET Framework would involve the class using the Service Locator to call a factory method passing a string key that indicates the type of object being requested and receiving as the return value an object of type Object that would have to be cast to the appropriate interface.

The introduction of generics into the .NET Framework has led most current libraries that provide an implementation of the pattern to make use of a generic factory method that returns a strongly typed object of the appropriate interface. One example of a library that provides a Service Locator implementation is the Common Service Locator library, which is a collaborative effort on CodePlex (http://commonservicelocator.codeplex.com/), allowing for a common Service Locator to be used across various Inversion of Control libraries. This independence is desirable because the Service Locator has to be known to the class requesting collaborators; it could become very easy to find you are locked in to a particular Inversion of Control solution because changing Inversion of Control providers would require substantial change to the application code.

The order processing class that you used with Dependency Injection may look like the following when modified to use the Service Locator pattern (assuming you have an installed and configured Service Locator implementation):

```
public class OrderProcessor
{
    public void OrderProduct(int productId, string creditCardNumber, Customer customer)
    {
        IInventorySystem inventory = ServiceLocator.GetService<IInventorySystem>();
        ICreditCardProcessor cardProcessor =
                            ServiceLocator.GetService<ICreditCardProcessor>();
        IShippingSystem shipping = ServiceLocator.GetService<IShippingSystem>();
        ProductInventoryInfo product = inventory.GetProduct(productId);
        if(product.IsAvailable == true)
        {
            cardProcessor.ProcessPayment(creditCardNumber, product.Price);
            shipping.ScheduleShipment(productId, customer);
        }
        else
        {
            inventory.Backorder(productId, customer.CustomerId);
        }
    }
}
```

As you can see from the sample code, the code that makes use of the order processor class now does not need to know what collaborators are required for the order processor to complete its responsibility successfully; you need for the Service Locator to know only how to resolve all of the collaborators' interfaces.

■ **Note** While the Common Service Locator project is used widely in .NET Framework projects, at the time of this writing, it has not yet been updated for compatibility with Windows Runtime applications. Before attempting to use it in a Windows Runtime application, you should check to see whether Windows Runtime support has been added.

Selecting an Inversion of Control Method

The Service Locator and Dependency Injection patterns clearly take a much different approach to achieving Inversion of Control, and these differences often lead to philosophical discussions about which is better. Rather than tag either as "better," it is much better to look at the advantages and disadvantages that each brings to the table and understand that at different times and in different scenarios each will assert an edge over the other that makes it the most appropriate choice for that scenario.

One of the biggest advantages that I see in using Dependency Injection (at least when constructor injection is used as opposed to property injection) is that the component provides a very clear advertisement in the form of constructor arguments as to what external services it needs in order to complete its job. This also allows the component to be independent of the mechanism used to provide Inversion of Control because it does not need to be aware of any IoC container or Service Locator implementation. If you're not using some sort of framework that is responsible for "building up" components and ensuring dependencies are resolved, the injection approach can also lead to having to invent ways to pass references down through several layers of application code in order to make the reference available to the code that depends upon it, which makes changes at the component level that require the introduction of a new dependency bubble changes through multiple levels.

The biggest advantage that I see in the Service Locator pattern is a direct counter to the advantage of using Dependency Injection. Because the component does not advertise the dependencies that it has on external services to complete its work, the code adheres more closely to the concept of encapsulation. By advertising external dependencies required to complete work, it can be said that the components using Dependency Injection reveal a bit more of "how" the work is done instead of leaving the entire focus on "what" work is to be completed. Using the Service Locator approach, there is no need to ensure that service references are passed from layer to layer that may not need them. This advantage to some degree is countered by the fact that many developers using Inversion of Control will also be using some sort of framework that will handle the resolution of dependencies. Additionally, by removing the explicit advertisement of dependencies on object construction, the risk of finding that a necessary service has not been registered late in the process increases, and the component cannot "fail early."

All other things being equal, I find that my preferences lean to the explicit model provided with constructor injection and allow whatever IoC container that I am using to handle many of the drawbacks of this approach. This allows me to quickly look at the method signature of the constructor for any class that I have built using this model and understand what it needs to get its job done, which is a big advantage when trying to quickly understand problems with production code. There are some times when you find that your component *must* support a public constructor with no arguments and other times when it is not required but makes sense to do so. In these cases, the Service Locator becomes a valuable tool to make services available to your component.

Standing on the Shoulders of Giants

Throughout this chapter there have been allusions to the idea that if you are using Inversion of Control you will be using some library or framework to achieve Inversion of Control. This is because there are several really good libraries that have evolved over the last several years, and unless you are just trying to satisfy your own intellectual curiosity about how such a framework would be constructed, there's not a lot of justification to building your own Inversion of Control framework. To use the phrase that was popular when the .NET Framework 4.0 went live in April 2010, "You should be writing code that only you can write."

Some of these toolkits include the MVVM Light Toolkit, which is written by Laurent Bugnion of GalaSoft and is likely the first of the toolkits to be ported to Windows Runtime and the Unity application block, which is written and maintained by Microsoft's Patterns and Practices team.

■ **Note** At the time of this writing, the Patterns and Practices team had begun work on adding Windows Runtime support to Unity, but the implementation was not complete. Unity should be fully functional in Windows Runtime when the final Visual Studio 2012 product is released.

Conclusion

In this chapter, I introduced Inversion of Control. I discussed the motivation behind using Inversion of Control in applications and introduced two popular methods through which Inversion of Control is achieved. As you continue to build the sample application using the Model-View-ViewModel pattern, you will see Inversion of Control become a very important component of your application design to allow you to isolate collaborators.

■ ■ ■

CHAPTER 12

The Role of Service Agents

*Of all those in the army close to the commander none is more intimate than the secret agent;
of all rewards none more liberal than those given to secret agents; of all matters none is more
confidential than those relating to secret operations.*

—Sun Tzu

In Chapters 10 and 11 you learned about the Model-View-ViewModel pattern and the concept of Inversion
of Control. In this chapter, you will learn about Service Agents and how they are used to achieve Inversion of
Control when building applications using the Model-View-ViewModel pattern. Although simplistic both in
concept and in implementation, Service Agents are an integral part of achieving the separation that is a major
goal of the Model-View-ViewModel pattern. Building on what you have already learned, you should find the
concepts straightforward and easy to understand.

Introducing the Service Agent

So far, your exploration of the Model-View-ViewModel pattern has included a fairly simplistic view of the world
in which your applications will run. The user interacts with the View, the View binds to the ViewModel, and the
ViewModel handles communication with the real model (see Figure 12-1).

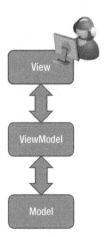

Figure 12-1. *Simplified view of Model-View-ViewModel*

This simplified view is great for communicating the general way that the Model-View-ViewModel pattern works, but it ignores some very critical factors. The first factor that is ignored (or at least not taken into account) when looking at the simplified view of MVVM is that very often a stark line should be drawn between ViewModel and Model because very rarely will the actual Model reside on the same machine on which the View and ViewModel are executing. This leaves a more realistic view of the pattern looking something like Figure 12-2.

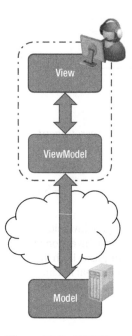

Figure 12-2. *MVVM expanded view*

If you were paying close attention in the previous chapter, you should see a problem with this view. Our ViewModel has a direct dependency on something that is running on a completely different machine. This not only makes it difficult to make changes to how the Model works but creates a situation where a lot of preconditions must be met before the ViewModel can be tested. In addition to the ViewModel being available, whatever service is exposing the Model must be running and accessible to the code testing the ViewModel. In many cases, the extra complexities introduced into the testing process makes people decide to forego automated testing altogether and hope that any bugs can be identified during manual testing.

Any time a design discourages automated testing, there's an opportunity (and I would argue a responsibility) to improve the design. In this case, we refactor the code to remove the responsibility of talking directly to the Model from the ViewModel and instead give that job to an intermediary that knows only how to talk to the Model. We call this intermediary a *Service Agent*. The introduction of the Service Agent is illustrated in Figure 12-3.

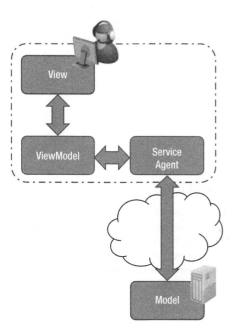

Figure 12-3. *MVVM with Service Agent*

Removing Dependency

By adding the Service Agent between the ModelView and the Model, you reduce the number of responsibilities of the ViewModel, but there is still the potential for the ViewModel to be dependent upon the specific service exposing the Model if you're not careful to use what you've learned about Inversion of Control. Consider the following code snippet that may appear within the Execute method of a command exposed by the ViewModel:

```
public void Execute(object arg)
{
    var agent = new ModelServiceAgent();
    this.Data = agent.GetData();
}
```

This code shows evidence that a Service Agent was introduced but is no less dependent upon the Model than it would have been with no Service Agent at all because it depends upon a specific Service Agent implementation. Very often you can identify this type of dependency by reviewing the code and looking for any time that the new operator is used. If the type that is being created with new exposes behavior that needs access to external resources, it should most likely be removed by introducing Inversion of Control to our ViewModel.

Extract the Service Agent Interface

The easiest way to begin updating your design to use Service Agents that fully decouple your ViewModel from any specific implementation of the service exposing the Model is to examine the interactions that will be necessary between the ViewModel and Model. These interactions can be used to determine the necessary operations that would need to exist on an interface that will be exposed by a Service Agent. This interface should include only the operations needed by the ViewModel or potentially by multiple ViewModels if the same Model is servicing multiple ViewModels within the application. In the case of the previous code sample, if this was the only interaction between the ViewModel and Service Agent, the Service Agent's interface would be defined as follows:

```
public interface IModelServiceAgent
{
    List<SomeDataType> GetData();
}
```

Refactor the ViewModel to Use the Extracted Interface

Once the Service Agent's interface has been defined, references to a specific implementation of the interface should be removed from the ViewModel and replaced with references to the interface. This can be accomplished a couple of different ways depending upon whether you have selected Dependency Injection or Service Locator as the method through which you are going to achieve Inversion of Control in your application. If using Dependency Injection, the typical approach is to maintain a class-level reference to an instance of an object exposing the Service Agent interface, which is passed to the constructor of the ViewModel. The relevant pieces of code from the ViewModel would read as follows:

```
public class MyViewModel
{
    private IModelServiceAgent _modelAgent;

    public MyViewModel(IModelServiceAgent modelAgent)
    {
        _modelAgent = modelAgent;
    }

    public void Execute(object arg)
    {
        this.Data = _modelAgent.GetData();
    }
}
```

If Service Locator has been selected instead of Dependency Injection, there is no need to maintain a reference to the class-level variable or to provide that instance to the constructor. Instead, whatever method is exposed by the Service Locator implementation that you are using to retrieve a reference to an object exposing a specific interface will be called in place of the line of code previously using the new operator. Assuming a Service Locator that is implemented as a static class with a generic GetService method, the original code modified to use a Service Agent and Service Locator might look like this:

```
public void Execute(object arg)
{
    var agent = ServiceLocator.GetService<IModelServiceAgent>();
    this.Data = agent.GetData();
}
```

As I mentioned in the previous chapter, the specific method chosen for Inversion of Control is largely left to personal preference. This bears mentioning again here because at first glance many developers who are not very familiar with exercises in removing or reducing external dependencies may see the two very simple code samples presented in this section and be struck by the additional setup required for the Dependency Injection route as opposed to the single line of code required to change the ViewModel to use a dynamic lookup provided by the Service Locator. The important thing not clearly spelled out in the code samples is that in the case of Dependency Injection, I have completely removed one source of external dependency by exchanging the use of a concrete class for an interface, while in the case of the code using the Service Locator, I have exchanged the use of a concrete Service Agent class for a lookup performed by a concrete `ServiceLocator` class. In both cases, I am left in a better position than had I not factored out the dependency on the specific service exposing the Model because it will be much easier to test; however, before using Service Locator, you should be careful to ensure that accepting a dependency upon whatever library is providing your Service Locator functionality will not overly limit future design decisions in your application.

Conclusion

This short chapter introduced a concept whose importance is easily belied by its simplicity. This pattern allows you to develop the View and ViewModel objects to run on the client device completely independent of any specific implementation of the Model and indeed with no Model whatsoever having been developed. This creates a very resilient environment in which it is very easy to create your own "fake" implementations of the Service Agent interface or to use a mocking framework to cut down on the number of Service Agent interface implementations that you have to create and maintain for the various testing scenarios necessary for your application. After all of the refactoring and removal of dependencies, you have a "secret agent" of your own that can keep you from knowing how to talk to the Model and are left with the only view of the pattern that really matters for this application (see Figure 12-4).

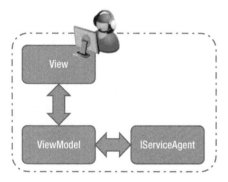

Figure 12-4. *MVVM with Service Agent interface*

CHAPTER 13

■ ■ ■

Asynchronous Programming Model

The only reason for time is so that everything doesn't happen at once.

—Albert Einstein

Windows applications are intended to be used in a connected world where having the application request data from a server halfway around the world is a common occurrence. To keep applications responsive, whether waiting for data from a remote server or from a file on the local hard drive, many of the WinRT libraries have been built around an asynchronous model. This chapter discusses that model and considerations that you must make as a developer to successfully program against it.

Laying Some Foundation

This chapter will rely heavily on some features of C# and the .NET Framework that center on using methods as a variable or passing a method as a parameter to another method. This is at the core of being able to specify code that runs asynchronously. If you're already comfortable with delegates, anonymous methods, and the Action<T> and Function<T> objects, feel free to skip ahead to the case study. Many of the code samples in this section will focus on standard console applications instead of graphical applications in order to allow you to focus on the coding concepts with minimal distraction. As you integrate data retrieved from web services into your service agents in Chapter 16, you will see asynchronous functionality in a graphical Windows application.

Delegates

Delegates are a language feature that has been in the .NET Framework since the initial release. They act like function pointers in other languages. Simply put, they allow you to have a variable that itself is a function. This allows scenarios where you can have code that knows only the "shape" of the method it's calling (the inputs and outputs) and is somewhat shielded from implementation details. The most recognizable example of delegates in the .NET world has to be events. When you write the Click handler for a button in a C# WinForms application, you are actually writing a delegate. At runtime, the code in Button checks to see whether its delegate has been set and then calls your code having no idea what your code will do—only that it is the required shape.

To use delegates, the first thing you need to do is to declare the delegate. The declaration specifies a name for the delegate, the return value, and any parameters and reads as follows:

```
private delegate void PrintSomething(string message);
```

After declaring the delegate, you're able to use it in your code, as demonstrated in this small console application:

```
class Program
{
    private delegate void PrintSomething(string message);
    static void Main(string[] args)
    {
        PrintSomething func;
        func = PrintSomethingToConsole;
        func("My Message");

        Console.ReadKey();
    }

    static void PrintSomethingToConsole(string message)
    {
        Console.WriteLine(message);
    }
}
```

You can really start to see possibilities when you think about using delegates as arguments to methods to make the method more dynamic, but there's one more really important characteristic about delegates that makes them useful even when other language constructs now do a similar job—they can be combined. What this means is that you can use C# + and += operators to assign multiple methods (all having a matching shape) to the delegate variable, and it will invoke each of the methods whenever it is called. Here's an example of using a single delegate variable to invoke multiple methods, sending its output to both the console and debug output windows:

```
class Program
{
    private delegate void PrintSomething(string message);
    static void Main(string[] args)
    {
        PrintSomething func;
        func = PrintSomethingToConsole;
        func += PrintSomethingToDebug;
        func("My Message");

        Console.ReadKey();
    }

    static void PrintSomethingToConsole(string message)
    {
        Console.WriteLine(message);
    }

    static void PrintSomethingToDebug(string message)
    {
        Debug.WriteLine(message);
    }
}
```

The C# delegate is a powerful construct, and as you move on to the next couple of sections, you should start to see a common theme in that the delegate really forms the base concept for a type-safe equivalent to function pointers.

Anonymous Methods

The problem with delegates in some cases is that having to create separate, named methods to describe the function to be performed can be a bit unwieldy in cases where the method being called is simple and will not be used other than by the delegate invocation. This brings me to a feature added in C# 2.0—anonymous methods. Anonymous methods distilled down to their simplest explanation are methods that are defined inline in code and are not given a name (at least not by the developer). An anonymous method is defined by using the delegate keyword and method parameters followed by the code block containing the method body. If you go back to the first delegate example and use an anonymous method, it could be written as follows:

```
class Program
{
    private delegate void PrintSomething(string message);
    static void Main(string[] args)
    {
        PrintSomething func;
        func = delegate(string message)
            {
                Console.WriteLine(message);
            };
        func("My Message");
        Console.ReadKey();
    }
}
```

The fact that you get the convenience of not being required to define a separate method is nice, but there's more than that to anonymous methods. Anonymous methods also provide language support for closures in C#. A closure is a programming construct that allows for a function to access variables that are outside of its typical scope. Basically, the local variables of the method containing the closure remain in scope for the executing delegate. This allows for anonymous methods to hit what I consider to be one of the real sweet spots for them in C# 2.0—filtering and sorting generic lists.

The List <T> class contains several methods that have names starting with *Find* and include on their argument list an argument of type Predicate <T>, which is a delegate type defined in the Framework libraries. Predicate <T> accepts a single argument of type T and returns a boolean. When the Find method of a List <T> object is called, the predicate is called for each element in the list until one returns true. If none of the predicate invocations returns true, the Find method returns null. Here's an example of how Find and the closure functionality can be used together to search a list of strings:

```
List<string> names = new List<string>(new[]{ "Sam", "Fred", "Bill" });
string searchTerm = "Fred";
string result = names.Find(
                delegate(string expression)
                {
                    return expression.Equals(searchTerm,
                    StringComparison.InvariantCultureIgnoreCase);
                });
```

■ **Caution**   The anonymous method can be a powerful tool in your tool belt to help make your applications easier to read, understand, and maintain. It can also do just the opposite. Be careful when using anonymous methods to ask yourself whether it adds or detracts from clarity. This is especially true when the anonymous method spans multiple lines of code.

Action and Func <TResult> Objects

As you've examined delegates and anonymous methods, you have for the most part been looking at some very simple code that involves a single class communicating with itself using a delegate. Each of these examples required the declaration of a delegate object to describe the shape of the method before a variable could be declared using that shape. This can become inconvenient and make you spend more time than necessary writing delegate declarations. To help remove the need for this repetitive work and allow you to focus on writing code that does something unique and interesting, the .NET Framework includes two related sets of objects that together cover most of the declaration needs for anything that acts like a function pointer.

The Action object is used to define a delegate that receives no arguments and has a void return type. Generic variants of Action keep the void return type portion of the signature but add method arguments, so the PrintSomething delegate that you've been using in the examples could be defined as Action <string> PrintSomething and not require its own type definition. Action variants can be used to describe void methods with many parameters. Looking at the previous anonymous method example, you can use Action <T> to remove the delegate declaration as follows:

```
class Program
{
    static void Main(string[] args)
    {
        Action<string> func;
        func = delegate(string message)
            {
                Console.WriteLine(message);
            };
        func("My Message");
        Console.ReadKey();
    }
}
```

The Func <TResult> object is used to represent a delegate that accepts no arguments and has a return type defined by TResult. As with Action, the Func <TResult> object has generic variants that allow specification of parameters. To determine the shape of the method signature, the last (or only) type in the type arguments list becomes the return type, and any preceding type arguments are used in the order they appear as arguments to the function. For example, the Round method of the Math class has the signature decimal Round(decimal d, int decimals), and an equivalent signature described with a Func object would be Func <decimal, int, decimal> Round.

You may or may not have noticed, but you have already seen Func <T, TResult> in use when you looked at anonymous methods. The LINQ extension methods defined for collection types very heavily make use of Action and Func variants, and you saw an example of that when you used the Find method to search the list of strings. The Find method accepts an argument that is a function that takes a single instance of whatever type is contained by the collection and returns a bool to indicate whether the object instance meets your criteria.

When Find is called on the collection, the code loops through each contained item, passing it to the method passed in by the caller. If that method call returns true, the instance is made the return value and processing stops. If all the items in the collection evaluate to false, the method returns null. If you were to use Func <T, TResult> to create your own implementation of the Find method, it would look something like this:

```
// assume we're in a class that holds a collection of strings
public string Find(Func<string, bool> predicate)
{
    foreach(string current in _myContainedStrings)
    {
        if(predicate(current) == true) return current;
    }
    return null;
}
```

Action and Func are used very heavily in the .NET Framework, and the way they are used can provide some excellent guidance for patterns you may want to follow in your own applications. If you want some more examples of this brought together in one place, take a look at the methods of the List<T> object in the Systems.Collections.Generic namespace in the .NET Framework Library Class Library Reference.

The Case Study

To frame up the discussion in this chapter, let's pretend you have been given the task of displaying books from an online catalog in a Windows application. In your application, you need to start by displaying a list of categories. When the user selects a category from the list, the user should be presented with a list of books within the selected category.

The catalog data is stored on a server that allows access to its data via a public web service. The web service has three methods that are pertinent to your requirements.

- The first method receives no input parameters and simply retrieves a listing of categories present in the catalog.

- The second method receives a category name as its only parameter and returns a list of ISBNs that identify books found within the specified category.

- The third method receives an ISBN as its only parameter and returns a data structure containing attributes of the requested book.

Breaking Out of Sequence

In this section, you will examine a number of solutions to solving the problem presented in the case study. You will begin be looking at the simplest solution, which is a single-threaded approach, and from there move through a series of multithreaded approaches that build upon each other to finally reach what is typically the ideal solution for a modern .NET application. Code samples presented in this section typically focus on narrow pieces of the solution to illustrate points, but you can download and run the complete solutions, which are available in the downloadable content for this chapter.

The Single-Threaded Solution

Developers and people in general think of algorithms in terms of a linear sequence of steps executed one at a time until the job is done. Approaching work with this mind-set makes for a solution that is easy to understand and is maintainable, if the need for a change to the algorithm is discovered in the future. Figures 13-1 and 13-2 illustrate the synchronous processing approach.

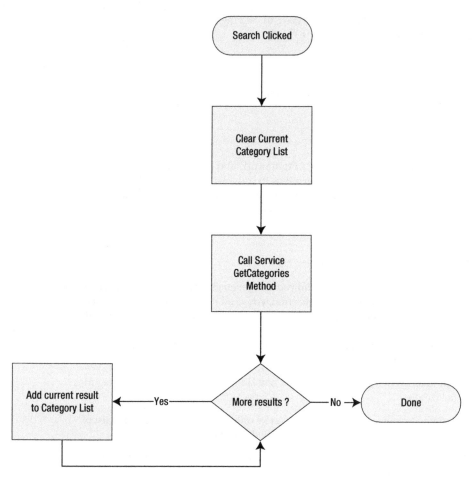

Figure 13-1. *Synchronous get categories*

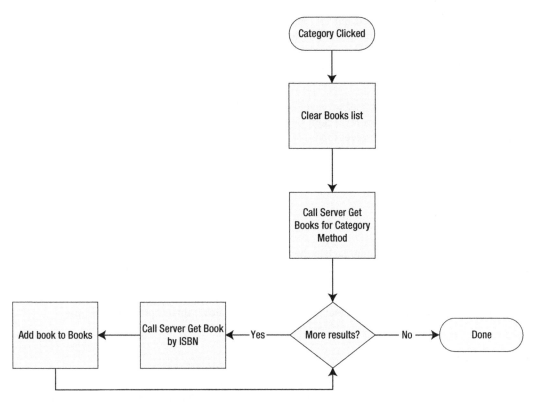

Figure 13-2. *Synchronous get books for category*

Using Observable collections that are bound to UI elements, the C# code would look something like the following (for the sake of illustration, I am assuming that a service proxy and relevant data objects have been defined, but you can browse and run the complete solution in the downloadable code for this chapter):

```csharp
public class BookSearchPage
{
    ObservableCollection<Category> _categories = new ObservableCollection<Category>();
    ObservableCollection<Book> _books = new ObservableCollection<Book>();
    private void getCategoriesButton_Click(object sender, RoutedEventArgs e)
    {
        // remove any existing entries
        _categories.Clear();

        var bookServerClient = new BookServerClient();
        var retrievedCategories = bookServerClient.GetCategories();
        foreach(var category in retrievedCategories)
        {
            _categories.Add(category);
        }
    }
}
```

```
// called from SelectionChanged event of whatever list is displaying categories
private void SelectCategory(string categoryName)
{
    // remove any existing entries
    _books.Clear();

    var bookServerClient = new BookServerClient();
    var retrievedIsbns = bookServerClient.GetBooksForCategory(categoryName);
    foreach(string isbn in retrievedIsbns)
    {
        Book book = bookServerClient.GetBook(isbn);
        _books.Add(book);
    }
}
}
```

The problem with the synchronous approach in this scenario is that when you execute all of the steps in sequence, you guarantee that the process will take as long to execute as the sum of the time to execute each step. In the worst case, this leaves the user staring at what appears to be a locked-up screen for a long time. At best, it leaves them watching some sort of animation designed to convince them that the application is not locked up. In either case, the user is left with an application that is not responsive, which is unacceptable to most users.

Multithreading

So, how do you keep your user from waiting? The answer is multithreading. When you get into the application flow in which a list of books within the category is to be displayed, instead of looping through the list, retrieving each book, and displaying the result, you will loop through the list and initiate the retrieval of each book asynchronously. When each asynchronous retrieval result is received, you will display the book that was retrieved. This breaks the Display Category flow into two separate flows, an Initiate Category flow and a Book Details Received Flow, which are shown in the now separate flows of Figures 13-3 and 13-4.

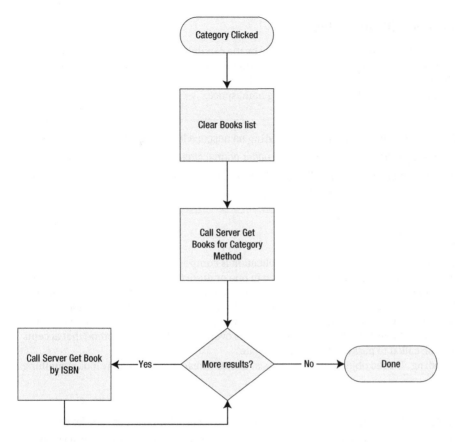

Figure 13-3. *Initiate category retrieval*

Figure 13-4. *Book received*

Using System.Threading.Thread Objects

Implementation of this asynchronous approach can vary greatly by the capabilities of the API, so let's start by assuming that the service API does not provide any of its own support for being used in an asynchronous manner. In this case, you have to take control of threading yourself and will use the basic threading functionality offered through the .NET Framework in the System.Threading namespace.

■ **Note** There is a great deal more to the objects in the Threading namespace than what I will cover in this book. Use of the threading objects directly is no longer recommended under normal circumstances because of the other alternatives that exist, so I'll give enough grounding so that you'll know where to look if you need more control over threading and appreciate that you normally won't have to go there.

System.Threading.Thread

The runtime execution environment for most any modern application is composed of a process in which memory resources are established and the program is managed in one or more threads of execution that perform the processing work for the application. In a .NET application, you can interact with these threads of execution using the Thread object. In its simplest usage, you instantiate a new Thread, using the constructor to pass a delegate that will be executed in its own thread, and call its Start method. The delegate can have the shape of either Action or Action <object>. When Action <object> is used, the overload of the Start method that accepts an object parameter should be called to pass a value to the delegate.

Using the System.Threading.Thread object, your first pass at a multithreaded solution may look something like this:

■ **Note** For reasons I'll discuss following the code sample, the Thread object is not exposed directly for Windows applications built on WinRT, and this example could not be used for building such an application, but it is good to gain a general understanding of the concept before moving on. The downloadable sample code for this chapter includes this example implemented as a WPF application, which will also provide an opportunity for you to see how similar Windows XAML applications are to their WPF ancestor.

```
public class BookSearchPage
{
    // Moved BookServerClient up here because we need to access it from several places now
    BookServerClient _bookServerClient = new BookServerClient();
    ObservableCollection<Category> _categories = new ObservableCollection<Category>();
    ObservableCollection<Book> _books = new ObservableCollection<Book>();
    private void getCategoriesButton_Click(object sender, RoutedEventArgs e)
    {
        // remove any existing entries
        _categories.Clear();

        var retrievedCategories = _bookServerClient.GetCategories();
        foreach(var category in retrievedCategories)
        {
            _categories.Add(category);
        }
    }
}
```

```
    // called from SelectionChanged event of whatever list is displaying categories
    private void SelectCategory(string categoryName)
    {
        // remove any existing entries
        _books.Clear();

        Thread worker = new Thread(SelectCategoryAsync);
        worker.Start(categoryName);
    }

    private void SelectCategoryAsync(object categoryName)
    {        var retrievedIsbns =
_bookServerClient.GetBooksForCategory(categoryName.ToString());
        foreach(string isbn in retrievedIsbns)
        {
            Thread worker = new Thread(GetBookAsync);
            worker.Start(isbn);
        }
    }

    private void GetBookAsync(object isbn)
    {
        Book book = _bookServerClient.GetBook(isbn.ToString());
        _books.Add(book);
    }
}
```

The illustrative code only begins to scratch the surface of the complexities involved with working with threads by showing the disconnected manner in which you have to work with different pieces of your algorithm. Rather than reading the code from top to bottom, you have to jump through multiple methods, keeping in mind what triggered the method call and the state of all your variables at the time. This code, which used to retrieve the list and then each book in the list, now becomes more of a supervisor that tells one thread to go get the list and then in turn for each book in the list tells another thread to go get it. It is much easier to comprehend the flow in Figure 13-2 than to jump back and forth between Figure 13-3 and Figure 13-4.

You should see now that your life starts to become much more complicated when you manually take control of threading within your application. You didn't even begin to deal with issues such as making sure you process the result back on the correct thread (with your collections bound to UI elements, you cannot modify them from background threads) or ensure that you don't overstep the processing capability of your machine by creating too many threads. These are more advanced topics that you can often shield yourself from needing to understand by taking advantage of higher-level objects that the .NET Framework provides for you.

Introducing Tasks

Multicore computers are becoming increasingly more common every day. Today's low-end consumer desktop computers typically have two cores as compared to higher-end consumer machines, with eight or more cores. Even many devices such as smartphones and tablets have multiple cores. This proliferation of multicore machines has driven developers to increasingly use threading in their applications and unfortunately has, in many cases, exposed end users to the result of a developer not dealing well with the complexities of managing an application across multiple threads. To help manage this complexity, the Task Parallel Library was introduced with the 4.0 .NET Framework as a layer above the low-level management of threads and state.

Task and Task <TResult> Objects

The Task and Task <TResult> objects can be thought of as multithreaded objects that serve a similar function to Action and Func in the single-threaded world. They allow you to specify code that is to be executed on another thread of execution and provide a mechanism for the result of the execution to be supplied back to the calling thread. As the developer, you specify what needs done asynchronously and the code that handles the result (if any), but you are not required to deal with any low-level scheduling or throttling requirements because that is handled for you.

Much like the Thread object, in the Task object's simplest usage pattern, you can create a Task object passing an Action to its constructor and then call its Start method to initiate it running on a separate thread. A simple console application using Task is shown here:

```
class Program
{
    static void Main(string[] args)
    {
        Action action;
        action = () =>
            {
                Console.WriteLine("In async method...");
                Thread.Sleep(500);
                Console.WriteLine("Leaving async method...");
            };
        Task task = new Task(action);
        Console.WriteLine("Initiating task");
        task.Start();
        Console.WriteLine("Task initiated and control returned to main thread");
        Console.ReadKey();
    }
}
```

The advantage in using Task over Thread in this case is that you don't have to worry about too many details of "how" the multithreading should be accomplished, only "what" is to be done off the main thread. In some cases—especially with long-running tasks—you will care to have a greater degree of control over the creation or behavior of the threads on which the Task will run. In these cases, the Task object also has constructors that support providing hints to the task scheduler and providing a token that can be used from your application code running on the main thread to send a signal to the running task that it should be canceled. This provides the opportunity to be shielded from these details by default but still have the functionality available when needed.

Task <TResult> is used when the code that will be running on another thread produces a result that needs to be communicated back to the thread that initiated the Task object. Because the calling code cares about the result of executing the task, it cannot have the "fire-and-forget" simplicity that comes with using the version of Task without a result. The calling code will typically perform its other processing and then wait for the IsCompleted property of the task to return true or call the Wait or Join method to enter a state where it's waiting for the task to complete. Here is one example of waiting for the task to complete before moving on:

```
class Program
{
    static void Main(string[] args)
    {
        Func <int> getRandomNumberAsync = () =>
            {
                Console.WriteLine("In async method...");
```

```
            Thread.Sleep(500);
            return new Random().Next();
        };

    Task<int> randomNumberTask = new Task<int>(getRandomNumberAsync);
    randomNumberTask.Start();
    while (! randomNumberTask.IsCompleted)
    {
        Console.WriteLine("waiting for result....");
        Thread.Sleep(50);
    }

    Console.WriteLine("Received result of {0}", randomNumberTask.Result);
    Console.ReadKey();
    }
}
```

When working with multiple tasks, it sometimes makes more sense to have a way to provide some orchestration to say "Go do this, and when you're done, take the result and do something else" rather than to have code that explicitly waits for the completion and then starts another task. The ContinueWith method is used to accomplish this and can make your asynchronous code easier to follow because it provides some of the readability you get when simply listing steps in a serial manner. Here's an example of how to change the previous sample to use ContinueWith instead of waiting in a loop:

```
class Program
{
    static void Main(string[] args)
    {
        Func<int> getRandomNumberAsync = () =>
            {
                Console.WriteLine("In async method...");
                Thread.Sleep(500);
                return new Random().Next();
            };

        Task<int> randomNumberTask = new Task<int>(getRandomNumberAsync);
        randomNumberTask.ContinueWith(completedTask =>
            {
                Console.WriteLine("Received result of {0}", completedTask.Result);
            });
        randomNumberTask.Start();
        Console.WriteLine("Task initiated.  Waiting for result...");
        Console.ReadKey();
    }
}
```

When you use this code, the task scheduler executes randomNumberTask and then passes it to another task that you did not name once it is complete. This second task can examine the Result property of the initial task, using it to perform further processing. If necessary, you can exercise the same level of control over the continuation task that is available to you in the initial task through the use of the ContinueWith overloads that accepts TaskContinuationOptions and/or CancellationToken.

Using the Task Parallel Library, the multithreaded solution starts to look a little bit more like the original single-threaded approach:

```
public class BookSearchPage
{
    BookServerClient _bookServerClient = new BookServerClient();
    ObservableCollection<Category>_categories = new ObservableCollection<Category>();
    ObservableCollection<Book>_books = new ObservableCollection<Book>();
    private void getCategoriesButton_Clicked(object sender, RoutedEventArgs e)
    {
        _categories.Clear();
        var retrievedCategories = _bookServerClient.GetCategories();
        foreach (var category in retrievedCategories)
        {
            _categories.Add(category);
        }
    }

    public void SelectCategory(string categoryName)
    {
        _books.Clear();
        var categoryRetrievalTask = new Task<IEnumerable<string>>((cat) =>
            {
                return _bookServerClient.GetBooksForCategory(cat.ToString());
            }, categoryName);
        categoryRetrievalTask.ContinueWith(result =>
            {
                foreach (string isbn in result.Result)
                {
                    var bookRetrievalTask = new Task<Book>( i =>
                    {
                        return _bookServerClient.GetBook(i.ToString());
                    }, isbn);
                    bookRetrievalTask.ContinueWith(b => _books.Add(b.Result));
                    bookRetrievalTask.Start();
                }
            });
        categoryRetrievalTask.Start();
    }
}
```

Async and Await

As you've just seen, the Task Parallel Library can be used to abstract away a good deal of the complexity involved with managing threads and can allow you to write code in a way that allows the developer of the code and anyone who reads it later to see the code as describing the linear algorithm used to solve the problem but at runtime allows the application to benefit from the multiple processor cores that are available. While the Task Parallel Library gets you a good deal of the way to just laying out the steps to solve the problem, you still see a fair amount of code relating to use of the Task Parallel Library in the solution. In C# 5, Microsoft addressed this by adding language support for tasks using the new async and await keywords, which further abstract asynchronous programming.

The async keyword is a language feature that essentially marks a method as behaving in an asynchronous manner. This allows the compiler to do the work of wrapping the method in a Task using the Task Parallel Library that you saw in the previous section. The async keyword does not by itself make the method asynchronous, so you will still find yourself writing asynchronous code or making use of method calls exposed by other classes that are in turn marked asynchronous (such as using the GetAsync method of the HttpClient object). The real power in the async keyword is that it serves as a marker for you to use the await keyword for code that calls the method marked as async. When calling code is marked using await, the method call is executed in the context of a task. This gets even better when the async method returns a value used by the calling code because the compiler will also take care of ensuring that the code following the method call is placed into its own continuation task, much like when you manually coded the continuation in the previous section's example. This means that most methods making use of the asynchronous keywords will participate in a chain of methods where each method in the chain is both marked async in the method signature and makes use of await somewhere in the body of the method.

By using async and await, you get even closer to having code that is expressed as a very simple sequence of steps where it is easy for the developer to express and where others can read the logical flow of the steps required to solve a problem, while the runtime execution of the program can happen with the full benefits of today's multicore and multiprocessor systems' ability to execute code in parallel. Here you see the example that you've been working on through this chapter nearly returned to the syntax of the original synchronous implementation:

```
public class BookSearchPage
{
    BookServerClient _bookServerClient = new BookServerClient();
    ObservableCollection<Category> _categories = new ObservableCollection<Category>();
    ObservableCollection<Book> _books = new ObservableCollection<Book>();
    private void getCategoriesButton_Clicked(object sender, RoutedEventArgs e)
    {
        _categories.Clear();
        var retrievedCategories = _bookServerClient.GetCategories();
        foreach (var category in retrievedCategories)
        {
            _categories.Add(category);
        }
    }

    public async void SelectCategory(string categoryName)
    {
        _books.Clear();
        var retrievedIsbns = await _bookServerClient.GetBooksForCategory(categoryName);
        foreach (string isbn in retrievedIsbns)
        {
            var book = await _bookServerClient.GetBook(isbn);
            _books.Add(book);
        }
    }
}
```

PUTTING IT TOGETHER

In this exercise, you'll use what you've learned in this chapter about asynchronous programming in the .NET Framework to build a working application that retrieves data asynchronously. The application will be focused on using the asynchronous patterns, and to keep as much focus as possible on the asynchronous nature of the call, the application will not use the MVVM pattern that you've been learning in other chapters or many other best practices that would be necessary in a real-world application. To work through the example, you will need Windows 8, any edition of Visual Studio 2012, and an active Internet connection.

1. To get started, open Visual Studio, and create a new project. The project type should be Blank App (XAML), which can be found in the Windows Store category under Visual C#. Name the project RssReaderCs.

2. Right-click the project in the Solution Explorer window, and select Add ➤ New Folder. Use Entities for the folder name.

3. Right-click the Entities folder you created in the previous step, and select Add ➤ Class. Name the new class FeedItem.cs.

4. Add the properties that you'll be using to the FeedItem class. You'll need Title, Link, PublicationDate, and Description properties. When you've added the properties, the class should look like this:

```
public class FeedItem
{
 public string Title { get; set; }
 public Uri Link { get; set; }
 public DateTime PublicationDate { get; set; }
 public string Description { get; set; }
}
```

5. Open MainPage.xaml.cs, and ensure that the following using statements appear in the using statement section at the top of the source file:

```
using System.Collections.Generic;
using System.Collections.ObjectModel;
using System.Xml;
using System.Xml.Linq;
using RssReaderCs.Entities;
using System.Threading.Tasks;
using System.Net.Http;
```

6. Now let's add the method that's going to do all the real work. This method will make use of the built-in HttpClient to retrieve a string from the RSS source. Once that asynchronous method completes, the results will be parsed to produce a list of the FeedItem class created in step 4, and that list will be returned to the calling code. In keeping with the recommended naming standard for asynchronous methods, you'll add the word Async to the end of the method name. Add the following method to MainPage.xaml.cs:

```
public async Task<List<FeedItem>> DownloadFeedAsync()
{
 const string feedUrl = "http://meta.stackoverflow.com/feeds";
HttpClient client = new HttpClient();
 client.MaxResponseContentBufferSize = int.MaxValue;
 // now asynchronously retrieve the feed from server
```

```
var response = await client.GetStringAsync(feedUrl);
// load the result into an XML document we can process
var doc = XDocument.Parse(response);
var atomNamespace = XNamespace.Get("http://www.w3.org/2005/Atom");
var entryNodeName = atomNamespace.GetName("entry");
var entryNodeName = atomNamespace.GetName("title");

return doc.Descendants(entryNodeName).Select(item =>
new FeedItem
{
Title = item.Element(titleNodeName).Value
}).ToList();
}
```

7. Now that you can retrieve data, let's create a bindable container to hold that data. Before the constructor in `MainPage.Xaml.cs`, add the following lines to set up the container:

```
private ObservableCollection<FeedItem> _feedItems =
 new ObservableCollection<FeedItem>();
public ObservableCollection<FeedItem> FeedItems
{
 get { return _feedItems; }
}
```

8. Now let's create the event handler for the button that will be created in the next step. Add the following method to `MainPage.Xaml.cs`:

```
private async void OnRetrieveButtonClicked(object sender, RoutedEventArgs e)
{
 _feedItems.Clear();
 var feedResults = await DownloadFeedAsync();
 foreach(var item in feedResults)
 {
 _feedItems.Add(item);
 }
}
```

9. Now let's create the user interface. In the markup of `MainPage.xaml`, replace the grid and contents with the following markup, creating a title block, a button, and the list that you'll bind results to:

```
<StackPanel Background = "{StaticResource
ApplicationPageBackgroundThemeBrush}">
 <TextBlock HorizontalAlignment = "Left" TextWrapping = "Wrap"
 Text = "Async Rss Reader" Style = "{StaticResource PageHeaderTextStyle}"/>
 <Button Content = "Retrieve Feed" HorizontalAlignment = "Left"
 Click = "OnRetrieveButtonClicked" />
 <ListView x:Name = "FeedList">
 <ListView.ItemTemplate>
 <DataTemplate>
 <TextBlock Style = "{StaticResource HeaderTextStyle}"
 Text = "{Binding Title}" />
```

```
    </DataTemplate>
  </ListView.ItemTemplate>
  </ListView>
</StackPanel>
```

10. Build the project, and then you have one more step. You need to bind the `ListView` to the `FeedItems` collection. For this example, you'll handle the task in the page's code-behind. Update the constructor in `MainPage.xaml.cs` to add this binding as follows:

```
public BlankPage()
{
 this.InitializeComponent();
 FeedList.ItemsSource = FeedItems;
}
```

11. That's it! Run the sample, and watch the list populate after you click the button.

In this exercise, you built a working application that retrieves an RSS feed from the Internet and displays the title for results in a list. You left a few fields in the `FeedItem` class that you did not display or populate. For extra reinforcement, use the `link`, `published`, and `summary` elements in the XML to fill the remaining fields and add controls to the `ListView`'s `DataTemplate` to display these values.

Conclusion

In this chapter, you learned about the necessity of keeping your application responsive to the user and to use threading when applicable to benefit from the multicore processing available on modern CPUs. You also got a brief glimpse into the complexities of thread management before learning about how the Task Parallel Library along with the async and await keywords can make many multithreaded scenarios as simple to code and read as a single-threaded approach. The skills gained in this chapter will help you deal with most common threading scenarios that you will encounter when developing Windows applications.

While you should now be equipped to handle common threading scenarios, it is important to realize that you will most likely encounter situations where async and await or even the Task Parallel Library are not sufficient to meet your needs. In these situations, I encourage you to first look to the Task Parallel Library to see whether there is a way it can be leveraged. If no solution is available in the Task Parallel Library, then tread carefully into the world of threading.

CHAPTER 14

■ ■ ■

Mocking the Service Agent

Reading furnishes the mind only with materials of knowledge; it is thinking that makes what we read ours.

—John Locke

When you last worked on the MovieBrowser sample application in Chapter 10, you completed an application that displayed data bound to a ViewModel and used events of that ViewModel to trigger navigation, giving the appearance of an application that is complete but with sample data. Since completing that work, you have learned about Inversion of Control, the asynchronous programming model, and service agents. In this chapter, I will discuss the design of the interface for your service agent, you will choose an approach for how the MovieBrowser service agent will do its job, and finally you will create a service agent and modify the ViewModel for the MovieBrowser application to use this service agent. The service agent that you create in this chapter still will not interact with real data, but the application will complete with the exception of creating the "live" service agent that you will implement in Chapter 16.

Craftsmanship and API Design

Throughout my career I have witnessed continuous tension between those who insist that developing software is an art and those who hold just as insistently that it is a science. I tend to think of it as a combination of both. A growing cultural trend in the software development community has been to view the work of those of us who build software as that of a craftsman. The trend has picked up steam, and many developers have chosen to sign the Manifesto for Software Craftsmanship at http://manifesto.softwarecraftsmanship.org. The manifesto reads as follows:

> *As aspiring Software Craftsmen we are raising the bar of professional software development by practicing it and helping others learn the craft. Through this work we have come to value:*
> *Not only working software, but also well-crafted software*
> *Not only responding to change, but also steadily adding value*
> *Not only individuals and interactions, but also a community of professionals*
> *Not only customer collaboration, but also productive partnerships*
> *That is, in pursuit of the items on the left we have found the items on the right to be indispensable.*
> *© 2009, the undersigned.*
> *this statement may be freely copied in any form, but only in its entirety through this notice.*

I think the "craftsman" moniker fits the developer role well because we produce a product that must often creatively solve problems but often must also fit together with other pieces of the puzzle in a harmonious manner. The craftsman in Figure 14-1 strives to make a violin that is a unique thing of beauty but must also meet exacting specifications in certain areas to ensure that the instrument can play alongside other instruments within an orchestra.

Figure 14-1. *Violin maker*

You may ask what craftsmanship has to do with service agents. This is the first time in this book that you are focusing on building an application programming interface (API) intended to be consumed by another piece of software; namely, you are creating the shape of the service that the ViewModel in the MovieBrowser application will use to communicate with the outside world. In this portion of the project, you decide what your objects should be called and how they will be organized. Those decisions will have a direct and lasting impact not only throughout the time that you spend developing the project but also throughout its usable life. It is estimated that of the costs that go into any development project, only 10 percent of the total cost is expended during the initial development and that 90 percent will be incurred after the initial completion of the project. A common analogy is that the initial development cost is only the tip of the iceberg (as shown in Figure 14-2). This means you or somebody else will spend far more time and effort trying to read, understand, and modify the code than you put into writing it in the first place.

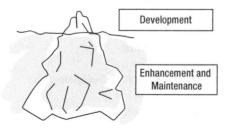

Figure 14-2. *Development vs. enhancement and maintenance*

The following are some of the more important pieces that can make or break the usability of an API design:

- *Naming*: The names of classes, methods, and parameters tell a lot about what your objects are supposed to do and what information is needed to make them successful in fulfilling their responsibility. The method signature bool a(string b, out int c) is functionally equivalent to bool TryParse(string s, out int result), but the latter is much more intuitive than the former.

- *Organization*: Namespaces are often used as a tool to help ensure that your classes do not having naming conflict with other classes, but they can also provide valuable clues as to the purpose of the classes they contain and make your API far more discoverable.

- *Avoid "setup" requirements*: When possible, operations of classes that are intended to provide an API should be self-contained rather than requiring developers who consume the API to call a sequence of operations in a predefined order to make the desired call successful. A frequently seen violation of this principle is when developers have to set certain properties of an object before calling a method. In these cases, a more usable API design would be to have additional parameters on the method receive all of the information required to successfully complete the desired operation.

Designing the MovieBrowser Catalog Service Agent

The requirements of the service agent used to help the MovieBrowser ViewModel retrieve data can largely be inferred by taking a look at the data model and how that data model is already integrated into the version of the application that was completed in Chapter 10. The ViewModel gets its data from the SampleMovieDataSource object, which is shown as a class diagram with the data that it exposes in Figure 14-3. The SampleMovieDataSource is meeting the needs of the ViewModel by exposing a single property: Genres. This property provides a gateway to the entire object graph representing the data displayed in the MovieBrowser user interface.

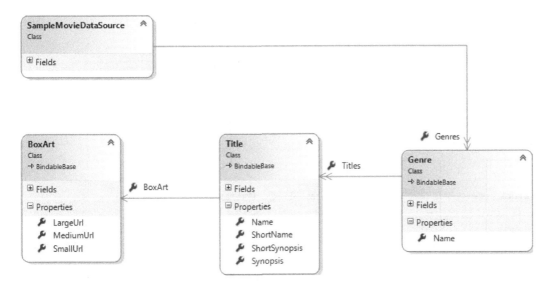

Figure 14-3. SampleMovieDataSource *class diagram*

Because you know that the SampleMovieDataSource object is meeting the needs of the ViewModel in the MovieBrowser application, you can safely assume that any service agent that provides access to a collection of Genre objects will also meet these needs. Agents are expected to interact with some external entity, so a method will be used as opposed to a property. I will call the method GetGenres, which is a method name that accurately describes exactly "what" the method does without giving any information as to "how" this is accomplished.

At this point, I believe that there will be a method named GetGenres, and the responsibility of this method will be to make a populated collection of Genre objects available to the ViewModel. A reasonable design choice might be to make the method signature read as follows:

```
public ObservableCollection<Genre> GetGenres()
```

This method signature clearly defines a method that meets the needs that have been identified and would be sufficient. However, it does introduce a characteristic that may not be immediately apparent if you are not accustomed to working in an asynchronous environment. Because the collection of Genre objects form the return value of the method, none of the Genre objects can be retrieved until all of the data has been retrieved. Figure 14-4 illustrates the flow when a fictional service requires consumers to first retrieve a list of Genre names and then each Genre one at a time by name.

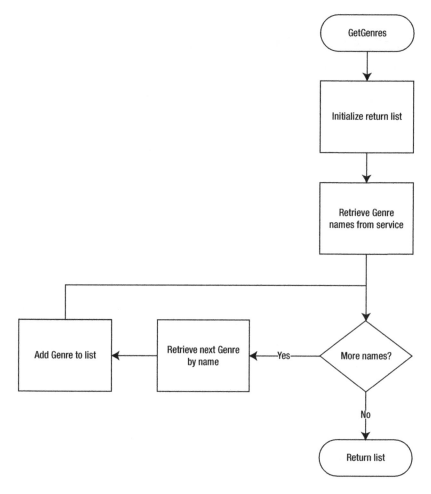

Figure 14-4. *Return all Genres at once*

As a critical thinker, you may think back to Chapter 13 and say, "Well, I would just execute it asynchronously." You could do this, but it wouldn't change the fact that no Genre objects would be available for the user to view until they all are. Running the flow in Figure 14-4 asynchronously would still potentially leave the user of your application staring at a blank screen (or a spinning ProgressRing) until suddenly all of the Genre objects appeared.

An alternative to requiring the service agent to provide all of the requested data at one time would be to make use of a construct known as a *callback method*. The callback method is used to provide code to be executed by the service agent when data is available. This is similar in concept to using events. Using the same fictional service depicted in Figure 14-4, a callback could be introduced, changing the flow to what is depicted in Figure 14-5. If you assume that the callback defined accepts a Genre object as its only argument and adds that Genre to the ViewModel's collection of Genre objects, then the data begins to be revealed to the user when the first Genre is returned.

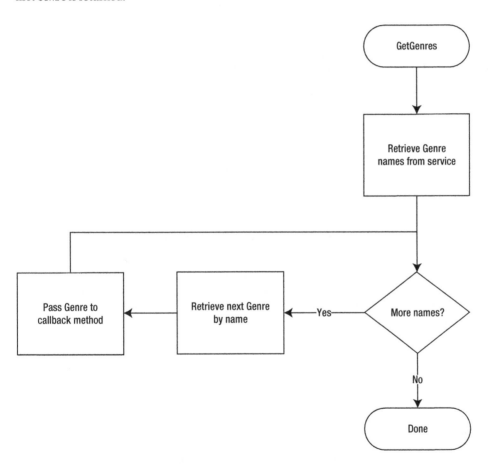

Figure 14-5. *Use a callback method to return one Genre at a time*

While the example of having to retrieve the Genre objects one at a time is not typical of a service that is designed for bulk retrieval, it is not the least bit unusual for services to implement paging mechanisms that limit the amount of data retrieved in a single call, possibly allowing the data to be retrieved only in batches of tens or hundreds. Because of the flexibility inherent in using the callback method and the potential for it to allow your application to appear more responsive and performant, the callback method will be used for the GetGenres method. The method's signature will appear as follows:

```
public void GetGenres(Action<Genre> genreAvailableCallback);
```

Going back to the concept of craftsmanship and that names matter, it is a good idea to take the opportunity to "measure twice and cut once," as experienced carpenters tell aspiring craftsmen in that trade. Upon critical review of the name GetGenres, especially because the method no longer returns a collection of Genre objects and is designed specifically to account for the possibility (but not requirement) of asynchronous execution, the name no longer seems to be the best fit for the functionality. Instead, InitiateGenreRetrieval seems more appropriate, so the updated method signature will read as follows:

```
public void InitiateGenreRetrieval(Action<Genre> genreAvailableCallback);
```

Building the Movie Catalog Service Agent

Now that the appropriate layout of the interface used by the ViewModel in the MovieBrowser application to retrieve catalog has been decided upon, it's time to implement the service agent. These are the steps to complete this implementation:

1. Create the interface.

2. Create an implementation of the interface.

3. Update the ViewModel to use the service agent.

EXERCISE: IMPLEMENT SERVICE AGENT IN MOVIEBROWSER

In this exercise, you will create the interface and an implementation of this interface for the service agent used by the MovieBrowser sample application. Additionally, you will update the ViewModel of the application to make use of the service agent. To complete this exercise, you will need the completed MovieBrowser exercise from Chapter 10 and need Windows 8 and any edition of Visual Studio 2012.

■ **Note** If you did not complete the exercise from Chapter 10 and want to complete this exercise, you can start with the MovieBrowser project available in the downloadable source code for Chapter 10.

---

1. Open the MovieBrowser solution as updated in Chapter 10.

2. Right-click the project in the Solution Explorer, and select Add ➤ New Folder. Name the folder Interfaces.

3. Right-click the Interfaces folder created in the previous step, and select Add ➤ New Item. From the Code section, select Interface, and name the interface IMovieCatalogServiceAgent.cs. Click OK when the Add New Item dialog appears, as shown in Figure 14-6.

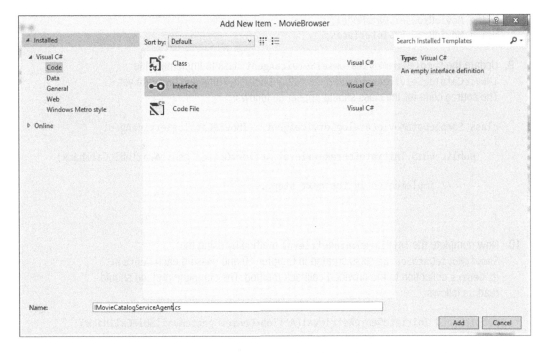

Figure 14-6. *Adding the IMovieCatalogServiceAgent interface*

4. Open IMovieCatalogServiceAgent.cs, and update the using statements at the top of the code file to include the following:

```
using System;
using MovieBrowser.DataModel;
```

5. Update the interface definition of IMovieCatalogServiceAgent to have public visibility, and include the InitiateGenreRetrieval method. The completed interface definition should read as follows:

```
public interface IMovieCatalogServiceAgent
{
    void InitiateGenreRetrieval(Action<Genre> genreAvailableCallback);
}
```

6. Right-click the project in the Solution Explorer, and select Add ➤ New Folder. Name the folder ServiceAgents.

7. Right-click the ServiceAgents folder created in the previous step, and select Add ➤ Class. Name the class SampleDataMovieCatalogServiceAgent.cs.

8. Update the using statements at the top of the SampleDataMovieCatalogServiceAgent.cs source file to include the following:

```
using System;
using MovieBrowser.Data;
```

```
using MovieBrowser.DataModel;
using MovieBrowser.Interfaces;
```

9. Update the `SampleDataMovieBrowserServiceAgent` class to implement the `IMovieCatalogServiceAgent` interface without actually retrieving any data yet. The source code for the class should appear as follows:

```
class SampleDataMovieCatalogServiceAgent : IMovieCatalogServiceAgent
{
    public void InitiateGenreRetrieval(Action<Genre> genreAvailableCallback)
    {
        // implemented in the next step...
    }
}
```

10. Now complete the `InitiateGenreRetrieval` method by using the `SampleMovieDataSource` class created in Chapter 10 and passing each `Genre` in its `Genres` collection to the provided callback method. The complete method should read as follows:

```
public void InitiateGenreRetrieval(Action<Genre> genreAvailableCallback)
{
    var catalog = new SampleMovieDataSource();
    foreach(var genre in catalog.Genres)
    {
        genreAvailableCallback(genre);
    }
}
```

At this point, you have a functioning implementation of the service agent. In the next several steps, you will modify the ViewModel to remove its dependency upon `SampleMovieDataSource` and instead make use of the service agent.

11. Open `MovieBrowserViewModel.cs`. Add the following lines to the `using` statements at the top of the source code file:

```
using MovieBrowser.Interfaces;
using MovieBrowser.ServiceAgents;
```

12. Find the property definition for `Genres` in `MovieBrowserViewModel.cs`. Modify it to read as follows:

```
public ObservableCollection<Genre> Genres
{
    get;
    private set;
}
```

13. Find and delete the following line of code from `MovieBrowserViewModel.cs`:

```
private SampleMovieDataSource _catalog = new SampleMovieDataSource();
```

14. Update the `MovieBrowserViewModel` class constructor to accept an instance of `IMovieCatalogServiceAgent`. The constructor's method signature should read as follows:

```
public MovieBrowserViewModel(IMovieCatalogServiceAgent catalogServiceAgent)
```

15. Update the `MovieBrowserViewModel` class constructor to initialize the `Genres` property and then call the `catalogServiceAgent` parameter's `InitiateGenreRetrieval` method, specifying that each `Genre` object provided through the callback method should be added to the `Genres` collection. The following code should be added to the beginning of the constructor:

```
Genres = new ObservableCollection<Genre>();
catalogServiceAgent.InitiateGenreRetrieval(Genres.Add);
```

At this point, you have updated the `MovieBrowserViewModel` class to remove its dependency on `SampleMovieDataSource` and instead depend upon any implementation of `IMovieCatalogServiceAgent`. You have also, however, removed the parameterless constructor required to be able to create an instance of the class in XAML. In a real-world application, a dependency injection framework would be used to help bridge this gap, but for the sake of simplicity, you will add a parameterless constructor that will invoke the dependency injection constructor, passing an instance of the only existing implementation of the service agent interface.

16. Create a new parameterless constructor for the `MovieBrowserViewModel` class. This method should contain no code in its body but should invoke the overload of the constructor that contains an `IMovieCatalogServiceAgent` parameter, passing a new instance of `SampleDataMovieCatalogServiceAgent`. The new constructor should read as follows:

```
public MovieBrowserViewModel() : this(new SampleDataMovieCatalogServiceAgent())
{
}
```

17. Build and run the application. You should see the same result as when you completed Chapter 10.

You have completed updating the MovieBrowser application to use a service agent.

Conclusion

In this chapter, I briefly discussed software craftsmanship and API design, and then you learned how to design and implement the service agent interface for the MovieBrowser sample application. If the idea of software craftsmanship resonates with you, I encourage you to read further online at http://manifesto. softwarecraftsmanship.org/. For further guidance in designing software that will be consumed as an API, see the "Design Guidelines for Developing Class Libraries" topic on Microsoft's MSDN Library (http://msdn.microsoft.com).

CHAPTER 15

Connecting to Data in the Cloud

We love standards—that's why we have so many of them.

—Author Unknown

Modern applications are increasingly connected, often storing little or no permanent data on the device running the application and instead relying on one or more external services to handle storage, retrieval, or manipulation of data. This implies that communication has to take place between the client and server in order for the application's job to get done. Communication of any sort requires not only the parties involved in the exchange to exchange data but for that data to be exchanged in a way that allows it to be understood by all parties and allowed to become information. In this chapter, I will cover some vocabularies and protocols that are used to exchange information between connected machines today, and I will give you an in-depth look at the Open Data Protocol (OData), which is increasingly popular because of its capability to communicate in a very simple manner.

Connecting Applications

Applications haven't always been connected across a network, and the earliest applications were not even able to communicate with other applications running on the same machine. Each application had its own set of code to handle every action that needed to be performed for the application to meet the goal of its user. A great example of this was older word processing applications that were capable of printing only to specific print devices for which they had been programmed. Each application that needed to print included its own code for how to open a communications port and send properly formatted commands to the specific printers. For example, if a program needed to print the text "Hello World!" to the printer, it would have to send the following for a Hewlett-Packard PCL printer:

```
<ESC>&l1L<ESC>&l0E
<ESC>*p100x207Y<ESC>(10U<ESC>(s1p9v0s3b16602THello World!
```

For many Zebra printer models, it would have to send the following:
```
N
A10,10,0,PL,5,5,5,N,"Hello World!"
P1,1
```

The list of printer models each with their own printing dialect goes on to become quite exhaustive, and everybody needs for programs to be able to print to the printer that they own, so you can imagine that there were a lot of printing subroutines required even for the most trivial of programs. This had developers spending a lot of time writing the same code that other developers had written many times over, instead of writing code that was unique and brought value to their application; this went on until the concept of a reusable printing system was introduced. That's when developers could use an API to specify what it was that they wanted to print rather than how to print it, leaving the specific implementation details for any given printer to the printing subsystem. Following this introduction, the developer may have had only to write code like this:

```
Printer.Print "Hello World!"
```

The underlying system would handle generating the appropriate commands to send to whatever printer the user had configured as their default printer.

Just as reusable components brought applications significant value in the area of printing and other low-level utility functions, developers started wanting to leverage code that others had written in order to perform other actions such as interacting with databases and writing spreadsheets or word processing documents. Vendors exposed APIs for interacting with their product typically by providing header files that could be linked statically with a compiler, but this solution was too brittle, and a more flexible solution was needed. Microsoft's Component Object Model (COM) and the Object Management Group's Common Object Request Broker Architecture (CORBA) emerged as competing standards to define a way for applications to communicate with each other first on the local machine and later over a network, in the case of Distributed Component Object Model (DCOM).

COM and CORBA each defined an ecosystem in which application developers could choose to have their application participate, but these binary protocols were difficult to bridge (as illustrated in Figure 15-1), and in an increasingly distributed world, people started to look toward eXtensible Markup Language (XML) as the answer to their integration needs. XML evolved in the mid-1990s as a text-based, human-readable exchange format that could easily be extended to take on vocabularies that allow it to be virtually limitless in the type of information that can be exchanged as long as both sender and receiver have agreed on the vocabulary. It was picked up as a proposed recommendation by the Worldwide Web Consortium (W3C) in 1997, and by 1999 the benefit of allowing applications to communicate using a text-based format that works well with HTTP and could easily traverse firewalls was widely recognized and XML-RPC (for Remote Procedure Call), which would later evolve into Simple Object Access Protocol (SOAP) and its related family of standards.

Figure 15-1. *COM and CORBA interoperability challenge*

Fostered by the Organization for the Advancement of Structured Information Standards (OASIS), SOAP is an XML dialect that is specifically targeted to providing a mechanism for invoking operations on and receiving results from services exposed on servers across a network. Often these services are accessed using the Internet and the HTTP protocol but may also be on the local network using other transport options such as raw TCP/IP or various queuing options available from vendors such as Microsoft, IBM, and Oracle. SOAP provides a dialect for describing the services that are exposed, the operations exposed by these services, and the format of the request and response messages used by the service.

Battling Complexity with REST

As is alluded to by Figure 15-2, SOAP does not work alone. Very sophisticated interactions with regard to messaging patterns, security, transactions, and other orthogonal concerns can be defined using the suite of standards supporting SOAP web services that are under the stewardship of OASIS. While this makes SOAP services very flexible and powerful, it also creates a situation where it is easy to become mired in complex standards when needing to meet simple data access needs for a variety of clients. This is where the REpresentational State Transfer (REST) architectural style comes into play. You should note that REST is referred to as an *architectural style* as opposed to a protocol. This is because the concept behind REST is to make use of the capabilities defined in the well-supported HTTP protocol instead of inventing another protocol. Simply put, REST is a bit of an amorphous term that is used to characterize when architects and developers choose to make use of HTTP's addressing scheme, request methods, and response codes to define interactions for their services.

Figure 15-2. *The variety of SOAP standards can create confusion*

The use of HTTP as an application protocol ensures that a wide range of clients already speak at least the vocabulary of the protocol itself if not the particular dialect of the data being transferred. I'll discuss the data in a bit, but first let's dig deeper into the capabilities and characteristics of HTTP used when using the REST style to connect applications.

Use of URI

The first capability defined by HTTP is the concept of the Uniform Resource Identifier (URI), which is a string that uniquely identifies a resource on the Internet. The URI is most commonly thought of as a web address and includes the protocol used to access the resource, the server on which the resource is located, optionally a port on the server (if none is specified, then the default for the protocol is assumed), and the path to the resource on the server. For example, look at the following URI for a resource made available on a server:

```
http://lburns.example.com:459/sites/home.html
```

The URI includes the following information to address the requested resource:

- Communication protocol: HTTP

- Server: lburns.example.com

- TCP port: 459

- Path to requested resource: /sites/home.html

You have now seen URIs used to address files on a web server for well over a decade, and this should not be a new concept to anyone who regularly uses computers on the Internet, but people often think of addressing files as the sole purpose. The name Uniform Resource Identifier was chosen very carefully instead of Uniform File Identifier because its goal was to view the World Wide Web as a connected collection of resources as opposed to a big file store. These resources might be stored in a text file on the server as is often the case with static content, but they could also be any other content and are often textual representations of data stored in a database. If I am developing an HTTP-enabled human resources management application, I may choose an addressing scheme that assigns the following URI to the employee with an employee number of 5, as illustrated in Figure 15-3.

```
http://mycompany.com/employee/5
```

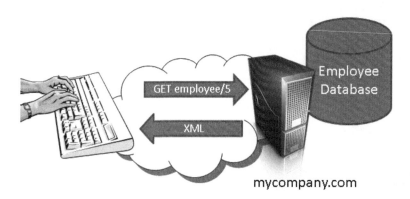

Figure 15-3. *HTTP GET*

The important considerations in the addressing scheme are that the scheme be consistent within each application to maintain predictability in the addressing of resources and that the scheme is designed in such a way as to avoid any naming collisions that would cause ambiguity about the actual resource (or entity) represented by any given address. This can be accomplished effectively by using "folders" in the path to establish unique namespaces in which to organize entities. Although URI addressing does provide for sequences that allow you to include special characters or whitespace within the address for resources (such as %20 for a space), it is important to realize that the URI will often be shared and seen by users of the application, so it is a good practice to avoid creating a naming scheme that requires these escape sequences.

One method to avoid using these escape sequences is to take a cue from the news publishing industry and their practice of "pluggifying." The term *plug* comes from a spacer that used to be placed between words in a printing press, and brought forward to Internet usage, pluggifying a term usually means converting the term to all lowercase letters, removing any special characters, and replacing spaces with a hyphen. Often in online news outlets you see this in a resource naming scheme where resources representing news articles are addressed using the date of the article as a namespace and the pluggified title of the article as the resource name. If mynewspaper.com published a story on May 5, 2012, titled "Pre-teen Boy Ties Shoes before Leaving House," the URI would likely be as follows:

```
http://mynewspaper.com/2012/05/05/pre-teen-boy-ties-shoes-before-leaving-house
```

In addition to providing a "friendly" resource name, the practice dictates that when naming a resource, nouns should be given preference over verbs. This is because the URI should reference the entity itself and not an action being performed upon the entity. You'll learn how to specify actions in the next section. If you look back to the example retrieving employee number 5, this was expressed as a noun using the URI syntax:

```
http://mycompany.com/employee/5
```

Expressed as a verb, the URI syntax would be similar to the following:

```
http://mycompany.com/getemployee?id=5
```

■ **Note** In an online world, your URIs become a very visible and important component of your "brand," so choose them wisely.

HTTP Methods

Just as a URI defines which entity the requestor has an interest in for an HTTP request, an HTTP method defines the specific action to be taken upon the entity. In many cases, you will hear the HTTP method referred to by the alternate term *HTTP verb*. Many developers who have built even simple web pages have some level of familiarity with the GET and POST methods, but there is actually a comprehensive set of verbs defined by the standard that covers most scenarios encountered in a Create Read Update Delete (CRUD) application.

GET

The GET method is the most commonly used HTTP method used when making requests to servers on the Internet. It represents a request to retrieve the indicated resource such as the request shown earlier in Figure 15-3. When specific options are present in the request header (discussed later), the GET method can become a little more dynamic, specifying conditions under which the retrieval request should be honored, most often centering upon the date and time at which the resource was most recently updated.

POST

The POST HTTP method is often used in web applications and over the years has been viewed as the only alternative to the GET method. It has been most often used when needing to submit all but the most trivial of data to the server for processing; it has been favored primarily, because when using this method, the data being submitted is hidden from the end user inside the HTTP request body instead of clearly visible in the user's browser address bar as part of the URI. While it has been used beyond the bounds of its intent, the HTTP protocol actually defines POST as indicating that the request body contains data that is to be persisted as a new child of the indicated URI. In the case of our HR system, this would mean the URI would be `http://mycompany.com/employee` (note no employee ID is specified) because the result of the request would be that a new record is saved in the employee database. Figure 15-4 illustrates this interaction.

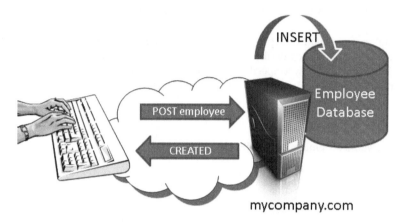

Figure 15-4. *HTTP POST*

PUT

While the POST method is intended to create a new entity, the PUT method is primarily intended to overwrite the entity at the specified URI. I say primarily because in practice the server response to a PUT request is to execute logic where an existing entity at the specified URI will be updated, and if no entity exists at the specified URI, a new one will be created. In the case where a new entity is created, the primary difference between the POST and PUT methods is that the request for the POST method will specify the parent container of the entity, and the PUT method directly specifies the intended URI for the created entity. Figure 15-5 shows a PUT request for the employee with an ID of 5.

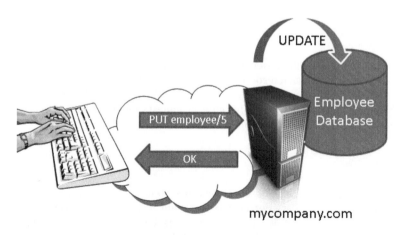

Figure 15-5. *HTTP PUT*

DELETE

The DELETE verb is used to request that the server delete the entity represented by the requested URI. The intent of this verb is that if the server responds with a successful return code, the entity specified should no longer be available. This could mean either that the entity was physically deleted or that it was moved, marked inactive, or in some other way caused to become inaccessible to future requests. The actual manner in which the server application ensures the resource is no longer accessible is up to the developer of the application. From an HTTP perspective, the only thing that is important is that once the DELETE request is successfully executed, the resource can no longer be accessed. Figure 15-6 shows a DELETE request for the employee with an ID of 5.

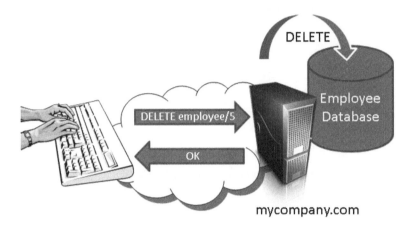

Figure 15-6. *HTTP DELETE*

PATCH and MERGE

The PATCH method is not part of the HTTP specification, but its addition is a proposed change documented in the Internet Engineering Task Force document RFC 5789. PATCH is intended to fill a gap, whereas the PUT method defines a method to overwrite an entity in its entirety, but some update scenarios involve only submitting updates capable of changing portions of the entity. For example, if I want to update the Title field of my employee entity using PUT, I need to retrieve the entire entity, update the Title field, and PUT the result back to the server. Not only does this use bandwidth that does not necessarily need to be used for the data transfer, but it also leaves the record more exposed where two individuals update different fields within a short period of time causing the first updater's changes to be lost.

Consider the following scenario where entities are updated only with PUT:

1. Users 1 and 2 simultaneously retrieve employee 5 with the following attributes:

   ```
   ID = 5
   Name = John Doe
   Title = Accountant
   Hire Date = 12/9/1999
   ```

2. User 1 updates the Name field and executes a PUT with the following data:

   ```
   ID = 5
   Name = Jim Doe
   Title = Accountant
   Hire Date = 12/9/1999
   ```

3. User 2 then updates the Title field and executes a PUT with the following data:

```
ID = 5
Name = John Doe
Title = Programmer
Hire Date = 12/9/1999
```

In this scenario, User 1's updates are overwritten and completely lost, and the data becomes corrupt. Let's take a look now at how PATCH could be used to reduce this risk.

1. Users 1 and 2 both retrieve employee 5 with the following attributes:

```
ID = 5
Name = John Doe
Title = Accountant
Hire Date = 12/9/1999
```

2. User 1 updates the Name field and executes a PATCH request with the following data:

```
Name = Jim Doe
```

3. User 2 updates that Title field and executes a PATCH request with the following data:

```
Title = Programmer
```

In this scenario, each user updated only their intended fields, and the final result combines the work of the two to look like this:

```
ID = 5
Name = Jim Doe
Title = Programmer
Hire Date = 12/9/1999
```

The MERGE method is similar in semantics and intent to PATCH but is neither part of the HTTP specification nor the subject of an RFC. It is mentioned here because it is used by some Microsoft-based services.

Others

In addition to the HTTP methods I have covered are some other methods that I will list here for the sake of being complete, but I will not discuss them in depth because they do not have any significant bearing on the coverage of REST and OData. The methods that are part of the HTTP standard but are not covered in this chapter are CONNECT, HEAD, OPTIONS, and TRACE.

HTTP Headers

HTTP defines headers in which the request from the client and the response from the server can both contain additional metadata to describe characteristics of the request. These headers can include predefined attributes with special meaning defined by the standard as well as headers that are not included within the specification but have some agreed-upon meaning to the client and server. When headers are included in an HTTP message, they take on the following form:

```
Header-Name: Value
```

The best way to convey a general understanding of HTTP headers is to look at a simple interaction between a client and server and examine the headers transferred to complete the interaction. To facilitate this inspection, I will utilize the free tool the Fiddler Web Debugger, which is written by Eric Lawrence and available at www.fiddler2.com.

■ **Note** One of the keys to being a successful developer on any platform is to have a good understanding for the tools that are available. I strongly encourage any .NET developer who has not already done so to review the list of essential tools and utilities compiled by Scott Hanselman at www.hanselman.com/tools.

EXERCISE: EXAMINE HTTP HEADERS

In this exercise, you will use the Fiddler Web Debugger to capture HTTP headers produced as the client and server interact to perform a Bing search. To complete the exercise, you will need a web browser such as Microsoft Internet Explorer and the Fiddler Web Debugger, which can be downloaded freely from www.fiddler2.com. For detailed instructions on the installation and use of Fiddler, please refer to the documentation on the Fiddler web site.

1. Make sure that Fiddler is configured and running.

2. Using your web browser, navigate to www.bing.com.

3. In the Fiddler window, examine the left pane, and find an entry with a host of www.bing.com and a URL of /. Your screen should be similar to the one shown in Figure 15-7.

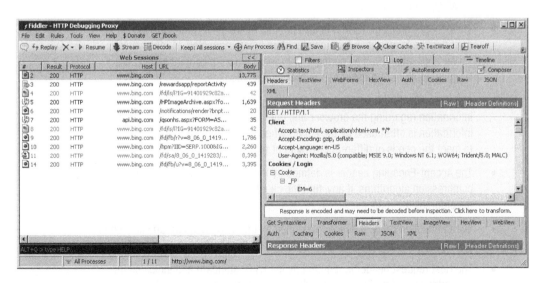

Figure 15-7. *Fiddler*

■ **Note** When looking for the main web request, you may notice that there are a lot of requests showing in the left pane. Between scripts, images, and social integration, even the simplest web interaction now often includes interaction with numerous servers.

---

4. Examine the Fiddler request window in Raw view. The result should look similar to the following:

```
GET http://www.bing.com/ HTTP/1.1
Accept: text/html, application/xhtml+xml, */*
Accept-Language: en-US
User-Agent: Mozilla/5.0 (compatible; MSIE 9.0; Windows NT 6.1; WOW64; Trident/5.0;
MALC)
Accept-Encoding: gzip, deflate
Connection: Keep-Alive
Host: www.bing.com
Cookie: <omitted>
```

The first line of the header indicates the HTTP method and URI being requested and the version of the HTTP standard for which the request is being produced. The remaining lines each represent headers that give the server additional information about the client request.

- The Accept header is defined by the HTTP standard and indicates the Multimedia Internet Mail Extension (MIME) type or types that are acceptable to the client for a response. In this case, text/html and application/xhtml+xml are explicitly spelled out as being acceptable, but the */* also indicates that any MIME type will be accepted.

- The Accept-Language header is also defined by the HTTP standard and specifies the language/culture combination being requested. In many cases, server applications will be configured to serve different content based on the language/culture requested by the client application.

- The User-Agent request header is defined by the HTTP standard and contains information regarding the browser and operating system of the client. This information is often used by the server when different content must be served to meet the needs of different browsers or platforms.

- The Accept-Encoding header is defined by the HTTP standard and defines the compression algorithms, if any, that the client can support if the server chooses to compress the response.

- The Connection request header is defined by the HTTP standard and is used to specify connection options being requested by the client.

- The Host request header is required by the HTTP standard and indicates the host address and port number to which the request should be sent.

- The Cookie request header is not defined by the HTTP standard but is commonly used and understood by most clients and servers. This field contains the cookie values stored by the client for this host.

5. Examine the Fiddler response window in Raw view. The result should begin with text that looks similar to the following:

```
HTTP/1.1 200 OK
Cache-Control: private, max-age=0
Content-Type: text/html; charset=utf-8
X-UA-Compatible: IE=9
P3P: CP="NON UNI COM NAV STA LOC CURa DEVa PSAa PSDa OUR IND"
Vary: Accept-Encoding
Content-Encoding: gzip
Date: Fri, 11 May 2012 21:29:04 GMT
Content-Length: 12628
Connection: keep-alive
Set-Cookie: _SS=SID=12345; domain=.bing.com; path=/
```

The first line of the response header indicates the HTTP version used by the server to produce the response followed by the numeric HTTP response code and a text description for the response code. The remaining lines each represent headers that give the client (or proxy servers between the client and server) additional information about the server's processing of the request.

- The Cache-Control response header defined by the HTTP standard is a directive telling any proxies how caching of this response is to be handled. For relatively static content, this header can be used to help ensure that caching proxies will serve up cached copies of content, significantly reducing bandwidth and processing requirements on the server serving the content.

- The Content-Type response header is defined by the HTTP standard and indicates the MIME type and character set used in the response. The Content-Type should be compatible with the Accept header supplied by the client in the request.

- The X-UA-Compatible header is not defined by the HTTP standard and was introduced by Microsoft with the release of Internet Explorer 8 to provide a mechanism through which content providers could provide a directive that their content is to be rendered in Internet Explorer Compatibility mode.

- The P3P header is not part of the HTTP specification but is used by another W3C initiative, the Platform for Privacy Preferences (P3P).

- The Vary response header is used to tell any caching proxy which field or fields must match in order to serve up a cached version of the content. In the case of this response, the directive is given that Accept-Encoding request headers must match for the proxy to be allowed to serve its cached copy to another client.

- The Content-Encoding response header is part of the HTTP standard and indicates which compression method, if any, has been applied to the content being served. The Content-Encoding provided by the server should be compatible with the Accept-Encoding requested by the client.

- The Date response header is defined by the HTTP standard and indicates the date and time at which the server originated the message.

- The Content-Length response header is defined by the HTTP standard and is used to indicate the length of the message body.

- The Connection response header is defined by the HTTP standard and is used to specify any connection options between server and client.

- The Set-Cookie is not part of the HTTP standard but is commonly used and understood by most servers and user agents as a mechanism through which the server directs the user agent to store cookie values.

6. You're done. If you're interested, continue to explore the request and response of other requests.

HTTP Response Codes

Anyone who developed applications when COM was the prevalent method to create Windows applications will remember the HRESULT. This was a numeric return from any COM method call that indicated the success or failure of the call. This varies from the .NET exception-based system where if a method completes without having thrown an exception, it should be considered by the calling code to have succeeded, and the similar method SOAP uses with faults instead of exception, but it is very similar to the HTTP concept of response codes.

As you saw in the exercise examining HTTP headers, every HTTP response begins with a line that includes a numeric response code (formally referred to as *status code*) and a textual description for the response code. The response codes are divided into subsets based on the first of three digits.

- 1xx status codes indicate an informational response.

- 2xx status codes indicate successful processing of requests.

- 3xx status codes indicate that redirection is necessary and the client should request a different resource than what was requested.

- 4xx status codes indicate an error with the client request.

- 5xx status codes indicate that a server error occurred attempting to process the request.

Many standard and nonstandard status codes exist (including my favorite, 418 – I'm a TeaPot, which is defined in RFC 2324 as an IETF April Fool's joke in 1998). Tables 15-1 through 15-5 include only those status codes defined in the HTTP standard.

Table 15-1. *1xx: Informational*

Code	Description
100 – Continue	This status code is used when the client has sent a partial request and the server needs to indicate that the client should continue and send the rest of the request.
101 – Switching Protocols	This status code is used as a response to the client including a request (via the Upgrade request header) that the interaction between the client and server use a different protocol and indicates that from that point forward the requested protocol will be used.

Table 15-2. *2xx: Success*

Code	Description
200 – OK	This is the most commonly encountered success status code and indicates that the request was successfully processed with no additional information provided.
201 – Created	This status is used to indicate that an entity was successfully created as a result of the request submitted using the POST or PUT method.
202 – Accepted	This status code is used only to indicate that the server successfully accepted the request from the client but not that the request has been successfully processed. This code may be encountered in a situation where the client and server expect requests to be processed asynchronously in a "fire-and-forget" mode where only delivery of the message is guaranteed before the client moves on. For example, if a request is made to a web server to initiate a complicated set of calculations that may take minutes or hours to complete, the server may return a 202 response to indicate to the client that the request was accepted by the server and the client should not wait for further response.
203 – Non-Authoritative Information	This status code is used to indicate that the information that has been successfully retrieved and is being returned in the response body should not be considered as having come from the original source or the source that is designated as the authority. It indicates that there is no guarantee as to the accuracy of the information.
204 – No Content	This status code is used to indicate that the request was successfully processed on the server, but there is no content in the message body to send to the client.
205 – Reset Content	This status code is similar to 204 in that there is no data in the accompanying message body, but it also provides direction to the client that the user interface elements used to generate the request should be reset, such as clearing form fields.
206 – Partial Content	This status code is used in conjunction with the client having submitted its request using the Range request header and is used to indicate that only a certain range within the complete result is being returned. This can be useful in situations where the paging of results is desired.

Table 15-3. *3xx: Redirection*

Code	Description
300 – Multiple Choices	This status code indicates that multiple resources may meet the criteria of the request, and it is necessary for the client to select the appropriate resource. Typically the body of a message returned with a 300 status code will include the list of potential matches, but the standard does not define how this list is to be presented.
301 – Moved Permanently	This status code is used to indicate that the requested resource is no longer located at the requested URI and that this and future requests for the resource should be directed to an alternate URI. When this status code is returned by a server, the alternate URI will be specified in the Location HTTP response header.
302 – Found	This status code is similar to the 301 status code in that the user-agent is directed to retrieve the requested resource from an alternate URI found in the Location HTTP response header, but the redirection is not considered a permanent move, and future requests should continue to use the URI originally requested by the client.

(continued)

Table 15-3. (*continued*)

Code	Description
303 – See Other	This status code indicates that the user agent should request an alternate URI found in the Location HTTP response header but specifies that the method used to request the alternate resource be GET. This status code can be useful in situations where a PUT or POST is processed and the user should be redirected to a static HTML page indicating that data was updated successfully.
304 – Not Modified	This status code is most often used in conjunction with requests that specify via headers that the resource should be returned by the server only if it has been modified since a specific date, indicating that the client has one version of the resource and wants to download another version only if one that is newer exists. This can save data transfer bandwidth and processing time on both the client and server. When the 304 status code is returned by the server, no data should be expected in the body of the message.
305 – Use Proxy	This status indicates that the requested resource must be retrieved through a specific proxy server. The Location HTTP response header will contain the URI of the appropriate proxy server when this status code is returned.
306 – Not Used (used to be Switch Proxy)	Under the HTTP 1.0 standard, the 306 status code was a direction that subsequent requests should use a specified proxy. The Switch Proxy definition is no longer applied to this code, but it remains in the current standard as unused and reserved for future use.
307 – Temporarily Moved	This status code is similar to the 301 status code in that the user agent is directed to retrieve the requested resource from an alternate URI found in the Location HTTP response header, but the redirection is not considered a permanent move, and future requests should continue to use the URI originally request by the client.

Table 15-4. *4xx: Client Error*

Code	Description
400 – Bad Request	This status code indicates that because of errors in the syntax of the client request, the server could not understand the request well enough to know what was being asked of it.
401 – Unauthorized	This status code indicates that the user is requesting access to a resource that requires authorization, but either the user has not yet been authenticated or authentication has occurred and the authenticated user does not possess authorization necessary for the resource.
402 – Payment Required	This status code exists in the standard as a placeholder and has not yet been defined beyond its textual description, but it can be useful when developing the API for a subscription-based service as long as the client and server both know what to expect. This expectation would be set by some sort of agreement outside the control of standards and would be handled on an application-by-application basis by the designer of the service. As with any "reserved for future use" item, if you do choose to use this status code, it should be with the full understanding that when "future use" comes, it may turn out to be used in a manner that breaks your application.

(*continued*)

Table 15-4. (*continued*)

Code	Description
403 – Forbidden	This status code is used to indicate that the server is refusing to service the request. According to the HTTP standard, this status code should be used only when access to the resource is being denied in such a way that the client cannot successfully gain access to the resource by modifying the request or obtaining authorization.
404 – Not Found	This status code is used to indicate that the client has requested a resource that cannot be found at the specified URI and that the server is not aware of an alternate URI from which the resource may be successfully accessed.
405 – Method Not Allowed	This status is used to indicate that the method used in the request header when attempting to access a resource is not permissible for that resource. When this method is used, the response will also contain an Accept response header that will specify the methods that are acceptable for the requested resource.
406 – Not Acceptable	This status code is used to indicate that the server cannot provide a representation of the requested resource that meets the characteristics specified in the headers sent by the client with the request. An example of this could be that the user-agent has specified an Accept-Language header with a value of fr-FR to indicate that the response should be in the French language with the appropriate culture applied for France, but the server is capable only of providing a response appropriate for the en-US language/culture combination.
407 – Proxy Authentication Required	This status code indicates that the client must first authenticate with the proxy server before the request can be fulfilled. Successful authentication with the proxy will be evidenced by the existence of the Proxy-Authenticate HTTP request header.
408 – Request Timeout	This status code indicates that the client did not complete its request within the time allotted for client requests by the server.
409 – Conflict	This status code is used to indicate that the request cannot be carried out because it would cause a conflict. This status code is most often associated with requests that modify data and could be used to indicate that the user requested a modification to what is no longer the current version of an entity and that the client's copy of the entity should be refreshed before attempting to resubmit any modifications.
410 – Gone	This status code is used to communicate that the requested resource is known to have been previously available at the specified URI but is no longer available at any known URI and that condition is permanent.
411 – Length Required	This status code indicates that the client did not provide a Content-Length HTTP request header with its message and that the server will not process a request without this field present.
412 – Precondition Failed	This status code is used to indicate that one or more preconditions specified in the client request headers did not pass when evaluated and the requested action will not be performed.
413 – Request Entity Too Large	This status code is used to indicate that the server will not process the request because the body of the message is larger than the server has been configured to allow. Restricting the size of client requests is often used to prevent clients from accidentally or deliberately rending the service and making it useless because it is bogged down trying to process very large messages.

(*continued*)

Table 15-4. (*continued*)

Code	Description
414 – Request URI Too Long	Because of security flaws that can be exploited on many servers by providing specially crafted URIs that are very long, many servers are now configured to refuse processing of requests where the URI exceeds a specified length. This status code is used to indicate that the maximum allowable length has been exceeded.
415 – Unsupported Media Type	This status code is used to indicate that the entity represented in the body of the request message is not in a format that is usable by the server.
416 – Requested Range Not Satisfiable	This status code is used in conjunction with requests that have specified in the request headers that a certain range is desired and is used to indicate that data was not available to satisfy the range requested.
417 – Expectation Failed	This status code is used in conjunction with the client having used an Expect request header to communicate the expectation that the server act in a certain way and is used to communicate that the server cannot satisfy the expectation.

Table 15-5. *5xx: Server Error*

Code	Description
500 – Internal Server Error	This status code is used to indicate "something went wrong" and is generated when an exception occurs during the processing of a request that does not map to one of the other server error codes.
501 – Not Implemented	This status code is used to indicate that the server does understand what is being asked of it but does not provide the functionality to meet the request.
502 – Bad Gateway	This status code is most often seen when requests are being forwarded to other servers and is used to indicate that the server received an unexpected or bad response from a server further down the chain.
503 – Service Unavailable	This status code is used to indicate that the service is under maintenance or some other temporary condition such as high request volume has made the server stop accepting and processing requests.
504 – Gateway Timeout	This status code is most often seen when requests are being forwarded to other servers and is used to indicate that the server times out waiting for a response from a server further down the chain.
505 – HTTP Version Not Supported	This message indicates that the HTTP version specified in the client request is incompatible with what the server is configured to allow. In practice, most existing web servers and clients all use version 1 as the major protocol version, so until a 2.x standard is adopted, this error should never be seen.

As you can see from these tables, the HTTP standard provides a comprehensive set of status codes capable of communicating to a fine detail the result of both read and write requests for resources. This capability is utilized by REST-ful services to avoid the creation of yet another exception-reporting mechanism.

OData Protocol by Example

At this point, you've taken a pretty deep dive into HTTP, and you should have a pretty solid working understanding for the pieces of HTTP. Coverage of SOAP would have either required a book of its own or just barely scratched the surface and left you without nearly the level of knowledge that you have of HTTP. That's the point of REST; it's a simple architectural style that builds on the simplicity and capability of HTTP. The downside of REST as a style instead of a standard is that there can be and are many variations of this style that all fit under the same umbrella description of REST, so if you are conversant in one REST implementation, you may not have the slightest familiarity with some other implementation. OData seeks to level this out to some degree by formalizing a REST style that incorporates the semantics of HTTP requests and responses and AtomPub or JSON to provide common message formats.

Because you will be working in an environment that plays well with XML, I will be covering only the AtomPub message format in this chapter, but you should also be aware that developers working in JavaScript can take advantage of the JavaScript Object Notation (JSON) support that is built into the OData protocol to allow it to be used more easily from browser-based tools such as jQuery. In addition to defining a common set of message formats, OData provides the semantics for requesting CRUD operations on a data model. In this section, you will work mostly by example to learn about the OData protocol.

AtomPub

One of the message formats supported by OData is the XML-based AtomPub format, which is defined by IETF RFC 4287. The purpose of AtomPub is to provide an XML dialect specialized in communicating sets of related entities. This specification was written with use cases such as newsfeed publishing in mind, and those roots are evident in some of the syntax, but the format is also very well suited for retrieving lists or single records along with the necessary information to navigate to related information through the use of link tags. Being a relatively simple format, AtomPub's use in OData can probably be best understood through a simple practice of navigating a live data set exposed as an OData service.

EXERCISE: VIEWING A LIVE ODATA SERVICE

In this exercise, you will use a web browser to navigate an example data service exposed on the OData.org website. To complete this exercise, you can use any web browser, but I have found Internet Explorer 9 to be less suitable for viewing OData because it attempts to intelligently display the feed and cannot. I will be using Google's Chrome web browser and recommend you do the same.

1. Using your selected web browser, navigate to `http://services.odata.org/ OData/OData.svc/`. Your browser should display the following result:

```
<?xml version="1.0" encoding="iso-8859-1" standalone="yes"?>
<service xml:base="http://services.odata.org/OData/OData.svc/"
         xmlns:atom="http://www.w3.org/2005/Atom"
         xmlns:app="http://www.w3.org/2007/app" xmlns="http://www.w3.org/2007/app">
  <workspace>
    <atom:title>Default</atom:title>
  <collection href="Products">
     <atom:title>Products</atom:title>
  </collection>
  <collection href="Categories">
     <atom:title>Categories</atom:title>
  </collection>
```

```
          <collection href="Suppliers">
            <atom:title>Suppliers</atom:title>
          </collection>
        </workspace>
      </service>
```

The document communicates that there are three different data sets, or *collections* in the Atom terminology, exposed by the service. These collections include information on the URI at which to access the collection as well as a friendly title to represent the collection.

2. Now that you've viewed the collections exposed by the service, navigate to
   `http://services.odata.org/OData/OData.svc/Products`. The browser should
   display an XML document representing a list of products. I won't delve too deeply
   into the format in this step other than to note that each entry includes an ID element
   that is the URI for the specific entity in the list.

3. Use the ID element of the first product in the list to obtain the URI
   `http://services.odata.org/OData/OData.svc/Products(0)`, and navigate
   to the entity in the web browser. The following XML should be displayed:

```
<?xml version="1.0" encoding="iso-8859-1" standalone="yes"?>
<entry xml:base="http://services.odata.org/OData/OData.svc/"
       xmlns:d="http://schemas.microsoft.com/ado/2007/08/dataservices"
       xmlns:m="http://schemas.microsoft.com/ado/2007/08/dataservices/metadata"
       xmlns="http://www.w3.org/2005/Atom">
  <id>http://services.odata.org/OData/OData.svc/Products(0)</id>
  <title type="text">Bread</title>
  <summary type="text">Whole grain bread</summary>
  <updated>2012-05-15 T14:29:53Z</updated>
  <author>
    <name />
  </author>
  <link rel="edit" title="Product" href="Products(0)" />
  <link rel="http://schemas.microsoft.com/ado/2007/08/dataservices/related/Category"
        type="application/atom+xml;type=entry"
        title="Category" href="Products(0)/Category" />
  <link rel="http://schemas.microsoft.com/ado/2007/08/dataservices/related/Supplier"
        type="application/atom+xml;type=entry"
        title="Supplier" href="Products(0)/Supplier" />
  <category term="ODataDemo.Product"
            scheme="http://schemas.microsoft.com/ado/2007/08/dataservices/scheme" />
  <content type="application/xml">
    <m:properties>
      <d:ID m:type="Edm.Int32">0</d:ID>
      <d:ReleaseDate m:type="Edm.DateTime">1992-01-01 T00:00:00</d:ReleaseDate>
      <d:DiscontinuedDate m:type="Edm.DateTime" m:null="true" />
      <d:Rating m:type="Edm.Int32">4</d:Rating>
      <d:Price m:type="Edm.Decimal">2.5</d:Price>
    </m:properties>
  </content>
</entry>
```

Examine the XML and note the way that link elements are used to provide navigation to related elements such as the category and supplier of the product, which are contained in other collections you saw in the first step. Also note the `content` element, which is the extensibility point of the AtomPub format being leveraged by OData. The `content` element allows a MIME type to be specified, and in this case, you are specifying that the contents will be XML. Inside the content, the Microsoft schema's defining data service types and metadata are referenced, and several fields are expressed as child elements of a `properties` element. Each field has its name as the tag name, a `type` attribute to indicate the data type of the value, and the element's content is the value of the property.

4. Using the navigation link
   `http://services.odata.org/OData/OData.svc/Products(0)/Category`,
   navigate to the `category` entity referenced in the product. Examine the resulting
   XML to view the similarities and differences between the category and product.

In this exercise, you have used a web browser to request data from an OData service. You should now have a basic understanding for how AtomPub is used and extended to represent collections of data and individual entities along with conveying relationships between entities in the OData protocol.

URI Format

In addition to defining a common way to use AtomPub for describing the data exposed by services, OData also brings consistency in the way that these collections and entities are requested by defining a common URI format. The basic syntax of the URI format is the service root URI (`http://services.odata.org/OData.svc` in the case of this example) followed by the path to the resource (`/Products(0)` for the product with an ID of 0). Additionally, the path to the resource can be followed by a query string specifying any options such as filtering, sorting, and limiting the number of results. If instead of addressing the `Products(1)` entity directly, I wanted to filter for the product with an ID of 1, I would use the URI `http://services.odata.org/OData/OData.svc/Products?$filter=ID eq 1`.

The URI request format includes many options that control the way that data is returned and a comprehensive set of query operators to satisfy very granular filtering needs. For more information on the complete set of operations available, see the URI Conventions link at `www.odata.org/documentation`.

EXERCISE: USING QUERYSTRING TO CONTROL OUTPUT

The OData URI format allows for fine control over the data requested from an OData service. In this exercise, you will make use of query string options to control the data that is returned as a result of a query. To complete this exercise, you can use any web browser, but I have found Internet Explorer 9 to be less suitable for viewing OData because it attempts to intelligently display the feed and cannot. I will be using Google's Chrome web browser and recommend you do the same.

1. As in step 2 of the previous exercise, navigate your web browser to
   `http://services.odata.org/OData/OData.svc/Products`. Note that the
   fields for each product are present in its entry's `content` element and that the link
   elements for `Category` and `Supplier` contain no content.

2. Having the address for `Category` and `Supplier` included in the result, needing to
   make a separate request for this data when dealing with a large list of products,
   and needing to include the name of the Category with the output would result in
   an extremely "chatty" client that is inappropriate for applications connected over a

network, especially when the client and server are across the Internet. To overcome this chatty nature, in this step you will direct the service to include the category data itself instead of providing just a link. Update the URI in your web browser to read `http://services.odata.org/OData/OData.svc/Products?$expand=Category`. Note that the category link that used to read as follows:

```
<link rel="http://schemas.microsoft.com/ado/2007/08/dataservices/related/Category"
type="application/atom+xml;type=entry" title="Category" href="Products(0)/Category" />
```

now reads as follows:

```
    <link rel="http://schemas.microsoft.com/ado/2007/08/dataservices/related/Category"
type="application/atom+xml;type=entry" title="Category" href="Products(0)/Category">
      <m:inline>
      <author>
        <entry>
          <id>http://services.odata.org/OData/OData.svc/Categories(0)</id>
          <title type="text">Food</title>
          <updated>2012-05-15 T17:46:45Z</updated>
          272103_1_En
            <name />
        </author>
          <link rel="edit" title="Category" href="Categories(0)" />
          <link
rel="http://schemas.microsoft.com/ado/2007/08/dataservices/related/Products"
type="application/atom+xml;type=feed" title="Products" href="Categories(0)/Products" />
          <category term="ODataDemo.Category"
scheme="http://schemas.microsoft.com/ado/2007/08/dataservices/scheme" />
          <content type="application/xml">
            <m:properties>
              <d:ID m:type="Edm.Int32">0</d:ID>
              <d:Name>Food</d:Name>
            </m:properties>
          </content>
        </entry>
      </m:inline>
    </link>
```

3. In addition to expanding the amount of data that can be included in a result set, you can specify that only certain fields are of interest. This is especially helpful in cases where the entity contains many fields and you want to conserve network bandwidth. In this case, let's assume you are interested only in creating a price list for the products, so update the URI in your browser to read `http://services.odata.org/OData/OData.svc/Products?$select=Price`. Note that the navigation links for Supplier and Category are now gone and that the only field present in the contents element is Price.

In this exercise, you saw a little bit of what can be done to control data output using query string options in OData URIs. Spend a little bit of time with the sample service and the URI conventions documentation to see what you can do to affect the data output.

Connecting to OData Services from Windows Apps

From what you've already learned in this chapter, you may have surmised at this point that it would be very easy to use classes available in the .NET Framework to submit HTTP requests to an OData service and then parse the AtomPub XML that is returned by the service into something usable by your application. You may also have identified that this functionality would be a great candidate for its own class library to keep you from writing the same code over and over again. In both cases, you would be correct, but it gets even better than that.

The .NET Framework includes a utility designed to spare you from having to handle your own connection to OData services and from having to parse the results. This utility is called DataSvcUtil. Its job consists of two tasks:

- Read metadata from either a live OData service, a conceptual data model stored as XML in a CSDL document, or an entity design model stored as XML in an EDMX file.

- Produce code representing structures to correspond to each entity and a class to act as a service proxy.

The utility allows you to specify the file or URI from which to read the model, the path of the output file to which the code should be written, the target language for the code output (C# and VB are supported), the OData protocol version supported, and whether the collections generated by the utility should derive from DataServiceCollection. DataServiceCollection is an observable collection that will provide CollectionChanged events and also provides for its own change tracking, so unless you are going to be using the data as read-only and do not intend to data bind, DataServiceCollection is usually your best bet.

EXERCISE: CONSUME ODATA FROM .NET APPLICATION

In this exercise, you will learn to use the DataSvcUtil utility to generate a service proxy and supporting data objects and then make use of the generated code from a .NET application. To keep a narrow focus on OData-specific code, you will create a console application in this exercise. To complete the exercise, you will need any edition of Visual Studio 11.

1. Before you do any work within Visual Studio, you need to generate the file that will provide your service proxy and data objects. For this step, I will be using a working directory of C:\Temp because it is easy to navigate to from the command line, and it will be easy to find my output file later. From the Windows 8 Start screen, open the Developer Command Prompt application. If this application is not showing on the Start screen, use the Search charm to find it. Once at the command prompt, use the following commands (note the line wrap):

```
cd \
cd temp

DataSvcUtil /out:OData.cs /uri:"http://services.odata.org/OData/OData.svc"➥
/DataServiceCollection /version:2.0
```

2. Observe that the output of the command includes Generation Complete -- 0 errors, 0 warnings.

3. At this point, your code file OData.cs should be in the C:\Temp directory, and you're ready to work in Visual Studio. Open Visual Studio and create a new Windows console application named ODataClientSample. The New Project dialog should appear similar to Figure 15-8.

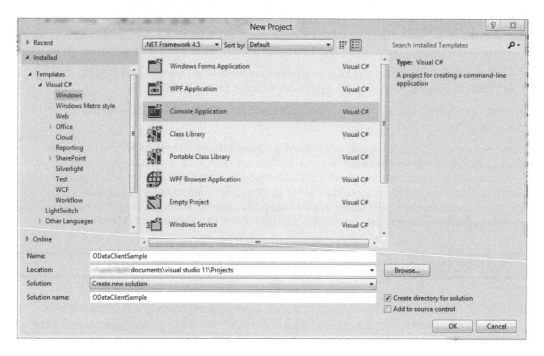

Figure 15-8. *Creating a console application*

4. Right-click the References folder in the Solution Explorer, and select Add Reference. Add a reference to the System.Data.Services.Client assembly.

5. Right-click the ODataClientSample project in the Solution Explorer, and select Add ➤ Existing Item. Navigate to the OData.cs file created in step 1.

6. Open Program.cs, and update the Main method as follows:

```
static void Main()
{
    var service=new ODataDemo.DemoService(new
                    Uri("http://services.odata.org/OData/OData.svc"));
    service.Products.ToList().ForEach(p =>
        Console.WriteLine("{0} - {1}", p.Name, p.Price));
    Console.ReadLine();
}
```

7. Press F5 to run your application, or click the Start arrow in the toolbar and observe data coming back from the service. You've just written your first OData client application, and the tools available in the .NET platform did most of the heavy lifting for you! The DataSvcUtil tool downloaded metadata from the OData sample service and generated a class representing each collection exposed by the service as well as the class used to interact with these collections.

In this exercise, you created a very simple OData client. You may find yourself using OData in more sophisticated ways, but the steps required to interact with the service and data objects will remain simple.

Available Services

A growing number of organizations are choosing to make their data available to developers through REST services using OData, creating a self-perpetuating cycle of the protocol becoming more popular because it is more popular. Notable producers of OData services include Netflix, eBay, and Windows Live. The best way to look for a producer providing data that you may be interested in is either by following the "ecosystem" link at www.odata.org or browsing the growing list of free and paid options available at the Windows Azure MarketPlace (http://datamarket.azure.com).

For the MovieBrowser sample application, you will be using the services exposed by Netflix at http://odata.netflix.com/. This service provides a rich variety of data to allow you to create a useful and interesting application with use cases that are likely to resemble requirements you may find in your own applications.

Conclusion

In this chapter, you looked at the motivation behind building reusable software components and the need for simplicity when exposing these components on the Internet to a variety of client platforms. You learned about the rich functionality available in the HTTP standard that is already understood by many user agents and how REST builds upon this to create an architectural style well suited for applications connected via the Internet. Finally, you learned how the OData protocol can provide a common implementation style and message format to allow consistency among REST services and how to access these services from a .NET client. You should now be ready to consume OData services in your own applications.

CHAPTER 16

Completing the Service Agent

Long is the road from conception to completion.

—Moliere

Over the course of the past several chapters you have been progressively applying new concepts to build the MovieBrowser sample application. In Chapter 14, you created a service agent that provided hard-coded sample data to the ViewModel. In this chapter, you will utilize the OData catalog provided by Netflix to create a service agent for the application that retrieves its data from a live service running in the cloud. In creating this service agent, you will also apply what you learned about asynchronous programming in Chapter 13.

Asynchronous Programming and the UI Thread

While the tools, frameworks, and technologies surrounding Windows programming have changed considerably over the years, the most fundamental concept of managing an event-based programming environment has remained unchanged. Windows applications utilize a procedure known as a *message pump*, which is essentially an endless loop that polls an input queue for messages from the operating system that are generated by user interaction such as input on the mouse and keyboard. These messages are then sent, or *dispatched*, to the application for processing as events. Once the application has completed processing the message, the cycle begins again. Figure 16-1 shows a conceptual representation of the message pump.

Figure 16-1. *Message pump*

Using a message pump is an effective and simple way to manage an event-driven environment, but it has one inherent weakness: the code written in event handlers executes inline with the message loop, as illustrated with an event handler calling a long-running service method in the sequence diagram in Figure 16-2. While the object responsible for invoking events, known as the Dispatcher, waits for the method call on the service to return, additional messages are being placed in the queue and waiting to be processed. This leaves the end user at best feeling like the application is sluggish and at worst seeing portions of the window that can't redraw or receiving a "not responding" message from Windows.

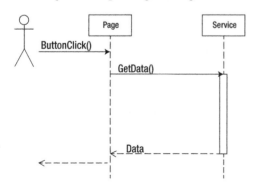

Figure 16-2. *Event with synchronous service call*

If you read Chapter 13, you may immediately recognize an opportunity to leverage asynchronous programming to allow the Dispatcher to continue processing other messages while code on another thread waits for a response from the service call. This is exactly what you will do in the service agent that communicates with the Netflix OData service, but there is a catch. User interface controls are not considered *thread safe*, which means they do not guarantee that access from multiple threads will not corrupt their data. To protect this data, the .NET Framework prevents any thread from interacting with a control, even indirectly, except for the thread that created it. Using data binding and the Model-View-ViewModel pattern, this can be problematic when a secondary thread attempts to update a property of the ViewModel because the property changed notification will fire on the thread that updated the object, and an exception will occur.

In a Windows application built on WinRT, you can avoid attempting to update UI components from the wrong thread by making use of the `CoreDispatcher` object, which is responsible for marshaling code execution to the UI thread. This is done by calling the `CoreDispatcher` object's `RunAsync` method, which accepts an enumerated value indicating the priority the method call should be given and the method that should be executed. The method must have a `void` return type and accept no parameters. You will see the `CoreDispatcher` object in action as you complete the service agent for the MovieBrowser application.

Choosing How to Call the Service

In Chapter 13 you called a service running in the cloud using the `HttpClient` class. In Chapter 15 you learned about OData, which uses the HTTP protocol and saw how the DataSvcUtil program can be used to create classes that allow you to interact with the OData service without having to explicitly handle making the HTTP call and parsing the result. Because OData is a REST service that uses HTTP, either calling the service using the `HttpClient` class or generating a service proxy with DataSvcUtil will produce a working result. In the case of the MovieBrowser application, consideration must be given to what the application needs from the service.

- A listing of genre names
- For each genre, a listing of the titles classified within the genre

These requirements represent a small subset of the functionality exposed by the service, and translation is necessary to get the data from the form in which it would be exposed through the generated service proxy. Therefore, I have chosen to use the `HttpClient` class directly, accepting that the trade-off is that I must parse the XML returned by the service, a task that you will find more mundane and repetitive than complicated. This parsing will be performed within helper methods to help ensure that the main logic performed by the service agent remains easy to read and understand.

■ **Note** "Hiding" code that is complicated or distracts from the logical flow of the application is a common practice to help produce maintainable code.

┌───┐
│   **EXERCISE: CREATING THE LIVE SERVICE AGENT**   │
└───┘

In this exercise, you will create the service agent that communicates with the live Netflix OData service along with its supporting code and update the application to use this service agent. To complete the exercise, you will need the completed MovieBrowser exercise from Chapter 14, Windows 8, any edition of Visual Studio 2012, and an active Internet connection.

■ **Note** If you did not complete the exercise from Chapter 14 and want to complete this exercise, you can start with the MovieBrowser project available in the downloadable source code for Chapter 14.

---

1. Open the MovieBrowser solution as updated in Chapter 14.

2. Right-click the project, and select Add ➤ New Folder. Name the folder `Utility`.

3. Right-click the `Utility` folder, and select Add ➤ Class. Name the class `NetflixXmlHelper.cs`. As the name suggests, this class will contain functionality used in parsing the XML returned by the Netflix OData service.

4. Update the `using` statements at the top of the `NetflixXmlHelper.cs` source file to include the following statements:

```
using System;
using System.Net.Http;
using System.Threading.Tasks;
using System.Xml.Linq;
using MovieBrowser.DataModel;
```

The main job of the `NetflixXmlHelper` class is to parse XML. Referencing the nodes that you need to query from the document returned by this query will require them to be fully qualified, including their XML namespace. The namespaces that will be used can be identified by retrieving a genre listing from `http://odata.netflix.com/v2/Catalog/Genres` and looking at the declarations at the top of the file. These include the following:

- atom: `http://www.w3.org/2005/Atom`

- d: `http://schemas.microsoft.com/ado/2007/08/dataservices`

- m: `http://schemas.microsoft.com/ado/2007/08/dataservices/metadata`

The `NeflixHelper` class will include definitions for these namespaces as well as each of the fields that will need to be parsed using its namespace-qualified name.

5. Add a field to the `NetflixXmlHelper` class for each of the needed namespaces. Use the following code:

```
private static readonly XNamespace AtomNamespace =
    XNamespace.Get("http://www.w3.org/2005/Atom");
private static readonly XNamespace DataServiceNamespace =

XNamespace.Get("http://schemas.microsoft.com/ado/2007/08/dataservices");
private static readonly XNamespace MetadataNamespace =

XNamespace.Get("http://schemas.microsoft.com/ado/2007/08/dataservices/
metadata");
```

In the next few steps, you will add nested classes to organize fully qualified element names used in parsing the XML. Each set of element names will be organized into a nested class containing only element names from a single XML namespace.

6. Create a nested class within `NetflixHtmlHelper` to hold the element names that will be referenced from the Atom namespace. Use the following code:

```
public static class AtomNodeNames
{
    public static readonly XName Entry = AtomNamespace.GetName("entry");
    public static readonly XName Title = AtomNamespace.GetName("title");
    public static readonly XName Id = AtomNamespace.GetName("id");
}
```

7. Create the nested class within `NetflixHtmlHelper` to hold the element names that will be referenced from the Data Services Metadata namespace. Use the following code:

```
public static class MetadataNodeNames
{
    public static readonly XName Properties = MetadataNamespace.
GetName("properties");
}
```

8. Create the nested class within `NetflixHtmlHelper` to hold the element names that will be referenced from the Data Services namespace. Use the following code:

```
public static class DataServiceNodeNames
{
    public static readonly XName Name =
DataServiceNamespace.GetName("Name");
    public static readonly XName ShortName =
DataServiceNamespace.GetName("ShortName");
    public static readonly XName Synopsis =
DataServiceNamespace.GetName("Synopsis");
    public static readonly XName ShortSynopsis =
        DataServiceNamespace.GetName("ShortSynopsis");
    public static readonly XName BoxArt =
DataServiceNamespace.GetName("BoxArt");
    public static readonly XName SmallUrl =
DataServiceNamespace.GetName("SmallUrl");
    public static readonly XName MediumUrl =
DataServiceNamespace.GetName("MediumUrl");
    public static readonly XName LargeUrl =
DataServiceNamespace.GetName("LargeUrl");
}
```

9. Create the `ParseTitle` method in `NetflixXmlHelper`. This method will accept an `XElement` as its only parameter and will return a `Title` object that has been populated from the data within the element. Use the following code:

```
public static Title ParseTitle(XElement titleElement)
{
    Title title = new Title();
    XElement propertiesElement =
titleElement.Element(MetadataNodeNames.Properties);
```

```
        title.Name =
propertiesElement.Element(DataServiceNodeNames.Name).Value;
        title.ShortName =
propertiesElement.Element(DataServiceNodeNames.ShortName).Value;
        title.Synopsis =
propertiesElement.Element(DataServiceNodeNames.Synopsis).Value;
        title.ShortSynopsis =

propertiesElement.Element(DataServiceNodeNames.ShortSynopsis).Value;

        BoxArt boxArt = new BoxArt();
        XElement boxArtElement =
propertiesElement.Element(DataServiceNodeNames.BoxArt);
        boxArt.SmallUrl =
boxArtElement.Element(DataServiceNodeNames.SmallUrl);
        boxArt.MediumUrl =
boxArtElement.Element(DataServiceNodeNames.MediumUrl);
        boxArt.LargeUrl =
boxArtElement.Element(DataServiceNodeNames.LargeUrl);

        title.BoxArt = boxArt;

        return title;
    }
```

10. Create the `GetGenresXml` method in `NetflixXmlHelper`. This method will asynchronously retrieve an XML document containing the genres in the catalog. For the sake of limiting the amount of data requested from the service, the `$top` query string parameter will be assigned a value of 10 to indicate that only ten records should be returned by the call, and the `$select` parameter will be used to indicate that the properties element should include only `Name`. Create the method using the following code:

```
public static async Task<XDocument> GetGenresXml()
{
    using(var webClient = new HttpClient())
    {
        var response = await webClient.GetStringAsync(

"http://odata.netflix.com/v2/catalog/Genres?$select=Name&$top=10");
        return XDocument.Parse(response);
    }
}
```

■ **Note** Notice how the use of `async` and `await` allow this asynchronous method to read as if it were synchronous.

11. Right-click the `ServiceAgents` folder, and select Add ➤ Class. Name the class `NetflixMovieCatalogServiceAgent.cs`.

12. Update the `using` statements at the top of `NetflixMovieCatalogServiceAgent.cs` to include the following statements:

```
using System;
using System.Collections.ObjectModel;
using System.Linq;
using System.Net.Http;
using System.Threading.Tasks;
using System.Xml.Linq;
using MovieBrowser.DataModel;
using MovieBrowser.Interfaces;
using MovieBrowser.Utility;
using Windows.ApplicationModel.Core;
using Windows.UI.Core;
```

13. Change the class declaration for `NetflixMovieCatalogServiceAgent` to have public visibility, and implement the `IMovieDataCatalogServiceAgent` interface. The class declaration should read as follows:

```
public class NetflixMovieCatalogServiceAgent : IMovieCatalogServiceAgent
```

14. Create the `ProcessGenre` method in `NetflixMovieCatalogServiceAgent`. The method will receive the XML element containing a genre record and a callback method of type `Action<Genre>`. The method will parse the `Name` out of the `Genre` XML and will retrieve the related titles from the Netflix OData service using the techniques you used with `Genre` to limit the amount of data being passed back. Once the titles have been retrieved, the assembled `Genre` instance will be passed to the supplied callback. Remember that the `MovieBrowserViewModel` is supplying the callback and will add the `Genre` to its `Genres` collection. This will indirectly update UI elements, so you have to ensure that the callback method is executed using the `Dispatcher`. Use the following code to implement this method:

```
const string titleUrlFormat =
"{0}/Titles?$top = 20&$expand = BoxArt&$select = Name,ShortName,Synopsis,
ShortSynopsis,BoxArt";
private async Task ProcessGenre(XElement genreElement
    , Action<Genre> genreAvailableCallback)
{
    string titleResponse;
    string titleListingUrl = string.Format(titleUrlFormat
        , genreElement.Element(NetflixXmlHelper.AtomNodeNames.Id).Value);
    using(var titleClient = new HttpClient())
    {
        titleClient.MaxResponseContentBufferSize = int.MaxValue;
        titleResponse = await
titleClient.GetStringAsync(titleListingUrl);
    }
    var titleDoc = XDocument.Parse(titleResponse);

    var titleObjects =
titleDoc.Descendants(NetflixXmlHelper.AtomNodeNames.Entry)
        .Select(element =>
```

```
        {
            return NetflixXmlHelper.ParseTitle(element);
        });

    var genre = new Genre();
    genre.Name =
genreElement.Element(NetflixXmlHelper.AtomNodeNames.Title).Value;
    genre.Titles = new ObservableCollection<Title>();
    foreach(var title in titleObjects)
    {
        genre.Titles.Add(title);
    }

    CoreApplication.MainView.CoreWindow.Dispatcher.RunAsync(CoreDispatcherPri
ority.Normal
        , () =>
        {
            genreAvailableCallback(genre);
        });
}
```

15. Implement the `InitiateGenreRetrieval` method in
    `NetflixMovieCatalogServiceAgent`. Because the method will be making use of
    the `await` keyword to consume `async` methods, it must also be marked `async`. Use
    the following code to implement the method:

```
public async void InitiateGenreRetrieval(Action<Genre>genreAvailableCallback)
{
    var genreDoc = await NetflixXmlHelper.GetGenresXml();

    foreach(var entryNode in
genreDoc.Descendants(NetflixXmlHelper.AtomNodeNames.Entry))
    {
        await ProcessGenre(entryNode, genreAvailableCallback);
    }
}
```

At this point, you have completed the implementation of your service agent that retrieves live catalog
data from the Netflix OData service. The final step is to update the parameterless constructor of the
`MovieBrowserViewModel` class to use this service agent instead of the `SampleDataMovieDataServiceAgent`
implementation.

16. Open `MovieBrowserViewModel.cs` in the `DataModel` folder.

17. Update the parameterless constructor to use the new service agent. The updated
    code should read as follows:

```
public MovieBrowserViewModel()
    : this(new NetflixMovieCatalogServiceAgent())
{
}
```

■ **Note**   Remember that in a "real-world" application a framework such as Unity or MVVMLight that includes dependency injection libraries would be used to alleviate this hard-coded dependency.

You have now completed the MovieBrowser sample application. Run the application and see your data coming back from the cloud. The completed application should appear similar to what is shown in Figure 16-3.

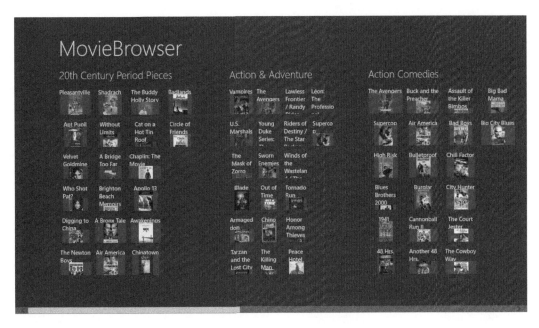

Figure 16-3. *Completed MovieBrowser application*

Conclusion

In this chapter, you applied what you learned in the previous chapters and completed the MovieBrowser sample application as a fully functional application to browse titles in the Netflix catalog. Seeing the screens populated with live data no doubt has you thinking of changes that you would make to the user interface. Make the application your own by experimenting with the data templates to achieve a look that you prefer.

CHAPTER 17

■ ■ ■

Interacting with Windows Search and Share

Teamwork is the ability to work together toward a common vision. The ability to direct individual accomplishments toward organizational objectives. It is the fuel that allows common people to attain uncommon results.

—Andrew Carnegie

One of the key design goals of Windows applications is to create a completely immersive experience for end users, one where for the time they are using your application, it remains the center of their world. One way that this is achieved is by following the "Win as One" design principle and by building applications where the user moves seamlessly between your application and the operating system. In this chapter, I will cover contracts that can be exposed by Windows applications to allow the application to extend the functionality of Windows 8 and become a fully participating member of an ecosystem of applications.

Contracts

Outside of the development world, a *contract* is a formal agreement that typically defines a set of expectations and obligations between two or more parties and involves some end goal that will provide mutual benefit. In the development world, a contract is really no different; it is a way for a component to announce needs, capabilities, or a data format in a formal manner that allows other components to know how to interact with that component. The formal declaration is necessary because simply possessing a capability is not enough to get the full benefit of reusability if potential consumers of that capability have no idea of how to tap into it, as depicted in Figure 17-1.

Figure 17-1. The lack of a formal contract prevents reuse

Two of the most common ways to communicate the characteristics of a contract in modern software are the use of XML and interfaces. XML is very useful for capabilities that can be configured as well as instances where interactions may span components that have been implemented using different technology stacks. A simple contract might look like the following snippet:

```
<capabilities>
    <capability> search</capability>
</capabilities>
```

The important thing is that all participants in interactions using XML contracts agree on the format and meaning of the XML that will be used to express the contract, and this is usually where formal schema definitions using XML Schema Definition (XSD) come into play.

When .NET applications are going to be interacting solely with other .NET applications, interfaces are most certainly the most common way to communicate a contract. The use of interfaces can succinctly communicate capabilities and expectations in a way that both other developers and the compiler can understand. Continuing with the example started in Figure 17-1, an interface to help with this interaction might look like this:

```
public interface ISearcher
{
    SearchResult SearchFor(string term);
}
```

Using this interface, the consumer knows that it requires a component with a method called SearchFor that accepts a single string parameter, so if the component providing the search capability implements this interface, the consumer can make use of it without any knowledge of how it is completing the job. Now that you have a contract, your interaction can look much more like what is depicted in Figure 17-2.

Figure 17-2. *A formal contract allows components to communicate and work together*

At this point, you may be saying, "Didn't you already talk about Inversion of Control?" If so, that's great, and you're really getting it. If you weren't asking yourself that or if the mention of it did not set off a spark of recognition, you may want to review Chapter 11 and make sure you are really comfortable with the concept, because in the next section you will see how crucial Inversion of Control is to completely integrating applications into Windows 8.

Application Contracts

In the previous section, I reviewed the role of contracts in ensuring that applications can communicate with each other. Now it is time to look at how contracts fit into the Windows 8 world. Microsoft defines a number of contracts that define ways for applications to expose capabilities that are in turn coordinated by Windows so that applications can share functionality and data with each other and with Windows without having to know anything about each other. These contracts include the Search, Share, Settings, Play To, and Cached File Updater contracts. They are exposed in your application through a combination of setting up a declaration in the XML manifest file for your application (`Package.appxmanifest`) and then implementing any required operations to fulfill the contract. The advantage of integrating these contracts into your application is that they make your application accessible to interaction with the operating system, such as through the Search and Share charms shown in Figure 17-3. I will discuss the Search and Share contracts in this chapter because they are the contracts that you will most commonly expose or consume in your Windows applications.

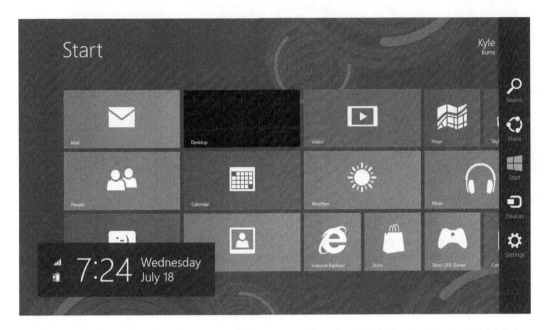

Figure 17-3. *Start screen with Search and Share charms*

Because the application contracts can be much more fully understood by actually using them, the rest of the chapter will consist of a brief introduction to each contract followed by a detailed exercise in which you will follow along and actually implement the contract.

Search Contract

The Search contract is used to advertise that your application has the capability of integrating with the Search functionality exposed in Windows 8 through the Search charm. When the Search charm is activated by a user wanting to perform a search, the left side of the screen is used as a results pane, and the right side displays a text box into which the user types search terms, a button to perform the search, and a listing of all the installed applications that expose the Search contract, as shown in Figure 17-4.

Figure 17-4. *Search activated*

When the user selects an application from the list of searchable applications, that application is activated, search-related events are sent to the application, and the application is put in control of the display for the results section of the screen. Some applications, such as the Apps application, will dynamically filter the results as the user is typing search terms, while other applications that require network calls or some other expensive resource may opt to wait until the user explicitly activates the Search button before performing any search.

EXERCISE: BUILD A SEARCHABLE APPLICATION

In this exercise, you will build a fully functional application that integrates with Windows 8 and performs a search. To help make the search more relevant and realistic, you will use the freely accessible OData service provided by Netflix to search their online library. To complete the exercise, you will need any version of Microsoft Visual Studio 2012 and Internet access.

1. To get started, open Visual Studio and create a new project. The project type should be Blank App (XAML), which can be found in the Windows Store category under Visual C#. Name the project SimpleSearchProvider.

2. Double-click the file Package.appxmanifest in the Solution Explorer, and select the Declarations page. You're not going to make any changes at this point, but observe that there are no items in the Supported Declarations section and that your screen looks similar to Figure 17-5.

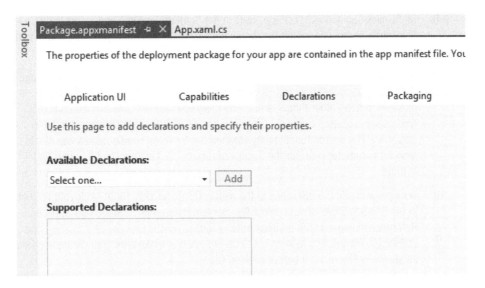

Figure 17-5. Manifest declarations before adding Search contract

3. Right-click App.xaml in the Solution Explorer, and select View Code. You're not going to make any changes at this point, but observe that the code module includes the following methods:

   - App (the constructor)
   - OnLaunched
   - OnSuspending

4. Add the Search contract by right-clicking the project in the Solution Explorer and clicking Add ➤ New Item. In the dialog that displays, select the Search Contract item under Windows Store and change Name to SearchResultsPage.xaml before clicking Add.

5. If you are prompted to include missing files, click Yes. Once Visual Studio has finished adding files, build the application to prevent any problems viewing the new page.

6. Double-click the file Package.appxmanifest in the Solution Explorer, and select the Declarations page. Observe that in the Supported Declarations section, and your screen now contains Search.

7. Right-click App.xaml in the Solution Explorer, and select View Code. Observe that in addition to the methods shown in step 3, the module now contains the method OnSearchActivated.

At this point, Windows is able to interact with your application and successfully communicate search requests, but you haven't added any code to actually perform a search. The next couple of steps will add the ability to interact with the Netflix online catalog in order and do the actual work of searching.

8. Right-click `SearchResultsPage.xaml` in the Solution Explorer, and select View Code. Read through the comments that begin with TODO to see where you still need to add your own functionality.

9. Before you go any further, take a look at the declaration of the `SearchResultsPage` class and notice that it inherits a class called `LayoutAwarePage`. This class provides, among other things, a property called `DefaultViewModel`, which is of type `ObservableMap <string, object>` and essentially functions as a bindable dictionary. The search functionality stubbed out by Visual Studio makes use of this map for parameters and for the display of results, so it is important to know that it is there.

10. Now you will add the reference to the Netflix OData service. Right-click your project in the Solution Explorer, and select Add Service Reference.... In the Add Service Reference dialog, use the address `http://odata.netflix.com/v2/Catalog`, and update the namespace to `NetflixCatalogService`. Make sure your dialog appears as shown in Figure 17-6 before clicking OK.

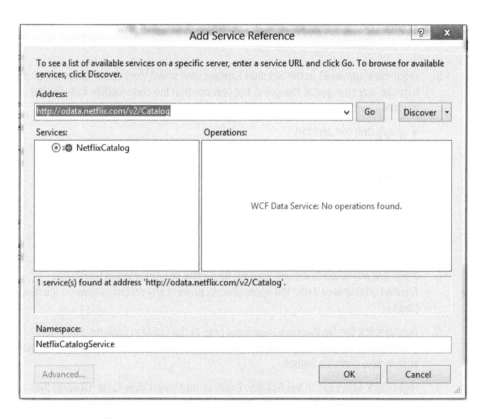

Figure 17-6. *Netflix OData service reference configuration*

11. Whenever you instantiate the service proxy that will communicate with the Netflix OData service for you, the URI of the service must be provided. If you do not still have SearchResultsPage.xaml.cs open from step 8, right-click SearchResultsPage.xaml in the Solution Explorer, and select View Code. Add the following line of code immediately after the class declaration:

```
private readonly Uri NetflixServiceUri = new
Uri("http://odata.netflix.com/v2/Catalog");
```

■ **Note** While we are using a hard-coded constant for the service URI in this exercise, it is important to remember that production applications should always favor storing data such as service URIs and database connection strings in a configuration file so that they can be updated without having to recompile and deploy the application.

12. In SearchResultsPage.xaml.cs, find the Filter_SelectionChanged method. This is the method that responds when the user submits updated search criteria. Replace all of the code between the TODO comment and the comment that reads Display informational text when there are no search results with the following code:

```
DefaultViewModel["Results"] = null; // clear previous result
var searchText = DefaultViewModel["QueryText"] as string;
if (!String.IsNullOrEmpty(searchText))
{
    NetflixCatalog catalog = new NetflixCatalog(NetflixServiceUri);
    var query = catalog.Titles.Where(t => t.Name.Contains(searchText)).
    Select(t => t);

    var queryResults = new DataServiceCollection<Title>();
    queryResults.LoadCompleted += (o, args) =>
        {
            if (queryResults.Continuation != null)
            {
                queryResults.LoadNextPartialSetAsync();
            }
            else
            {
                DefaultViewModel["Results"] = queryResults.Select(t =>
                new
                {
                    Title = t.Name,
                    Subtitle = t.ShortName,
                    Description = t.ShortSynopsis,
                    Image = t.BoxArt.MediumUrl
                }).ToList();

                // Ensure results are found
                object results;
                ICollection resultsCollection;
```

```
            if (this.DefaultViewModel.TryGetValue("Results", out results) &&
                (resultsCollection = results as ICollection) != null &&
                resultsCollection.Count != 0)
            {
                VisualStateManager.GoToState(this, "ResultsFound", true);
            }
        }
    };

    queryResults.LoadAsync(query);
}
} // this is the closing brace for null filter check
```

This code begins by setting any preexisting value for the search results to null. If the user has provided search text, the code instantiates a service proxy to the Netflix OData service, establishes a container to hold results, and then builds a query that will be executed against the service. Because the service call must be executed asynchronously, a handler is set up to handle the `LoadCompleted` event. In this handler, the `Continuation` property is checked to see whether there is more data to retrieve. If more data is available, the `LoadNextPartialSetAsync` method is called to get the next chunk of results. If no more data is available, the result set is transformed into the format expected by the bindings on the page, which by default requires the following fields:

- Title

- Subtitle

- Description

- Image

While these fields are expected by the default code created by Visual Studio, you could skip this transformation by updating the binding on the UI elements to expect the property names that you mapped. The mapped collection is then used to update the ViewModel's property to which the result grid UI elements are bound and the `VisualStateManager` is instructed to transition to the ResultsFound state, which is defined in XAML as ensuring the results grid is visible.

13. Notice you are retrieving `QueryText` from the ViewModel in step 12. The default implementation of the search functionality generated by Visual Studio stores the `QueryText` value in the ViewModel for the purpose of binding it to a `TextBlock` in the header section of the page surrounded by quotes. You need to use the value without these quotes, so you're going change this code to no longer save the quotes to the ViewModel. Find the `LoadState` method, and change the line of code that reads as follows:

```
this.DefaultViewModel["QueryText"] = '\u201c' + queryText + '\u201d';
```

to the following:

```
this.DefaultViewModel["QueryText"] = queryText;
```

■ **Note** The change you just made to the way you populate the QueryText property of the ViewModel will make it usable for your search, but it removes the desirable effect of displaying the value as quoted in the bound TextBlock. How could a ValueConverter be used to allow for storing the raw value and displaying the value formatted with quotes? If necessary, refer to Chapter 8 for a refresher on ValueConverters.

14. Run the project. Because you did not provide content for the application's MainPage, it should initial display a blank screen. With this screen displayed, swipe from the right side of the screen to activate the charm bar, select the Search charm, enter some text into the search TextBox, and then click the magnifying glass to submit the search. "No Results Found" should display while the search is being performed, and then after a short pause (depending on how broad your search term was and how many results returned), you should see results similar to what is shown in Figure 17-7.

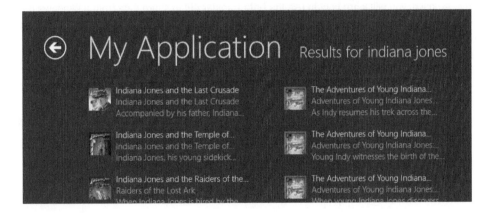

Figure 17-7. Search results

In this exercise, you learned the basics of exposing your application's data to Windows search. For further exercise, consider the following questions and see whether you can come up with a solution:

- How can I start showing results as soon as I receive the first chunk of data rather than waiting for it all to be retrieved? One possible answer would involve populating the ViewModel's Results field with an ObservableCollection instead of a List.

- Having "No Results" display while the search is going on in the background is not very user friendly. What could be done to avoid this? One possible answer would be to add an IsSearching property to the ViewModel and bind the visibility of the TextBlock based to the property.

Share Contract

The Share contract enables data to be shared from applications that are developed to be sources to applications that are developed to be targets. In this section, I will discuss each role and give you an exercise demonstrating how to integrate the role into your applications.

Sharing Source

The sharing source role is fairly easy to set up because this role does not actively advertise the role of producer to the Windows API in the way that Search does. Instead, your application will subscribe to the DataRequested event of a DataTransferManager object, which is fired when the end user activates the Share charm on the charm bar. When the event fires, your application fills a data container that has been handed to it, and Windows then makes this container available to a consuming application, known as the *share target*.

EXERCISE: SHARING DATA

In this exercise, you will learn how to use the Data Transfer API to share data from a Windows 8 application. Because it is a readily available source of data to share, you will extend the SimpleSearchProvider application that you created in the previous exercise. To complete the exercise, you will need any version of Microsoft Visual Studio 2012 and Internet access.

1. Open the SimpleSearchProvider project created in the "Build a Searchable Application" exercise.

2. In the Solution Explorer, right-click SearchResultsPage.xaml, and select View Code.

3. The important objects used to manage sharing are present in the Windows.Application.Data namespace. Add the following line to the using statements at the top of the code module:

   using Windows.ApplicationModel.DataTransfer;

4. Now you will write the code that does the real work of sharing data. You'll place it in a method that is suitable for wiring up as an event handler in a later step. Add the following method to the SearchResultsPage class:

```
private void OnShareDataRequested(DataTransferManager sender, DataRequestedEventArgs e)
{
    var request = e.Request;
    var queryText = DefaultViewModel["QueryText"] as string;
    if(string.IsNullOrEmpty(queryText))
    {
        request.FailWithDisplayText("No Search String");
        return;
    }

    var package = new DataPackage();
    package.Properties.Title = "Shared from My Application";
    package.Properties.Description = "Information regarding disposition of search";
```

```
package.SetText(string.Format("Search for \"{0}\" yielded {1} result(s)"
    , queryText, resultsGridView.Items.Count));

request.Data = package;
}
```

In this method, you evaluated whether a condition existed in which you should communicate an error message to the end user and abort sharing. When this occurs, the Share user interface will take the string provided to the `FailWithDisplayText` method and present it to the user. After making the determination that you should actually share data, the code creates an instance of a `DataPackage` object. The `DataPackage` object is aptly named because it serves to contain the data being transferred along with some related metadata. In this case, you are choosing to transfer textual data, so you use the `SetText` method to populate the item, but methods to share many other formats are available including the following:

- `SetBitmap`: Shares a stream representing a bitmap image
- `SetHtmlFormat`: Shares HTML-formatted text
- `SetRtf`: Shares RTF-formatted text
- `SetStorageItems`: Shares items implementing the `IStorageItem` interface such as files and folders
- `SetUri`: Shares a URI

In addition to the standard supported formats, `SetData` can be used to transfer user-defined formats, but these formats must be understood by both the source and destination applications. Once the `DataPackage` is populated, it is set as the `Data` property for the sharing request, and the work of your application is done.

5. With the hard work of actually producing the shared data behind you, you need to handle making sure that this code gets executed when the user selects the Share charm. Create the following method in the `SearchResultsPage` class:

```
private void InitializeSharing()
{
    var transferManager = DataTransferManager.GetForCurrentView();
    transferManager.DataRequested += OnShareDataRequested;
}
```

This method retrieves the `DataTransferManager` object, which is responsible for handling coordination between the Windows Share charm and the current view. Once you have a reference to this object, you indicate that your `OnDataShareRequested` method should be invoked when the user invokes the Share charm on this page.

■ **Note** When searching multiple times, Visual Studio may break the program execution because of an unhandled exception on the line of code setting the `DataRequested` event to your `OnShareDataRequested` handler. This exception will be handled within the framework, so it is safe to click Continue in this case.

---

6. As the final step of Share-enabling your application, you need to make sure that the `InitializeSharing` method is called when your page is initialized. Find the `SearchResultsPage` constructor, and add the following line after `this.InitializeComponents` is called:

    `InitializeSharing();`

7. At this point, your application is now enabled to be a source of shared data. Run the application, and perform a search. Once results are displayed on your screen, activate the Share charm on the charm bar. Notice that only a limited number of applications are available for selection as a target (in my case it was only Mail). These are the applications that have registered as targets when the data being shared is in the text format.

In this exercise, you learned how to share textual information. For further exploration, try experimenting with the other supported data types for sharing.

Sharing Target

The sharing target role takes a little bit more setup because in addition to writing code to respond to events in the Data Transfer API, the application's manifest must be updated to tell Windows that the application accepts data sharing and the format(s) that will be accepted.

EXERCISE: RECEIVING SHARED DATA

In this exercise, you will learn how to use the Data Transfer API to receive data shared from a Windows 8 application. Your application will be developed to receive shared URI data that you will then share from Internet Explorer. To complete the exercise, you will need any version of Microsoft Visual Studio 2012 and Internet access.

1. To get started, open Visual Studio, and create a new project. The project type should be Blank App (XAML), which can be found in the Windows Store category under Visual C#. Name the project SharingTargetSample.

2. Double-click the file `Package.appxmanifest` in the Solution Explorer, and select the Declarations page. You're not going to make any changes at this point, but observe that there are no items in the Supported Declarations section.

3. Right-click `App.xaml` in the Solution Explorer, and select View Code. You're not going to make any changes at this point, but observe that the code module includes the following methods:

    - `Constructor`
    - `OnLaunched`
    - `OnSuspending`

4. Add the Share Target contract by right-clicking the project folder that you created in the previous step and clicking Add ➤ New Item. In the dialog that displays, select the Search Contract item under Windows Store, and change Name to `ShareTargetPage.xaml` before clicking Add.

5. If you are prompted to include missing files, click Yes. Once Visual Studio has finished adding files, build the application to prevent any problems viewing the new page.

6. Double-click the file `Package.appxmanifest` in the Solution Explorer, and select the Declarations page. Observe that in the Supported Declarations section on your screen now contains Share Target and that with the Share Target selected in the Supported Declarations, the Data formats section lists text and uri. Click Remove for the text format, leaving only uri.

7. Right-click `App.xaml` in the Solution Explorer, and select View Code. Observe that in addition to the methods shown in step 3, the module now contains the method `OnShareTargetActivated`.

8. Right-click `ShareTargetPage.xaml`, and select View Code. Note the `Activate` method, which is called from the `OnShareTargetActivated` method in `App.xaml.cs`. This method sets ViewModel properties that are bound to controls on the page and then ensures that the page becomes the application's active view. At this point, the application has been activated and is displaying the data that is to be shared but has not yet actually consumed the data. This gives the user of your application the opportunity to evaluate the data that has been proposed for sharing and potentially choose not to complete the operation. The `ShareOperation` object that is present in the method's argument is saved to a class variable named `_shareOperation` so that it remains available when the user chooses to complete the operation.

9. Examine the code in the `ShareButton_Click` method in the `ShareTargetPage` class. This is the code that executes when the user chooses to accept the data being transferred to your application. The important thing in this method is the way that the `_shareOperation` variable is interacted with. The `ShareOperation` class has a number of methods that are intended to provide feedback to Windows as to the status of the data transfer. These methods are as follows:

    •   `ReportStarted`: This method is used to indicate that the automated transfer of data has begun. At this point, Windows may close the sharing UI elements.

    •   `ReportDataRetrieved`: This method is used to indicate that the consuming application has successfully retrieved the data stored in the `ShareOperation`'s `Data` property. While not necessary to call when small amounts of data are being transferred, this method can be used to indicate resources can be freed in cases where the transferred data is a `Stream` or some other memory-intensive object.

    •   `ReportSubmittedBackgroundTask`: In some cases, the share operation may include instructions to retrieve the shared content rather than the content itself. Such is the case when the actual data transferred is the URI for a resource and the consuming application responds by actually downloading the resource. In this case, the consuming application will use one of the classes in the `Windows.Networking.BackgroundTransfer` namespace to perform the actual download and call the `ReportSubmittedBackgroundTask` method to let Windows know that the transfer is in progress but will be a long-running operation.

- ReportError: This method is used to indicate that the transfer operation could not be successfully completely. It accepts a string argument that is intended to hold a descriptive message indicating why the transfer could not be completed.

- ReportCompleted: This method is used to indicate that the transfer operation has completely successfully.

The ShareButton_Click method calls the ReportStarted method to indicate that data is being transferred and then calls ReportCompleted to indicate that the operation is complete. Between these calls is where your application would do real work with the data present in the Data property of _shareOperation such as copying the link to an email or posting it to a social networking site. In the case of this application, you won't actually do anything with the data.

10. Now it's time to see the application at work. Run the application by choosing the Start Without Debugging (Ctl + F5) option.

■ **Note**   It is important to start without debugging in this case because the Share functionality does not always behave as expected when running under a debugger. If the rest of this exercise does not behave as described, check first that you did not just press F5.

---

11. The application should open to the blank MainPage. Press the Windows key to return to the Windows Start screen.

12. Open Internet Explorer.

13. Swipe from the right edge, and activate the Share charm. Your application should appear in the list of targets, as shown in Figure 17-8.

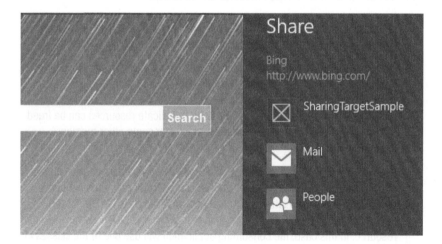

Figure 17-8. *Share activated*

14. Select SharingTargetSample from the list of available targets. Your application's sharing page should be displayed snapped in the right side of the screen, as shown in Figure 17-9. Notice that the fields bound to the ViewModel show property values that were copied from the `ShareOperation` in the page's `Activate` method.

Figure 17-9. *Sharing target selected*

15. Click Share to accept the data being shared and complete the data transfer.

You've completed your first application that consumes data produced and shared by another!

Conclusion

Windows is envisioned as a single ecosystem in which applications do a single job that is valuable to the user and perform that job well. By working together using the contracts defined by Microsoft, the output of the individual jobs performed by these applications can be shared and orchestrated by the end user to accomplish goals not even envisioned by the application developers. In this chapter, you learned the basics of how to integrate three scenarios that will be commonly encountered in Windows applications. For further learning opportunities, I encourage you explore the other application contracts and think of how they can be used in applications.

CHAPTER 18

Notifications and Tiles

The medium is the message.

—Marshall McLuhan

Windows 8 provides a rich environment in which you can create applications where it is difficult to discern the line between the operating system and your application, allowing your users to remain connected to your application even when they are not using it. Tiles and notifications are excellent examples of the integration. They provide opportunities for your application to communicate with users when your application is not running in the foreground. In this chapter, you'll examine tiles and notifications, learn how they compare, and look at how to determine which is the right choice for a given situation.

Toast Notifications

Toast notifications provide a way for your application to get information to the user quickly, regardless of what application your user is currently using. This is accomplished by producing a "pop-up" (hence the name *toast*) window that displays over the currently running application and can play a sound to provide audible notification as well. One common example of how toast notifications have been used successfully for many years is Microsoft Outlook's "new mail" notification. Unless users find this feature annoying and have turned it off (a point I'll return to), whenever a new e-mail message arrives, a small notification window appears just above the task tray showing the subject, the sender's name, and the first few words of the e-mail. This window is accompanied with a sound configured in Windows to further grab attention. If the user sees the notification and desires to read the message that they are being notified about, they can click the notification window and be taken to the full message. The scenario that I just described and that you are probably familiar with is very similar to the way that toast notifications work in Windows 8 applications.

Opt-in Model

Before diving into toast notifications, it is important to note that the ability to receive toast notifications is an opt-in model. Developers choose to have their applications receive toast notifications in the application's Package.appxmanifest file by setting the Toast Capable setting under Notifications to Yes, as shown in Figure 18-1. If this is not done, your application will not respond to toast notifications.

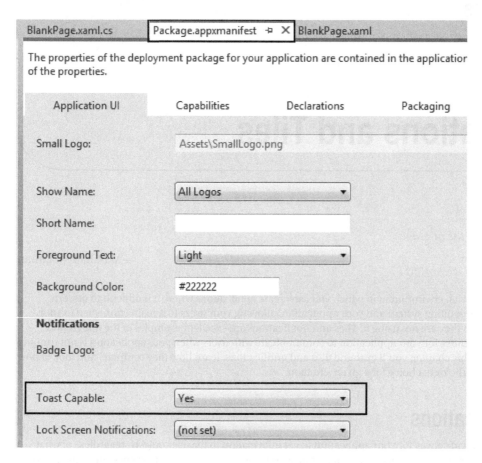

Figure 18-1. *Toast notification enabled*

Toast Templates

The visual and audio elements of toast notifications in Windows 8 applications are implemented as XML, with a number of templates from which the developer can choose to pick a format appropriate for a particular notification scenario. Table 18-1 describes the text-only templates, and Table 18-2 describes the templates with both text and an image. Figure 18-2 demonstrates the ToastText01, ToastText01, and ToastImageAndText01 templates for comparison.

Table 18-1. *Toast Text Templates*

Template	Description
ToastText01	This template contains a single text element that will display as up to three lines of text.
ToastText02	This template contains a text element that will display in bold as the first line and another text element that will display as up to two lines of text.
ToastText03	This template contains a text element that will display in bold as the first two lines and another text element that will display as the third line of text.
ToastText04	This template contains a text element that will display in bold as the first line, a text element that will display in bold as the second line, and another text element that will display as the third line of text.

Table 18-2. *Toast Text and Image Templates*

Template	Description
ToastImageAndText01	This template contains a single text element that will display as up to three lines of text and contains a large image displayed on the left side of the notification.
ToastImageAndText02	This template contains a text element that will display in bold as the first line, another text element that will display as up to two lines of text, and a large image that will display on the left side of the notification.
ToastImageAndText03	This template contains a text element that will display in bold as the first two lines, another text element that will display as the third line of text, and a large image that will display on the left side of the notification.
ToastImageAndText04	This template contains a text element that will display in bold as the first line, a text element that will display in bold as the second line, another text element that will display as the third line of text, and a large image that will display on the left side of the notification.

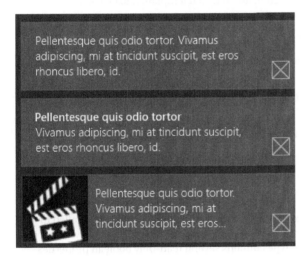

Figure 18-2. *Toast notifications*

Toast API

Now that you have an idea of the different types of messages available to you with the toast templates, let's take a look at how objects in the Windows Runtime allow you to use these templates and communicate with users. For using toast to communicate with users, the most important objects are the ToastNotification object, the ToastNotifier object, and the ToastNotificationManager object. The ToastNotification object represents the message to be sent to the user of the application. The ToastNotifier object contains the functionality of actually handling the showing or scheduling of notifications. As its name implies, the ToastNotificationManager object is used to manage toast notification operations. In this section, you will learn about each of these objects.

ToastNotification

The ToastNotification object is essentially a data container to hold information about a notification. The class has two properties: Content and ExpirationTime.

- Content is an XML document containing the information about which template is to be used and the visual and audio characteristics of the notification.

- ExpirationTime, if populated, indicates the time after which the toast should no longer be displayed.

ScheduledToastNotification

The ScheduledToastNotification object is similar to ToastNotification in that they both are data containers for notifications, but the ScheduledToastNotification object has many more properties, which are all read-only and are described in the following list. These properties are used to communicate information about a notification that has been scheduled to have Windows display at a later time. These can be thought of as analogous to an alarm.

- Content: XML document containing the information about which template is to be used and the visual and audio characteristics of the notification

- DeliveryTime: The time at which this notification is scheduled for display

- Id: A value specified by the developer scheduling the notification that is used to identify that notification

- MaximumSnoozeCount: The maximum number of times that this notification can be deferred by the user choosing to snooze

- SnoozeInterval: The amount of time to wait before displaying this notification again if the user chooses to snooze

ToastNotifier

The ToastNotifier object presents methods used to show and hide toast notifications, which are detailed in the following list. In addition to these methods, the object exposes a single property called Setting, which is of type NotificationSetting. The NotificationSetting type contains several read-only boolean properties communicating whether notification is enabled and, if not, the reason why it is disabled. Notification can be disabled by group policy, at the manifest level, by the application, or for the user.

- Show: Requests immediate display of the specified toast notification.

- Hide: Causes the specified toast message to no longer be displayed on the screen.

- AddToSchedule: Submits a toast notification for scheduling. The specified toast will be displayed by Windows at the scheduled time.

- RemoveFromSchedule: Cancels the previously scheduled display of the specified toast notification.

- GetScheduledToastNotifications: Retrieves a list of toast notifications that are scheduled for display by the ToastNotifier object's current application

ToastNotificationManager

The ToastNotificationManager object provides management functions for creating the templates that are used to initialize ToastNotification objects and for providing access to an appropriately initialized ToastNotifier object. The class includes the CreateToastNotifier method, which in its parameterless version creates a ToastNotifier object configured to send notification to the current application. CreateToastNotifier also has an overload that accepts a string containing an application ID. This version of the method returns a ToastNotifier configured to send notifications to the application with the specified application ID. Additionally, the ToastNotificationManager contains the GetTemplateContent method, which accepts a member of the ToastTemplateType enumeration and returns an XML document containing the designated template. This document is updated with the desired information to be contained in the notification and used to instantiate a ToastNotification object.

Creating and Sending Toast

The steps required to send a toast notification are relatively simple. First you retrieve the appropriate XML template using the ToastNotificationManager object's GetTemplateContent method. Once you have the XML, you update the document to reflect the message you want to send and use it to initialize a new ToastNotification instance. The last step is to retrieve an instance of a ToastNotifier object and call the Show method to display the toast.

EXERCISE: SENDING TOAST

In this exercise, you will create and show a toast notification. To complete the exercise, you will need Windows 8 and any edition of Visual Studio 2012.

1. To get started, open Visual Studio, and create a new project. The project type should be Blank App (XAML), which can be found in the Windows Store category under Visual C#. Name the project ToastSender.

2. Open MainPage.xaml.cs, and add the following to the using statements at the top of the file:

   ```
   using Windows.UI.Notifications;
   ```

3. Open MainPage.xaml, and add the following XAML inside the Grid element to create a Button:

   ```
   <Button Content="Send Toast" />
   ```

4. Double-click the Button in the designer. Visual Studio will automatically generate the Button_Click_1 event handler in MainPage.xaml.cs, and navigate to this method. Add the following code to the event handler:

   ```
   var templateType = ToastTemplateType.ToastText01;
   var toastTemplate = ToastNotificationManager.GetTemplateContent(templateType);
   var textNode = toastTemplate.GetElementsByTagName("text")[0];
   textNode.AppendChild(toastTemplate.CreateTextNode("Toast Message From My
   App"));
   var toast = new ToastNotification(toastTemplate);
   ToastNotificationManager.CreateToastNotifier().Show(toast);
   ```

5. Now you need to make sure Windows knows that your application serves toast. Double-click `Package.appxmanifest` in the Solution Explorer to open the manifest. On the Application UI tab, find the Toast Capable setting in the Notifications section, and set it to Yes.

6. Run your application. When you click the `Button`, a notification similar to the one shown in Figure 18-3 should appear.

Figure 18-3. *Toast notification*

You have now successfully created a toast notification from your application. If you'd like to explore further, try experimenting with some of the other template types.

You may find that the exercise you just completed looks too cluttered for your liking, with all of the code required to manipulate the XML document detracting focus from the code that is doing the work that you actually care about. If so, you're not alone, and the Microsoft team has included in the official SDK samples the Toast Notifications sample, which is a project that contains some very useful extension methods and objects to abstract away the direct XML manipulation. These samples are available in the Samples section of the Windows Store app dev center on MSDN (`http://msdn.microsoft.com`).

Considerations When Serving Toast

One of the most important things to remember when using toast in your application is that toast notifications are, by design, disruptive. They very effectively pull the user's attention away from whatever task they are currently performing and force them to give at least some of their attention to your application. Users also have the ability to disable notifications or to uninstall an application that they feel is too disruptive. For these reasons, it is important you choose what information to share via toast notification very carefully. Toast notifications should contain information that is crucial to deliver to the user immediately because it is time sensitive. A good example of this would be when the user has an incoming phone call for a telephony application or it is time for a scheduled appointment. A poor example would be an update on the current percent complete of a file being downloaded.

In addition to choosing whether to display a toast notification at all, you should also consider whether to use the default short duration notification or the long duration notification as well as whether to include an image with your notification. Typically you would use the short duration for most tasks that do not necessarily require an immediate action, such as indicating that it is time for a scheduled appointment; another example is when a file download has completed and you want to reserve use of the longer duration for those tasks that do require immediate notification, such as when a human is waiting for a response on an incoming call. Images should not be used to make the notification more interesting but should be used when they will actually add context to the message. Continuing with the telephony theme, an example of appropriate image use in toast notification would be to include a picture of the caller when notifying the user of an incoming call.

Tiles

The Start screen in Windows 8 (shown in Figure 18-4) is comprised primarily of a collection of squares and rectangles known as *tiles* that allow the user to launch applications. Many people coming from previous versions of Windows or other graphical operating systems are accustomed to the concept of a desktop with icons used to launch applications and will initially view tiles as being a big, touch-friendly version of the icons that they are used to seeing. Although tiles are big, touch-friendly replacements for icons, that is only half of the story. In addition to their roles of providing an easy-to-recognize graphic and launching applications, tiles can also provide rich communication to the user, allowing the Start screen to become a dashboard of sorts and to provide a single place where users can receive relevant information from the various applications on their system. Used well, this concept can help the user make decisions regarding which application they should open next.

Figure 18-4. *Windows Start screen*

Basic and Live Tiles

In Windows 8, tiles can be divided into two main categories: basic and live. Basic tiles are much more like how users will initially perceive tiles and are simply a static widget that can be clicked to launch their applications. The Internet Explorer icon in Figure 18-2 is an example of a basic tile. Live tiles are tiles that have been brought to life by the developer of their application, providing dynamic information and motion to draw the user back into the application. In Figure 18-2, the Weather application's tile is implemented as a live tile showing current weather updates for the user's location. While I make the distinction between live and basic tiles, it's important to note that Windows does not and that a tile being used as a basic tile can become a live tile simply by sending an update to the tile's contents.

Configuring the Application Tile

The `Package.appxmanifest` file contains options for configuring how the primary tile used for your application will look, as shown in Figure 18-5. These options allow you to specify the logo that will be displayed on the tile to represent your application as well as specify a shortened version of your application name designed to fit well as a tile overlay.

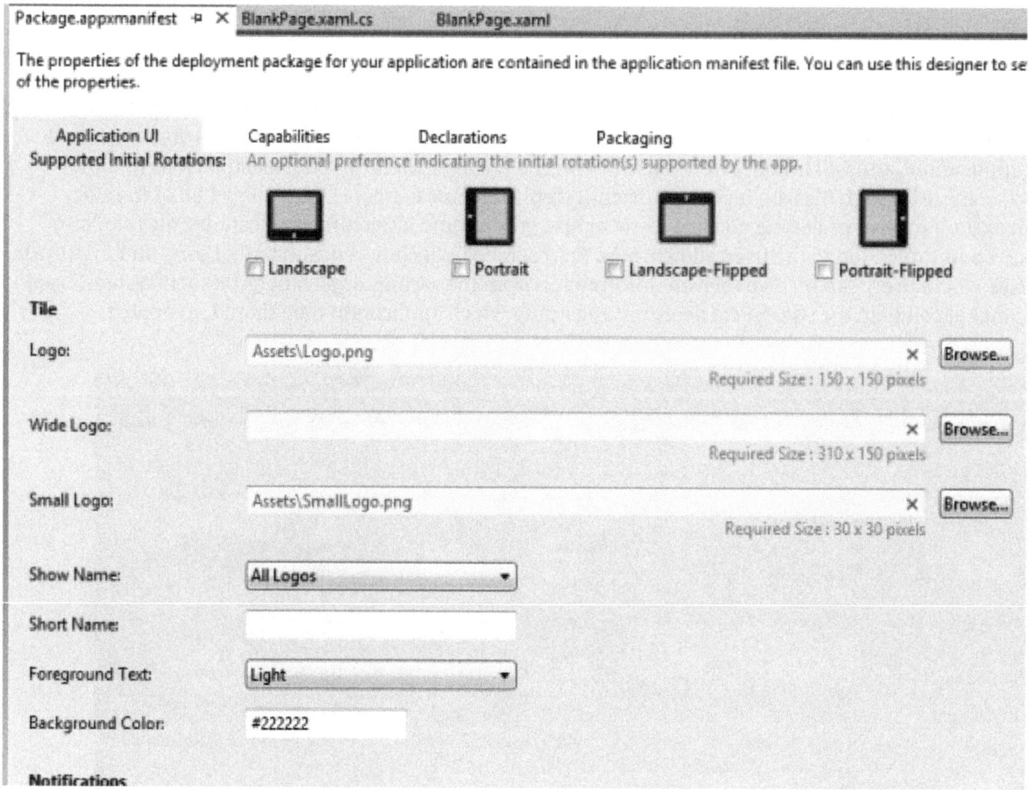

Figure 18-5. *Tile configuration*

At a minimum, an image should be provided for the Logo option, which defines the logo to be used on a square tile. This image should be 150 pixels wide by 150 pixels tall and can be either in JPEG or PNG format. If you decide that a wide tile is appropriate for your application (I'll talk about why to use wide tiles later in this chapter), you can also specify an image that is 310 pixels wide by 150 pixels tall to be used with the wide tile. The small logo will be used when Windows needs to display a list of applications (such as in the Search application) and needs to be 30 pixels wide by 30 pixels tall.

There also are several other options to configure:

- The Show Name option determines when the application's Display Name or Short Name (if configured) will be displayed as an overlay to the tile.

- The Foreground Text option specifies whether the text overlay should be light or dark.

- The Background Color option specifies the color of the tile.

Tile Templates

As with toast notifications, the look of a tile is based on a number of XML templates. Tiles do, however, provide far more template options because many of the templates have both square and wide versions and there are many more wide variations. Table 18-3 describes the square versions, and Table 18-4 describes a sampling of the wide tiles (to find the complete list with a picture of each, search MSDN for *choosing a tile template*). In the templates listed, the templates including *Peek* in their name all exhibit a behavior where the size of the tile as defined by the XML exceeds the actual size of the tile and the tile is animated to scroll up and down within a tile-sized viewport.

Table 18-3. *Tile Templates*

Template	Description
TileSquareBlock	This template is used to present a very short (two to three characters) string that will be rendered in a block of large text followed by an additional short string that will be rendered as a bold, regular-sized block of text.
TileSquareText01	This template is used to specify a string that is displayed in large text on the first line followed by three additional strings that are each displayed on their own line that does not wrap.
TileSquareText02	This template is used to specify a string that is displayed in large text on the first line followed by an additional string that is displayed wrapped across a maximum of three lines.
TileSquareText03	This template is used to specify four strings that are each displayed on their own line of text that does not wrap.
TileSquareText04	This template is used to specify a string that is displayed as regular text wrapped across up to four lines.
TileSquareImage	This template contains no text and displays a single image that fills the tile.
TileSquarePeekImageAndText01	This peek template combines TileSquareImage and TileSquareText01 for animation.
TileSquarePeekImageAndText02	This peek template combines TileSquareImage and TileSquareText02 for animation.
TileSquarePeekImageAndText03	This peek template combines TileSquareImage and TileSquareText03 for animation.
TileSquarePeekImageAndText04	This peek template combines TileSquareImage and TileSquareText04 for animation.

Table 18-4. *Wide Tiles*

Template	Description
TileWideText01	This template is used to specify a string that is displayed in large text on the first line followed by four additional strings that are each displayed on their own line that does not wrap.
TileWideText02	This template is used to specify a string that is displayed in large text on the first line followed by eight additional strings that are placed in a tabular display with four rows of two equally wide columns.
TileWideImage	This template contains no text and displays a single image that fills the tile.
TileWideImageCollection	This template contains no text and specifies one large image that fills a square area taking up the left half of the tile and an additional four smaller images that are displayed in a two-by-two grid that divides the right half of the tile into four even squares.

(*continued*)

Table 18-4. (*continued*)

Template	Description
TileWideImageAndText01	This template specifies a single image that is displayed using the full width of the tile and a string that is displayed wrapped across a maximum of two lines.
TileWideImageAndText02	This template specifies a single image that is displayed using the full width of the tile and two strings that are each displayed on their own line of text that does not wrap.
TileWideBlockAndText01	This template is used to specify four strings that are each displayed on their own line that does not wrap on the left side of the tile. On the right side of the tile, a fifth, very short, string is rendered as a large text block over a sixth string, which is displayed as a line of regular-sized bold text.
TileWideBlockAndText02	This template is used to specify a string that is displayed wrapped across up to four lines of text on the left side of the tile. On the right side of the tile, a second, very short, string is rendered as a large text block over a third string, which is displayed as a line of regular-sized bold text.
TileWideSmallImageAndText01	This template specifies a single small image that is displayed on the left side of the tile and a string that is displayed wrapped across a maximum of three lines of large text on the right.
TileWideSmallImageAndText02	This template specifies a single small image that is displayed on the left side of the tile. A string specifies text to be displayed in large text on the right side, and four additional strings each are displayed as nonwrapped regular lines under the larger line.
TileWidePeekImageCollection01	This peek template combines TileWideImageCollection and TileWideText09 for animation.
TileWidePeekImageCollection02	This peek template combines TileWideImageCollection and TileWideText01 for animation.
TileWidePeekImageAndText01	This peek template combines TileWideImage and TileWideText04 for animation.
TileWidePeekImageAndText02	This peek template combines TileWideImage and TileWideText05 for animation.
TileWidePeekImage01	This peek template combines TileWideImage and TileWideText09 for animation.
TileWidePeekImage02	This peek template combines TileWideImage and TileWideText01 for animation.

Figure 18-6 shows tiles using different templates to communicate or connect with an application's users. In this figure, the Travel application's tile is using a peek template; in the figure, the template is caught transitioning from the photo, which is sliding off the top of the tile, to the text, which is moving into position from below.

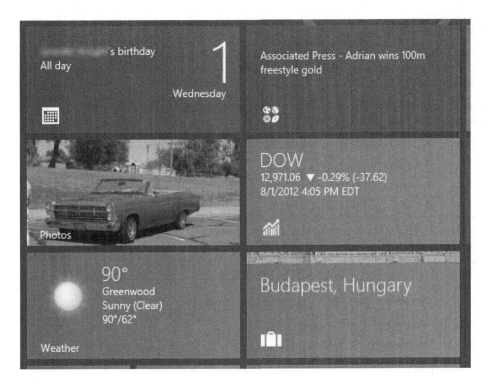

Figure 18-6. *Tiles connecting with the user*

Tile API

Now that you have seen the broad selection of templates available for creating tiles, you will learn how to use these templates to update tiles at runtime. The objects used in communicate with the user through tile updates is very similar to the set of objects used to communicate using toast notifications and include TileNotification, TileUpdater, and TileUpdateManager. The TileNotification object represents the tile update to be made. The TileUpdater object contains the functionality of actually handling the update or scheduling the update of tiles. As its name implies, the TileUpdateManager object is used to manage tile update operations.

TileNotification

The TileNotification object is essentially a data container to hold information about a tile update. The class has three properties: Content, ExpirationTime, and Tag.

- Content is an XML document containing the information about which template is to be used and the visual characteristics of the updated tile.

- ExpirationTime, if populated, indicates the time after which the tile should no longer be displayed.

- Tag is used when cycling between queued tiles to remove duplicates.

ScheduledTileNotification

The ScheduleTileNotification object is used to contain information about a tile update that has been scheduled to occur in the future. It is identical to the TileNotification object except that it adds two additional properties: Id and DeliveryTime.

- Id is a unique identifier for the tile update that can be used later to perform actions such as canceling the scheduled update.

- DeliveryTime is the time at which Windows should perform the tile update.

TileUpdater

The TileUpdater object presents methods used to update tiles and manage the update schedule, which are detailed in the following list. In addition to these methods, the object exposes a single property called Setting, which is of type NotificationSetting. The NotificationSetting type contains several read-only boolean properties communicating whether notification is enabled and, if not, the reason why it is disabled. Notification can be disabled by group policy, at the manifest level, by the application, or for the user.

- Update: Requests immediate update of the requested application tile

- Clear: Causes the tile to revert to its initial basic tile state

- GetScheduledTileNotifications: Retrieves a list of scheduled tile updates

- AddToSchedule: Adds a tile update to the schedule to be applied by Windows at a later time

- RemoveFromSchedule: Removes a specific scheduled tile update from the schedule

- EnableNotificationQueue: Enables a tile update feature with which Windows will cycle between up to five notifications

- StartPeriodicUpdate: Starts a timer updating the tile's contents with information from a specified URI at a designated interval

- StopPeriodicUpdate: Cancels the periodic updates started with a call to StartPeriodicUpdate

TileUpdateManager

The TileUpdateManager object provides management functions for creating the templates that are used to initialize TileNotification objects and for providing access to an appropriately initialized TileUpdater object. The class includes the CreateTileUpdaterForApplication method, which in its parameterless version creates a TileUpdater object configured to send notification to the current application. CreateTileUpdaterForApplication also has an overload that accepts a string containing an application ID. This version of the method returns a TileUpdater configured to send notifications to the application with the specified application ID, which must be included in the current application's package. CreateTileUpdaterForSecondaryTile is a method used when creating and managing secondary tiles, which is beyond the scope of this chapter. Additionally, the TileUpdateManager object contains the GetTemplateContent method that accepts a member of the ToastTemplateType enumeration and returns an XML document containing the designated template. This document is updated with the desired information to be contained in the notification and used to instantiate a TileNotification object.

Sending a Tile Update

The steps required to send a tile are relatively simple and very much like those used to send toast notifications. First you retrieve the appropriate XML template using the TileUpdateManager object's GetTemplateContent method. Once you have the XML, you update the document to reflect the desired tile content and use it to initialize a new TileNotification instance. The last step is to retrieve an instance of a TileUpdater object and call the Update method to display the updated tile.

EXERCISE: UPDATING TILES

In this exercise, you will create an application that sends tile updates. To complete the exercise, you will need Windows 8 and any edition of Visual Studio 2012.

1. To get started, open Visual Studio, and create a new project. The project type should be Blank App (XAML), which can be found in the Windows Store category under Visual C#. Name the project UpdateTiles.

2. Open MainPage.xaml.cs, and add the following to the using statements at the top of the file:

   ```
   using Windows.UI.Notifications;
   ```

3. Open MainPage.xaml, and add the following XAML inside the Grid element to create a Button:

   ```
   <Button Content="Update Tile" />
   ```

4. Double-click the Button in the designer. Visual Studio will automatically generate the Button_Click_1 event handler in MainPage.xaml.cs, and navigate to this method. Add the following code to the event handler:

   ```
   int counter = 10;
   var timer = new DispatcherTimer();
   timer.Interval = TimeSpan.FromSeconds(2);
   timer.Tick += (o, arg) =>
   {
       var templateType = TileTemplateType.TileSquareBlock;
       var tileTemplate = TileUpdateManager.GetTemplateContent(templateType);
       var textNode = tileTemplate.GetElementsByTagName("text")[0];
       textNode.AppendChild(tileTemplate.CreateTextNode((counter--).ToString()));
       var tile = new TileNotification(tileTemplate);
       TileUpdateManager.CreateTileUpdaterForApplication().Update(tile);
       if(counter < 0) timer.Stop();
   };
   timer.Start();
   ```

5. Run the application. When you click the Button and then go to the Start screen, you will see the application's tile counting down (assuming you get to the Start screen before the count reaches zero).

You have now created an application that updates its application tile. For further exploration, try experimenting with some of the other tile templates.

Considerations When Using Tiles

The main things to consider when communicating with your user via tiles is that the tile should at all times be relevant to your application and that the user is likely to view your tile only during the time that they have completed work in one application and are preparing to switch to another application. While the tiles are capable of providing the user with a dashboard, it is not likely that a user will actively monitor this dashboard for any length of time. One possible exception would be the case where the user is running Windows 8 on a mobile device and frequently glances at the Start screen tiles to see whether there is an application that requires attention.

Another consideration has to do with including time-sensitive information on any tile. Live tile updates can be suspended by the user or delayed for other reasons, so do not include any information in live tiles when it is critical that the user not be presented with stale data.

Conclusion

In this chapter, you learned the basics of working with toast notifications and tiles. The scenarios that I covered all center around creating and scheduling notification from a local application, but many more advanced scenarios are available; among them are the Windows Notification Service, secondary tiles, and badges. As you look to move beyond the basics of Windows 8 development, this would be an excellent area for a deep dive.

CHAPTER 19

■ ■ ■

Sensors, Devices, and the Location API

The torrent of centuries rolling over the human race has continually brought new perfections, the cause of which, ever active though unseen, is found in the demands made by our senses, which always in their turns demand to be occupied.

—Jean Anthelme Brillat-Savarin

In many ways, Windows 8 is about connection. Notifications and tiles connect applications to their users, Search and Share connect applications' data, and the use of web services connects to data in the cloud. In this chapter, you will learn about how sensors and other devices are used to connect Windows 8 computers with the physical world around them. I will discuss the accelerometer, inclinometer, compass, and ambient light sensors as well as the geolocation API and the Camera device. Because this book is not geared to advanced programming topics, I will not go beyond a brief introduction to each of these subjects; I will provide a simple exercise to give you some exposure to programming for each.

Windows 8 is found on a wide variety of hardware platforms ranging from standard desktops that used to be running Windows 2000 or Windows XP to state-of-the-art devices such as Microsoft's Surface tablet. This means that any given device may support all, none, or somewhere in between of the sensors that are discussed in this chapter. The simulator that ships with Visual Studio cannot in most cases be used to exercise code written for the sensor APIs when you don't have access to a sensor-equipped device. For these exercises, you may not be able to see the result without a device that is equipped with an appropriate sensor.

Physical and Virtual Sensors

Microsoft has a long history of creating software abstractions of hardware in order to help make sure that developers can write code on one Windows machine and have confidence that hardware changes will not impact the behavior of the application. One area where this has been very apparent is in the printing subsystem where the physical hardware that puts ink on paper is referred to as a *print device* and the actual object applications interact with is a software construct known as a *printer*. This abstraction continues and expands into the Windows 8 sensors world with a concept known as *sensor fusion*, where in addition to pieces of hardware being directly mapped to software abstractions, additional abstractions are created as a composite of hardware devices in order to keep developers from having to combine the raw data from multiple sensors to derive a meaningful result. The hardware accelerometer, gyrometer, and magnetometer devices' input values are combined by Windows to create the following:

- A virtual compass device that always points north

- A virtual inclinometer that determines the current position and rotation angle of the device in three-dimensional space

- A device orientation sensor that determines the device's orientation and rotation across four planes

These virtual devices create a value for developers by saving them the effort and potential for error of performing complex calculations on the raw sensor data. In the next several sections, I will discuss some of the more common sensors and devices on the Windows platform, and you will see the fusion of hardware and software in action.

Accelerometer

The accelerometer is a device that measures motion along three planes (as shown in Figure 19.1). This type of sensor has many modern applications including such devices as airbags in automobiles and the step counters distributed by many workplace wellness programs. Because the accelerometer is used to detect the rate of motion along these planes, it would be useful for scenarios such as using a shake gesture to clear the screen (you could build an Etch-a-Sketch) or a bump to get the ball moving in a game of pinball.

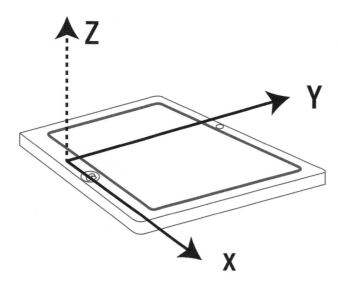

Figure 19-1. *Accelerometer planes*

To access the accelerometer data, an `Accelerometer` object is used. This object provides access to `AccelerometerReading` objects, which are data objects that contain the following properties:

- `AccelerationX`: Represents the G-force acceleration along the x-axis at the time of the reading

- `AccelerationY`: Represents the G-force acceleration along the y-axis at the time of the reading

- AccelerationZ: Represents the G-force acceleration along the z-axis at the time of the reading

- Timestamp: Indicates the time at which the sensor reading was captured

Access to the AccelerometerReading objects can be on demand by calling the GetCurrentReading method of the Accelerometer object, or you can subscribe to the ReadingChanged event in order to receive notification whenever the acceleration along any of the planes changes. In addition to the ReadingChanged event, the Accelerometer exposes a Shaken event to spare the developers of the effort of interpreting multiple ReadingChanged events to determine that a shake gesture has been performed.

EXERCISE: USING THE ACCELEROMETER

In this exercise, you will access data provided by the accelerometer sensor. To complete the exercise, you must have Windows 8 and any edition of Visual Studio 2012. To successfully run the completed example, your Windows 8 device must have an accelerometer sensor.

1. Open Visual Studio, and create a new project. The project type should be Blank App (XAML), which can be found in the Windows Store category under Visual C#. Name the project AccelerometerSample.

2. Open MainPage.xaml. Add the following XAML element inside the Grid on the page:

   ```
   <ListBox Name="accelerometerHistory" Height="500" Width="200" />
   ```

3. Open MainPage.xaml.cs. Ensure the using statements at the top of the source file include the following:

   ```
   using Windows.Devices.Sensors;
   using Windows.UI.Core;
   using Windows.UI.Xaml.Controls;
   ```

4. Add an event handler for an Accelerometer object's ReadingChanged event. This event will not be fired on the UI thread, so any interaction with UI controls has to be made using the RunAsync method of the page's Dispatcher. Use the following code to log the new entry:

   ```
   private void OnAccelerometerReadingChanged(Accelerometer sender,
     AccelerometerReadingChangedEventArgs args)
   {
     Dispatcher.RunAsync(CoreDispatcherPriority.Normal, () =>
       accelerometerHistory.Items.Add(
         string.Format("X: {0}, Y: {1}, Z: {2}"
         , args.Reading.AccelerationX
         , args.Reading.AccelerationY
         , args.Reading.AccelerationZ)));
   }
   ```

5. Declare a class-level Accelerometer variable. Place the following code at the top of the MainPage class definition before the constructor:

   ```
   private Accelerometer _accelerometer;
   ```

6. Initialize the `Accelerometer` instance, and subscribe to the `ReadingChanged` event. Update the constructor of `MainPage` to read as follows:

```
public MainPage()
{
  this.InitializeComponent();
  _accelerometer = Accelerometer.GetDefault();
  _accelerometer.ReadingChanged += OnAccelerometerReadingChanged;
}
```

7. Run the application. You should see the `ListBox` fill with reading entries.

You have now accessed data readings from the accelerometer sensor. For further investigation, try adding an event handler for the `Shaken` event.

Inclinometer

The inclinometer is used to measure rotation around three planes. These planes, illustrated in Figure 19.2, take their names from aeronautical terms and are referred to as *pitch*, *roll*, and *yaw*. There are many possible applications for inclinometer, but the first that consistently comes to mind for me is the game Labyrinth, where the player adjusts the incline of the game board in order to navigate a steel ball through a maze without allowing the ball to fall into holes placed throughout the maze.

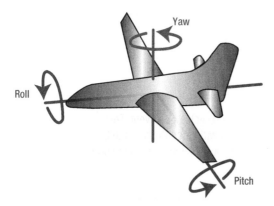

Figure 19-2. Pitch, roll, and yaw

The inclinometer sensor is typically a virtual sensor projected with sensor fusion, and the data is accessed through using an `Inclinometer` object to retrieve an `InclinometerReading` object. The `InclinometerReading` object contains the following properties:

- `PitchDegrees`: Represents the degree of rotation around the pitch plane

- `RollDegrees`: Represents the degree of rotation around the roll plane

- `YawDegrees`: Represents the degree of rotation around the yaw plane

- `Timestamp`: Indicates the time at which the reading was captured

Access to the InclinometerReading objects can be on demand by calling the GetCurrentReading method of the Inclinometer object, or you can subscribe to the ReadingChanged event in order to receive notification whenever the rotation around any of the planes changes.

EXERCISE: USING THE INCLINOMETER

In this exercise, you will access data provided by the inclinometer sensor. To complete the exercise, you must have Windows 8 and any edition of Visual Studio 2012. To successfully run the completed example, your Windows 8 device must support the inclinometer sensor.

1. Open Visual Studio, and create a new project. The project type should be Blank App (XAML), which can be found in the Windows Store category under Visual C#. Name the project InclinometerSample.

2. Open MainPage.xaml. Add the following XAML element inside the Grid on the page:

```
<StackPanel Orientation="Vertical">
  <StackPanel Orientation="Horizontal">
    <TextBlock Text="Pitch" />
    <TextBox Name="txtPitch" IsReadOnly="True" />
  </StackPanel>
  <StackPanel Orientation="Horizontal">
    <TextBlock Text="Roll" />
    <TextBox Name="txtRoll" IsReadOnly="True" />
  </StackPanel>
  <StackPanel Orientation="Horizontal">
    <TextBlock Text="Yaw" />
    <TextBox Name="txtYaw" IsReadOnly="True" />
  </StackPanel>
</StackPanel>
```

3. Open MainPage.xaml.cs. Ensure the using statements at the top of the source file include the following:

```
using Windows.Devices.Sensors;
using Windows.UI.Core;
using Windows.UI.Xaml.Controls;
```

4. Add an event handler for an Inclinometer object's ReadingChanged event. This event will not be fired on the UI thread, so any interaction with UI controls has to be made using the RunAsync method of the page's Dispatcher. Use the following code to update the TextBox controls with the current values:

```
private void OnInclinometerReadingChanged(Inclinometer sender,
  InclinometerReadingChangedEventArgs args)
{
  Dispatcher.RunAsync(CoreDispatcherPriority.Normal, () =>
```

```
        {
            txtPitch.Text = args.Reading.PitchDegrees.ToString();
            txtRoll.Text = args.Reading.RollDegrees.ToString();
            txtYaw.Text = args.Reading.YawDegrees.ToString();
        });
    }
```

5. Declare a class-level `Inclinometer` variable. Place the following code at the top of the `MainPage` class definition before the constructor:

    ```
    private Inclinometer _inclinometer;
    ```

6. Initialize the `Accelerometer` instance, and subscribe to the `ReadingChanged` event. Update the constructor of `MainPage` to read as follows:

    ```
    public MainPage()
    {
      this.InitializeComponent();
      _inclinometer = Inclinometer.GetDefault();
      _inclinometer.ReadingChanged += OnInclinometerReadingChanged;
    }
    ```

7. Run the application. You should see each `TextBox` updated as the rotation of your device changes.

You have now accessed data readings from the inclinometer sensor. Applications for this sensor could include the maze discussed earlier or a flight simulator that responds to you tilting the device. Think about other possible applications for the data this sensor provides and see what ideas you can come up with.

Compass

The compass sensor is another sensor that is typically exposed as a virtual sensor projected with sensor fusion. This sensor is responsible for reporting the orientation of the device in regard to the earth's magnetic and geographic north poles. This sensor is very valuable in creating navigation applications.

To access the compass data, a `Compass` object is used. This object provides access to `CompassReading` objects, which are data objects that contain the following properties:

*   `HeadingMagneticNorth`: Represents the orientation of the device measured in degrees clockwise from the earth's magnetic north

*   `HeadingTrueNorth`: Represents the orientation of the device measured in degrees clockwise from the earth's geographic north

*   `Timestamp`: Indicates the time at which the sensor reading was captured

Access to the `CompassReading` objects can be on demand by calling the `GetCurrentReading` method of the `Compass` object, or you can subscribe to the `ReadingChanged` event in order to receive notification whenever the device heading changes.

EXERCISE: USING THE COMPASS

In this exercise, you will access data provided by the compass sensor. To complete the exercise, you must have Windows 8 and any edition of Visual Studio 2012. To successfully run the completed example, your Windows 8 device must support the compass sensor.

1. Open Visual Studio and create a new project. The project type should be Blank App (XAML), which can be found in the Windows Store category under Visual C#. Name the project CompassSample.

2. Open MainPage.xaml. Add the following XAML element inside the Grid on the page:

   ```
   <TextBox Name="txtHeading" IsReadOnly="True" />
   ```

3. Open MainPage.xaml.cs. Ensure the using statements at the top of the source file include the following:

   ```
   using Windows.Devices.Sensors;
   using Windows.UI.Core;
   using Windows.UI.Xaml.Controls;
   ```

4. Add an event handler for a Compass object's ReadingChanged event. This event will not be fired on the UI thread, so any interaction with UI controls has to be made using the RunAsync method of the page's Dispatcher. Use the following code to update the TextBox with the new heading:

   ```
   private void OnCompassReadingChanged(Compass sender,
     CompassReadingChangedEventArgs args)
   {
     Dispatcher.RunAsync(CoreDispatcherPriority.Normal, () =>
       {
         txtHeading.Text = args.Reading.HeadingMagneticNorth.ToString();
       });
   }
   ```

5. Declare a class-level Compass variable. Place the following code at the top of the MainPage class definition before the constructor:

   ```
   private Compass _compass;
   ```

6. Initialize the Compass instance, and subscribe to the ReadingChanged event. Update the constructor of MainPage to read as follows:

   ```
   public MainPage()
   {
     this.InitializeComponent();
     _compass = Compass.GetDefault();
     _compass.ReadingChanged += OnCompassReadingChanged;
   }
   ```

7. Run the application. You should see the TextBox updated as the device's heading is changed.

You have now accessed data readings from the compass sensor. For further investigation, try updating the exercise to use geographic north instead of magnetic north. Remember that the HeadingTrueNorth property is nullable, so you will need to check for null before using its value.

Ambient Light

The ambient light sensor is responsible for detecting the brightness of the light surrounding a Windows 8 device. This sensor can be used in scenarios such as changing the size and contrast of screen elements to enhance readability or dimming the screen in order to help conserve power.

To access the ambient light data, a LightSensor object is used. This object provides access to LightSensorReading objects, which are data objects that contain the following properties:

- IlluminanceInLux: Represents the brightness reaching the light sensor measured in lux

- Timestamp: Indicates the time at which the sensor reading was captured

Access to the LightSensorReading objects can be on demand by calling the GetCurrentReading method of the LightSensor object, or you can subscribe to the ReadingChanged event in order to receive notification whenever the brightness of the ambient light changes.

EXERCISE: USING THE LIGHTSENSOR

In this exercise, you will access data provided by the ambient light sensor. To complete the exercise, you must have Windows 8 and any edition of Visual Studio 2012. To successfully run the completed example, your Windows 8 device must support the ambient light sensor.

1. Open Visual Studio, and create a new project. The project type should be Blank App (XAML), which can be found in the Windows Store category under Visual C#. Name the project LightSensorSample.

2. Open MainPage.xaml. Add the following XAML element inside the Grid on the page:

```
<TextBox Name="txtLux" IsReadOnly="True" />
```

3. Open MainPage.xaml.cs. Ensure the using statements at the top of the source file include the following:

```
using Windows.Devices.Sensors;
using Windows.UI.Core;
using Windows.UI.Xaml.Controls;
```

4. Add an event handler for a LightSensor object's ReadingChanged event. This event will not be fired on the UI thread, so any interaction with UI controls has to be made using the RunAsync method of the page's Dispatcher. Use the following code to update the TextBox with the new light measurement:

```
private void OnLightSensorReadingChanged(LightSensor sender,
  LightSensorReadingChangedEventArgs args)
{
  Dispatcher.RunAsync(CoreDispatcherPriority.Normal, () =>
    {
      txtLux.Text = args.Reading.IlluminanceInLux.ToString();
    });
}
```

5. Declare a class-level `LightSensor` variable. Place the following code at the top of the `MainPage` class definition before the constructor:

```
private LightSensor _lightSensor;
```

6. Initialize the `LightSensor` instance, and subscribe to the `ReadingChanged` event. Update the constructor of `MainPage` to read as follows:

```
public MainPage()
{
  this.InitializeComponent();
  _lightSensor = LightSensor.GetDefault();
  _lightSensor.ReadingChanged += OnLightSensorReadingChanged;
}
```

7. Run the application. You should see the `TextBox` updated as the light reaching the device's sensor changes, such as when you shade the device.

You have now accessed data readings from the ambient light sensor. For further investigation, try updating the exercise to change the size of the text in the `TextBox` using larger text with less ambient light and smaller text when there is more light available.

Geolocation

The geolocation API is considered a service as opposed to a sensor because of the various ways in which it can retrieve location information. Depending on the capabilities of the device and network availability, it may retrieve location from any or a combination of one of the following:

- WiFi signal

- IP information

- Cellular data connection

- GPS

Geolocation is unlike the sensors I discussed in that it has the ability to divulge information that is considered sensitive(namely, your location) to an application that could possibly either intentionally or inadvertently divulge this information to a malevolent party. For this reason, any application must declare that location information is accessed in the application manifest, and then a second level of authorization is required in which the user is prompted to grant the application permission to access location information.

Access to geographic location information is exposed through the GeoPosition class, which exposes the following properties:

- CivicAddress: Provides the civic (or postal) address associated with the current position

- Coordinate: Provides the latitude and longitude of the current position as well as altitude, heading, and speed if available

Access to the GeoPosition objects can be on demand by calling the GetGeoPositionAsync method of the GeoLocator object, or you can subscribe to the PositionChanged event in order to receive notification whenever a location change is detected.

EXERCISE: USING THE GEOLOCATION API

In this exercise, you will access data provided by the geolocation API. To complete the exercise, you must have Windows 8 and any edition of Visual Studio 2012. To successfully run the completed example, your Windows 8 device must have geolocation support through some means such as being actively connected to the Internet.

1. Open Visual Studio, and create a new project. The project type should be Blank App (XAML), which can be found in the Windows Store category under Visual C#. Name the project LocationSample.

2. Open MainPage.xaml.cs. Ensure the using statements at the top of the source file include the following:

```
using System;
using Windows.Devices.Geolocation;
using Windows.UI.Xaml.Controls;
```

3. Open MainPage.xaml. Add the following XAML element inside the Grid on the page:

```
<StackPanel Orientation="Vertical">
  <TextBox Name="txtLatitude" IsReadOnly="True" />
  <TextBox Name="txtLongitude" IsReadOnly="True" />
  <Button Content="Find Me!" />
</StackPanel>
```

4. Double-click the Button created in the previous step to generate a click handler. You will be using await to invoke an async operation within the code, so you will have to modify the method definition to include the async keyword. The completed method should use the following code:

```
private async void Button_Click_1(object sender, RoutedEventArgs e)
{
  Geolocator locator = new Geolocator();
  Geoposition position = await locator.GetGeopositionAsync();
  txtLatitude.Text = position.Coordinate.Latitude.ToString();
  txtLongitude.Text = position.Coordinate.Longitude.ToString();
}
```

5. Run the application. When you click the Find Me button, you will receive an `UnauthorizedAccessException`. This is because when creating the application, the manifest was not updated to declare that the application requests permission to use geolocation. Stop debugging, and I'll show how to fix this.

6. Open `Package.appxmanifest`. On the Capabilities tab ensure that Location is selected.

7. Run the application. Now when you click the Find Me button, you will be prompted to allow the application access to location information. Click Allow, and the `TextBox` instances are populated with latitude and longitude information for your current location.

You have now accessed location data using the geolocation API. For further investigation, try updating the exercise to display information from the civic address instead of coordinates.

Camera

The final device that I will discuss in this chapter is the camera. The camera is more than likely the most ubiquitous of the devices that allow interaction with the outside world, existing as an integrated piece of hardware in most laptops and tablets and as an inexpensive webcam for many desktop machines. As with geolocation, access to the camera is restricted to applications that both declare an intention to use the camera in the application's manifest and receive permission from the user the first time that the application attempts to access the device.

There are multiple ways to retrieve input from the camera, but the way that I will discuss and then you will practice in the exercise is to use the `CameraCaptureUI` object. This object displays a full-screen interface with which the user interacts to capture a still photo or video and then delivers the result to the application that initiated the capture. The process of capturing and displaying a photo that you will follow in the exercise consists of the following steps:

1. Create a `CameraCaptureUI` object.

2. Update capture settings with the characteristics you would like captured.

3. Instruct the `CameraCaptureUI` object to capture a photo, returning the result as a storage file.

4. Open the file and set it as the image source.

EXERCISE: USING CAMERACAPTUREUI

In this exercise, you will use the `CameraCaptureUI` object to capture a photo and then display that photo in your application. To complete the exercise, you must have Windows 8 and any edition of Visual Studio 2012. To successfully run the completed example, your Windows 8 device must have a camera.

1. Open Visual Studio, and create a new project. The project type should be Blank App (XAML), which can be found in the Windows Store category under Visual C#. Name the project CameraSample.

2. Open `MainPage.xaml.cs`. Ensure the `using` statements at the top of the source file include the following:

```
using System;
using Windows.Media.Capture;
```

```
using Windows.Storage;
using Windows.UI.Xaml;
using Windows.UI.Xaml.Controls;
using Windows.UI.Xaml.Media.Imaging;
```

3. Open `MainPage.xaml`. Add the following XAML element inside the `Grid` on the page:

```
<StackPanel Orientation="Vertical">
  <Button Content="Take Picture" />
  <Image Name="cameraCapture" Stretch="UniformToFill" />
</StackPanel>
```

4. Double-click the `Button` created in the previous step to generate a click handler. You will be using `await` to invoke an `async` operation within the code, so you will have to modify the method definition to include the `async` keyword. The completed method should use the following code:

```
private async void ButtonClick_1(object sender, RoutedEventArgs e)
{
  CameraCaptureUI captureManager = new CameraCaptureUI();
  captureManagerPhotoSettings.Format = CameraCaptureUIPhotoFormat.Png;
  var photo = await
  captureManager.CaptureFileAsync(CameraCaptureUIMode.Photo);
  if(photo != null)
  {
    var fileStream = await photo.OpenReadAsync();
    var bitmap = new BitmapImage();
    bitmap.SetSource(fileStream);
    cameraCapture.Source = bitmap;
    fileStream.Dispose();
  }
}
```

5. Open `Package.appxmanifest`. On the Capabilities tab ensure that Webcam is selected.

6. Run the application. Now when you click the Take Picture button, you will be prompted to allow the application access to the camera. Click Allow, and the UI will display for you to take a picture using your camera. When you are returned to your application, the photo you took in the camera UI will display on your page.

You have now used the `CameraCaptureUI` object to initiate capture of a photograph from your application.

Conclusion

In this chapter, you were exposed to some of the most common sensors and devices that help a Windows 8 device interact with the physical world around it. Sensors will be an important part of many Windows applications, so it is a good idea to become familiar with integrating them. It's likely that developers will continue to work on desktop machines because of the benefit that large and multiple monitors bring to the development workflow, so if you are going to get serious about developing with sensors, I recommend getting a sensor-equipped tablet for testing in addition to your primary development machine or looking at USB-connected external sensors.

CHAPTER 20

■ ■ ■

Sharing Apps in the Windows Store

There is no delight in owning anything unshared.

—Lucius Annaeus Seneca

Most craftsmen finishing a work don't want to tuck it away in a place where only they can see it—they want to share it with others who can appreciate it or get some value from it. This is as true for a software application as it is a work of art. Prior to Windows 8, if you were to ask "How do I share my applications with other people?" the answer would have invariably focused on the logistics of creating an installer package or the benefits of XCOPY deployment. The answer would most likely have lacked, however, any indication of how to make sure people knew about the application's availability or how to monetize the application if that is your goal. In this chapter, you will learn about the Windows Store, which is the primary method for distributing applications built for Windows 8. You will learn about giving your application a unique brand, packaging the application for distribution, and navigating the submission process. This chapter will not cover establishing a developer account or making use of in-app payment features enabled by the Windows Store APIs.

Branding Your Application

Throughout this book, you may have noticed that all of the sample applications showed the same rather nondescript splash screen that is pictured in Figure 20-1. This is because the splash screen image is one of several components that are required for all Windows applications and Microsoft includes a default for each of the required components with each new project in order to ensure the project can build and run immediately. Replacing these generic elements with alternatives that add the identity of your application through color, style, or imagery creates a better experience for the end user and does not leave them with the first impression that the developer of the application couldn't be bothered to change from the default. In this section, you will learn about the branding options in the Application UI section of the appxmanifest.xml file.

Figure 20-1. *Default application splash screen*

Display Name

The display name is used to identify your application. It is a string of up to 256 characters and displays in the Windows Store search results and app listings as well as search listings in Windows 8 and on application tiles when a short name has not been defined. Because this value is displayed publically to people who may be searching for an application, care should be taken to make it unique, descriptive, and enticing.

Default Language

The default language specifies the primary language for your application in the form of a two-digit language code followed by a hyphen and then a two-letter culture code. An application intended for English-speaking users in the United Kingdom would have a default language of en-UK, while English-speaking users in the United States would have a default language of en-US. Windows Store requirements require the primary language to be selected from a finite set of choices, so it may be a good idea to search MSDN for *Building the app package* and review the available language selection.

Supported Rotations

Applications in Windows 8 by default are expected to handle the user rotating the display however it suits them and still present an effective interface. Some applications will find themselves ill-suited to possible rotations, and the developer can select from a list of the following rotations (illustrated in Figure 20-2) to indicate what is supported by their application:

- Landscape
- Portrait
- Landscape-flipped
- Portrait-flipped

Figure 20-2. *Rotation options*

Splash Screen

The first thing a user sees when launching your application is the splash screen that displays as the application performs any necessary initialization. Applications must specify a splash screen image and may additionally specify a background color against which to display the image. Size and format requirements are very specific in that the image must be 620 x 300 pixels and must be in either PNG or JPG format. Figure 20-3 illustrates a splash screen that is more appropriate for the MovieBrowser sample application that you built in the exercises for this book.

Figure 20-3. *MovieBrowser splash screen*

Tile

Tile settings control how Windows displays various tiles shown for your application. These settings primarily revolve around various-sized logos but additionally include settings focused on the application's name display and colors.

The logo image is displayed on the square tile for your application in the Windows Start screen. This image is required because even if you intend to default to the wide tile on the Start screen, users can choose to display a square tile instead. Like the splash screen image, the logo must be in either PNG or JPG format. It also has specific size requirements in that it must be 150 x 150 pixels. In addition to the square tile logo, a 30 x 30 pixel small logo is required for Windows to use in the following places:

- In the search results on the Start screen

- In the full list of apps in the zoomed-out Start screen

- In the list of searchable apps

A 310 x 150 pixel logo is used when the application chooses to offer a wide tile.

In addition to specifying the logos to use for your application's tiles, you can also control the display of the application's name. These settings allow for an optional "short name" of up to 13 characters, which can provide a version of the application name shortened to fit onto tiles. If this setting is provided, the application's tiles and notifications will display using this value instead of the application's full name. Additionally, you can control under what circumstances the application's name (or short name if configured) should be displayed on the application tile. Choices include the following:

- All Logos

- Standard (square) Logo Only

- Wide Logo Only

When the application name is shown, you can additionally choose whether the text should be dark or light. Figure 20-4 shows a potential standard logo for the MovieBrowser sample application, and Figure 20-5 demonstrates the application's standard tile on the Start screen with the name configured to display using light text. As you can see, you need to be careful when making decisions regarding name display to ensure that your application's brand is maintained and that you don't end up with a logo and text combination that inhibits readability.

Figure 20-4. *MovieBrowser logo*

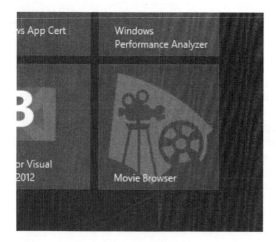

Figure 20-5. *MovieBrowser square tile*

Notifications

As you learned in Chapter 18, notification mechanisms such as live tiles and toast provide an opportunity for your application to connect with users while they are using other applications. When branding your application, you can indicate whether the application will make use of toast notification. Additionally, you can configure your application to present notifications when the lock screen is active. These notifications can be displayed either with a 24 x 24 monochrome badge image or as a wide tile toast notification. If the application is configured to show tile and text in the lock screen notification, then the wide tile logo must be specified in the tile branding options.

Navigating the Submission Process

It may seem a little bit out of order to discuss the process for submitting an application before I have described how to create the package that you will submit, but the submission process typically begins before you even start writing your application code and then resumes when the completed application package is ready for submission. In this section, I will discuss the different steps in the submission process.

App Name

The app name portion of the registration is one of the two most important reasons to begin the submission process prior to writing the application. In this step, you are able to specify the name that will identify your application in the Windows Store. Completing the step ensures that the name you have chosen is not already used or reserved and provides you with a one-year reservation on the name, during which time you can complete the application and submit it without worrying about whether somebody used your chosen name.

Selling Details

In the selling details step, you make selections regarding whether and how you want to make money from your application. This can include such options as making your application freely available, providing the availability of time- or feature-limited trial versions, or making money through advertising or in-app purchases. If you choose to sell your application, you must select a pricing tier for the application, which typically ranges from $1.49 US to $4.99 US. For the first $25,000 US in sales, Microsoft keeps a 30 percent store fee, and then the store fee reduces to 20 percent, leaving the developer with 80 percent of the net receipts.

Advanced Features

In the advanced feature step, you define whether the application should receive push notifications from a server and generate the identity information that will be used by the server to send notifications to your app. Besides the benefit of reserving a name, obtaining the values generated during this step to include in your application code is the second biggest reason to start the submission process prior to writing application code.

Age Rating

This step is used to specify the intended or appropriate age of your application's users. The Windows Store does not accept applications containing adult content. Applications that are assigned, or are unrated but merit, PEGI 16 or ESRB MATURE ratings are not allowed. You can upload third-party rating certificates or self-rate by assigning a Windows Store age rating.

Cryptography

In this step, you indicate whether your application makes use of cryptography. This is important because many nations have import/export restrictions around cryptographic software or software that makes use of cryptographic components, and your selection here will impact the geographic areas in which your application can be made available.

■ **Note**   The cryptography step is as far as you can go in the submission process before packaging your completed application for submission.

Packages

In this step, you upload the completed application package created in Visual Studio. The submission page allows you to either use a Browse button to navigate to the package on your computer or drag and drop the package from a Windows Explorer window to the browser page.

Description

In this step, you will enter a description for your application for each supported language. The description is required and will be used in the marketing of your application, so it is important that it describe what your application does in a way that encourages the prospective user to pick your application over others that may do the same or similar jobs. In this step, you will also be required to submit at least one screenshot for use in promoting your application, copyright information, and support contact information. In addition to these required elements, you may also choose to include the following:

- Descriptive bullet points

- Keywords

- Additional license terms

- Additional screenshots and promotional images

- Links to application website and privacy policy

Notes to Testers

Each application submitted to the Windows Store will be run through a series of automated tests to ensure conformance to Microsoft's guidelines and will also be manually reviewed for quality and content by Microsoft testers. If these testers need information such as login credentials in order to successfully exercise the application, you can provide notes for them here. The number of characters in this space is limited, so if your notes require more space than allotted, you could provide a URL to additional instruction. It's important to realize that the testers will likely have a lot of applications to test, so the easier you make the job on them, the better mood they will be in as they test your application.

Final Submission

After entering notes for the testers, you are given the opportunity to review and then finalize your submission. From this point forward, the process is out of your hands. The application will be run through automated tests and reviewed manually before a decision is made as to whether your application is accepted into the store. A dashboard within the developer portal can be used to view the current status of any submission that you have in progress.

■ **Note**   This chapter discusses the submission process but does not provide an in-depth look at the requirements against which your submission will be evaluated. To view the current requirements, search MSDN for the topic *Windows 8 app certification requirements*. This topic covers both technical and content-related requirements for Windows 8 applications.

Packaging Your Application

As described in the previous section, the first step of packaging your application for submission to the Windows Store is to reserve the application name in the store. Once the application name has been created, you can use the Associate App with the Store item in Visual Studio's Store menu (illustrated in Figure 20-6) to associate the current project with the Window's Store metadata for your reservation. This metadata includes the package display name, package name, publisher ID, and publisher display name.

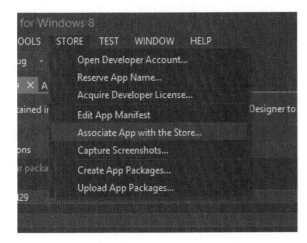

Figure 20-6. *Associating the app with Windows Store*

In addition to associating the project to a reserved application name in the Windows Store, the Store menu also provides a Capture Screenshots option, which launches your application in a simulator that includes its own screen capture tool. This is invoked using the camera icon shown in Figure 20-7. At least one screenshot must be captured for submission, and the images will be used in the Windows Store as well as any additional material Microsoft uses to promote your application.

Figure 20-7. *Camera icon*

Once you've completed the application and are ready to submit it to the Windows Store, the Create App Packages menu item initiates a short wizard that will create the necessary package files for you. Selecting Upload App Packages opens a web browser window to the developer portal and allows you to continue the application submission process at the Packages step, at which point you will upload the package you have created.

Conclusion

In this chapter, you learned how to communicate your application's unique brand and about the process for reserving names and submitting applications to be made available on the Windows Store. If you have an application to share with the world, you should open a developer account, reserve your name, and start using your skills to create the next great app.

Index

CPSIA information can be obtained at www.ICGtesting.com
Printed in the USA
LVOW011712231012

304104LV00001B/5/P